Anarchy, State, and Utopia

Though I heard him speak several times, I only met Robert Nozick once, and spent only one evening with him. In this far too brief acquaintance he impressed me as a person who was much as you see him in his writings: not merely brilliant but also charming and a delight to know. I would like to dedicate this little book to his memory.

Als ik kan.

Anarchy, State, and Utopia

An Advanced Guide

Lester H. Hunt

WILEY Blackwell

This edition first published 2015
© 2015 John Wiley & Sons, Inc.

Registered Office
John Wiley & Sons, Ltd, The Atrium, Southern Gate, Chichester, West Sussex, PO19 8SQ, UK

Editorial Offices
350 Main Street, Malden, MA 02148-5020, USA
9600 Garsington Road, Oxford, OX4 2DQ, UK
The Atrium, Southern Gate, Chichester, West Sussex, PO19 8SQ, UK

For details of our global editorial offices, for customer services, and for information about how
to apply for permission to reuse the copyright material in this book please see our website at
www.wiley.com/wiley-blackwell.

The right of Lester H. Hunt to be identified as the author of this work has been asserted in
accordance with the UK Copyright, Designs and Patents Act 1988.

Library of Congress Cataloging-in-Publication Data

Hunt, Lester H., 1946–
    Anarchy, state, and utopia : an advanced guide / Lester H. Hunt.
      pages   cm
    Includes bibliographical references and index.
    ISBN 978-0-470-67501-4 (hardback) – ISBN 978-1-118-88047-0 (paperback)   1. Nozick,
Robert. Anarchy, state, and utopia.   2. State, The.   3. Anarchism.   4. Utopias.   I. Title.
    JC571.H795 2015
    320.101–dc23
                                                          2015001990

A catalogue record for this book is available from the British Library.

Cover image: © Rike / iStockphoto

Set in 10/12.5pt Sabon by SPi Global, Pondicherry, India
Printed and bound in Malaysia by Vivar Printing Sdn Bhd

1   2015

Contents

Contents

Acknowledgments

Much of the writing of this book was done while on sabbatical leave from the University of Wisconsin at Madison during the fall of 2012. I thank the university for this much needed help. Of intellectual debts my greatest by far is to the many students, graduate and undergraduate, with whom I have discussed these issues since the spring of 1978 at the University of Pittsburgh. I thank one of these by name in an endnote, but I owe a similar debt to others, whom I cannot thank simply because I cannot sort out their contributions and attach names to them. I have also sharpened my thinking on a number of relevant points by discussing them with Nathaniel Hunt. Thanks are due to Molly Gardner for serving stint as my research assistant and to Deborah Katz Hunt, Nathaniel Hunt, and Joanna Pyke for proofreading and copyediting work. I would also like to thank the lifeguards at the Fireman's Park Swimming Beach on beautiful Goose Pond in Verona, Wisconsin for ignoring the man sitting under a tree and writing on his laptop during the summers of 2011–2014, and to the librarians at the Oregon Public Library in Oregon, Wisconsin for leaving in peace the one who was quietly writing in a corner of the library day after day during that same stretch of years. Perhaps it is needless to add that in both cases I was that man.

1

Nozick's Introduction and Preface

1. Why Read a Book about a Book?

Robert Nozick's *Anarchy, State, and Utopia* (hereafter ASU)[1] created a sensation when it appeared in 1974. It won the National Book Award in 1975 and in 2008 was listed by the *Times Literary Supplement* as one of the hundred most influential books since World War II. It is certainly, and by far, one of the most influential philosophical books of the twentieth century, having had a strong impact, not merely on the tiny world of academic philosophy, but on many people in the great world outside the academy as well. And yet Nozick once described this book as "an accident."[2]

As he told the story years later, he began writing it in the academic year of 1971–1972, which he spent at the Center for Advanced Study in the Behavioral Sciences near Stanford University. The original purpose for his stay there was to write on the problem of free will. Unfortunately, having come to California without having already worked out his views on the subject of fee will, he found himself spinning his wheels for several months. In early December, he was invited to give a talk to a student group at Stanford. In his talk he explained how he thought a state could arise out of conditions of anarchy. He then wrote these thoughts out. At about this time, his Harvard colleague John Rawls sent him a copy of his new book, *A Theory of Justice*.[3] Nozick had read an earlier draft of the book and discussed it in detail with the author. Finding that the published version was quite different from the draft he had seen, he read it and was moved to set down his reflections on why he still disagreed with Rawls' view. At the same time, he sketched out his own ideas on the subject of

Anarchy, State, and Utopia: An Advanced Guide, First Edition. Lester H. Hunt.
© 2015 John Wiley & Sons, Inc. Published 2015 by John Wiley & Sons, Inc.

Rawls' book: the problem traditionally known as that of "distributive justice." By this time the original project on free will must have seemed to be receding into the impossibly far distance. However, he noticed that the two pieces he had written that year seemed to fit rather nicely with a paper he had produced for a 1969 session of the American Philosophical Association in which he presented a new conception of utopia. If he just elaborated these writings and added some connecting material he would have a book – and something to show for his year at the Center. So he set to work and by the time his stay there was over in July he had hammered out a draft.[4] He then rewrote the whole work in the summer of 1973 (xv).

Nozick's book is often compared and contrasted – mainly contrasted – with the one he received in the mail that January, *A Theory of Justice*. Rawls' book does indeed have a very different history, and is a *very* different sort of book from Nozick's, despite their overlapping subject matter. Nozick's book came into existence rather suddenly and almost as an afterthought. In fact, it was only a few years earlier that he had first come to hold the radical point of view he defends there. On the other hand, Rawls' work on the ideas presented in his 1971 book goes back at least as far as his 1951 paper, "Outline of a Decision Procedure in Ethics."[5] These ideas were subjected to a long and laborious process of working and reworking. Several drafts of Rawls' book circulated widely in the philosophical community and were much commented upon. The book itself (the 1971 edition) is 607 pages long. In it, Rawls tries to forestall every misinterpretation of his views that he can think of, in addition to answering every sensible objection that comes to mind. (Notwithstanding all this work, people managed to disagree with it and even misunderstand it anyway.) Rawls' aim in writing his book was, clearly, to *establish* something.

Readers of Nozick's book soon realize that it is written with a sharply different end in view. It is not intended to present a closed system, nor to present irrefutable proofs that compel the reader's assent at every turn – very far from it. Instead of the rigorous proofs that we expect from an analytic philosopher, what we often find are jokes, paradoxes, outlandish examples, and curious digressions. Though the author does have strong – some would say extreme – views on many of the subjects he discusses, and though he does argue brilliantly for them, his ultimate purpose is to indicate lines of further fruitful research and to stimulate the reader to further reflection. The fundamental impression on the reader is that thinking about these issues on a high level of sophistication is interesting and fun, and that we ought to come along and think with him. Where the great virtue of Rawls' book is thoroughness, that of Nozick's is brilliance.

Where one strives for completeness, the other seeks to dazzle and amaze, even to amuse.

As we will see, Nozick's book has the shortcomings of one that was written in this accidental way: There are many loose ends, abrupt transitions, digressions vaguely or poorly integrated into the whole, and (for those who insist that this *is* a shortcoming) plenty of unfinished business. However, it is also clearly a work of genius and, as such, it has virtues that only an "accidental" book can have: an air of genuine freshness and spontaneity. Among the writings of philosophers, that is something one usually only finds in published notebooks, or in the works of philosophers who write aphorisms, such as Nietzsche and Wittgenstein. It is very hard to think of another book by an Anglophone analytic philosopher (with the possible exception of other books by the same author, of course) in which this feeling of openness and fresh air can be found at all.

I think a book on ASU must take a different approach to its subject matter from the one that would be appropriate if the subject were *A Theory of Justice*. Since Rawls is trying to establish something once and for all, the commentator's aim should be to say what it is that he is trying to establish, how he attempts to do so, and how close he comes to succeeding.

With Nozick, who is not trying to establish something once and for all, the approach must be different. My aim here is to support the further reflection Nozick is trying to stimulate, without (I hope!) completely euthanizing the sense of fun he instills. I will try to accomplish this by carrying out two broadly different functions. One is a matter of interpretation and explanation. ASU is at many points a rather difficult book to penetrate. Sometimes this is because of the complexity and profundity of the thoughts it expresses. At other times it is because the presentation of those thoughts is confusing, due, perhaps, to the rather hurried way in which it was written. In these cases I will do my best to straighten out the text and remove any difficulties that do not belong to the ideas themselves.

The other function I will be trying to carry out will be to engage critically with the text. We don't read a book like ASU for its literary beauties – though it is generally well and often brilliantly written. We read such a book to see if it can help us to get closer to the truth on the great issues with which it deals. In what follows, I will point out what I see as the strengths and weaknesses of Nozick's argument. I will indicate where the theory has explanatory power, where it is implausible, and where there are loose ends with further work to be done. I will also indicate ends that are not loose – that is, places where ideas are actually connected, sometimes in surprising ways, with ideas in other parts of the book. These connections often either explain or strengthen his argument. Sometimes I will suggest friendly amendments, so to speak: additions to a theory or argument that would make it stronger. Ultimately, my purpose will be neither to defend Nozick nor to attack him, but to try to indicate the wealth of things that can be learned by thinking about what he is saying.

Finally, I should say a word about the point of view from which I am writing this. In the first part of the book, Nozick attempts to show that a state can be both just and desirable. In the second, he presents reasons for thinking that no state more extensive than a "minimal state" is justified, in that such a state would necessarily violate individual rights. The third part, which is based on the paper on utopia, gives a reason why we should not mind the fact that, as he sees it, no more extensive state than a minimal one is justified. Rather, we should welcome it gladly. I think Nozick's justification of the state is a failure, though an extremely interesting and instructive one. As to the conception of distributive justice presented in Part II, I think that, though it stands in need of amendment and correction, the needed changes are more or less in the spirit of his enterprise and that the amended doctrine would have very similar political implications. Further, I think that Part III, which is almost ignored in the secondary literature, is one of the most interesting parts of the book. The interest here may be more political than purely philosophical, but it is no less substantial for that. He succeeds in making a strong case that the seemingly austere state that he seeks to justify can appeal to the idealistic side of human nature.

2. The Preface

Though Nozick's elegantly written preface needs no interpreting or straightening out, it might be useful to underscore some things he says there. He begins by straightforwardly revealing the platform upon which his argument will be based:

> Individuals have rights and there are things no person or group may do to them (without violating their rights). So strong and far-reaching are these rights that they raise the question of what, if anything, the state and its officials may do.

He also tells us plainly the conclusion he will draw from his argument:

> Our main conclusions ... are that a minimal state, limited to the narrow
> functions of protection against force, theft, fraud ... and so on is justified;
> that any more extensive state will violate persons' rights not be forced to
> do certain things, and is unjustified; and that the minimal state is inspiring
> as well as right. Two noteworthy implications are that the state may not use
> its coercive apparatus for the purpose of getting some citizens to aid others,
> or in order to prohibit activities to people for their own good. (ix)

Among the sorts of coercion that are not justified, then, are forced redistribution of wealth and paternalistic coercion. This would obviously rule
out many laws and policies now in effect.

He seems painfully aware that this is very far from the received view.
He points out that, in a way, this puts him at a certain logical disadvantage compared to the adherents of the received view:

> A codification of the received view ... need not use elaborate arguments. It
> is thought to be an objection to other views merely to point out that they
> conflict with the view which readers wish anyway to accept. But a view
> which differs from the readers' cannot argue for itself merely by pointing
> out that the received view conflicts with *it*! (x)

He is describing a rather odd sort of inference, one that always systematically aids the received view. If I react with horror to Nozick's views
because they are so "extreme" – supposing this means simply that they
are very different from views commonly held – then the inference seems
to be something like "your view is not the one commonly held, therefore
it is wrong." This is an inference that the critic of the common view
cannot effectively reverse. The reverse argument, the one that would say,
"well, the commonly held view is not mine, therefore *it* is wrong," would
obviously fall on deaf ears. And yet, from a purely logical point of view,
these are exactly the same sort of argument. If one is a good argument,
the other must be just as good, as far as their logic is concerned.

Some people would say, however, that they are not the same sort of
argument at all. David Hume, for instance, tells us that

> though an appeal to general opinion may justly, in the speculative sciences
> of metaphysics, natural philosophy, or astronomy, be deemed unfair and
> inconclusive, yet in all questions with regard to morals [a category in which
> Hume includes politics], as well as criticism [meaning criticism of the arts],

there is really no other standard, by which any controversy can ever be decided. And nothing is a clearer proof, that a theory of this kind is erroneous, than to find that it leads to paradoxes repugnant to the common sentiments of mankind."[6]

There is a simple and plausible line of reasoning that leads to the position that Hume is taking here, or at least one very similar to it. There is an obvious reason why appeals to "general opinion" are fallacious in science (what Hume is calling "natural philosophy"): In a field like astronomy, we evaluate any given opinion by consulting observations of certain objects in the world, the objects that the opinions are about. If the opinion does not conform to observations, we reject it. So there is no reason to take such opinions themselves seriously.

The case is very different with regard to moral, political, and aesthetic questions. Here there are no observations that can play the role that observations play in the context of scientific problems. The issue is not about the nature of some object but about what we should do, think, and feel about it. One very natural way to answer such questions is this. Based on our intuitive judgments about specific cases, we formulate a rule that seems to fit them. Someone finds a case where our immediate intuitive judgment conflicts with the rule – a counterexample to the rule. At that point, either the counterexample is neutralized (perhaps there is reason to doubt that intuitive judgment, for instance) or else the rule is abandoned or revised to avoid the counterexample. This approach – we might call it "methodological intuitionism" – would seem to tend in the long run to reinforce general opinions because those are the opinions that drive the intuitions of most people.[7] This, in fact, is the method that is typically used by "analytic" philosophers who deal with ethical and political issues. Perhaps it does not quite bring us to the position that Hume seems to be taking, which is that you and I ought to *substitute* these same generally held opinions for our own individual judgments, but it does seem, like Hume's position, to enthrone common opinion in a unique position of authority. It gives "moderate" views an enormous advantage over "extreme" ones.

This presents a potential problem for Nozick, due mainly to a feature of his book that he does not explicitly discuss in the preface, though he does hint at it there: Methodological intuitionism accounts for a good part of the way Nozick himself will argue for his views. He describes it in an elliptical and indirect way in a comment he makes immediately after one I quoted above, in which he describes the disadvantage borne by views that differ from those of most of his readers. He says that the heterodox view "will have to subject the received view to the greatest intellectual testing" by means of "scrutiny of its presuppositions, and presentation of a range of possible situations where even its proponents are uncomfortable with its consequences" (x). He is describing extremely briefly here two logical operations he will be performing throughout the book: The first consists of finding a rule that accounts for the judgments that people who hold the received view find intuitively appealing (if one begins by assuming this rule, then these particular judgments will follow as a matter of course), and the other consists of posing counterexamples to the rule. Both of these operations are instances of methodological intuitionism. Given that this intuition-driven method seems to be biased by nature in favor of orthodoxy, this raises the question of how Nozick will turn it instead to the support of heresy. On the face of it, it would seem impossible for a method that is based on intuitive judgments at every turn to support anything but the received view, unless there is some clever, sophistical trickery involved. What other possibility is there?

As we will soon see, there is an answer to this question. The answer is that Nozick turns common opinion against itself. More exactly, he divides it into two parts and knocks down the political portion of it by means of other common-sense opinions that are at least as widely held and more fundamental: widely held views that are not political but moral in nature.

Notes

1 Robert Nozick, *Anarchy, State, and Utopia* (New York: Basic Books, 1974). To minimize endnotes, all citations to ASU will be by page number, presented between parentheses in the text: e.g., (xi) or (134). All printings of ASU in English have the same pagination.
2 Robert Nozick, "Introduction," *Socratic Puzzles* (Cambridge, Massachusetts: Harvard University Press, 1997), p. 1.
3 John Rawls, *A Theory of Justice* (Cambridge, Massachusetts: Harvard University Press, 1971).
4 Nozick, "Introduction," p. 1.
5 John Rawls, "Outline of a Decision Procedure in Ethics," *Philosophical Review*, vol. 60, no. 2 (April 1951), pp. 177–198.
6 David Hume, "Of the Original Contract," in *Essays: Moral, Political, and Literary* (Indianapolis, Indiana: Liberty Classics, 1987), p. 486.
7 I call it "methodological" because it does not involve the metaethical theory that we have a faculty of intuition which by its very nature provides us with correct conclusions. Having written this, I see that Jan Narveson uses the phrase "methodological intuitionism" in pretty much the same sense that I am using it here in

his book *The Libertarian Idea* (Philadelphia, Pennsylvania: Temple University Press, 1988), pp. 115–117. He argues there that it is a bad method because it amounts to presenting opinions as if they constitute evidence of their own truth. I think it is obvious what Nozick's answer to this should be: that the method only takes common-sense judgments as a starting point and does not treat them as beyond question. The logical driving force is the search for a coherent set of principles that would justify those opinions. One must be ready to discard opinions that cannot fit into such a framework.

2

Ethical Bearings

1. Foundations, Such as They Are

As I have just said, though ASU is a work of political philosophy, the political argument is based on ethical ideas. Nozick argues from the moral to the political. Upon what are his ethical assumptions based?

This is clearly a question of fundamental importance. It is perhaps best to discuss it now, though that means departing from the order in which Nozick discusses these issues in ASU. The relevant material for this topic is mainly in his Chapter 3. I will not be dealing with his Chapter 2 until my Chapter 4.

Nozick clearly believes that his ethical point of view in this book is deeply rooted in ordinary common sense. Yet his point of view is quite distinctive and in fact is incompatible with some very influential ethical theories. Throughout the book, he treats utilitarianism as his chief philosophical opponent. He clearly believes that if utilitarianism is right, his ethical position is wrong, and vice versa. As we will see, he is surely right about that.

The argument of ASU is based on the idea that, as he says in the first sentence in the book, "[i]ndividuals have rights" (ix). These rights are clearly natural rights, in the sense that they are not bestowed on the individual by the state or any other human agent. Rather, one has them because one is a person. This is one of the points of agreement between Nozick and the political philosopher whose views are closest to his, the eighteenth-century English philosopher John Locke, whose most developed and mature statement of his views is his *Two Treatises of Government*. This work, especially the *Second Treatise*, is mentioned and

Anarchy, State, and Utopia: An Advanced Guide, First Edition. Lester H. Hunt.
© 2015 John Wiley & Sons, Inc. Published 2015 by John Wiley & Sons, Inc.

discussed a number of times in ASU, with such care and respect that it is quite obvious that Nozick was influenced by it. As we will see (below, in Chapter 5) there are similarities – though important differences as well – between their accounts of the state. For the present I should probably point out that there are a couple of important differences, though with an obvious similarity, on the issue of rights. Though both think that some rights are natural in the sense just explained, Locke, unlike Nozick, commits himself to a theory that natural rights have a certain structure. He holds that one has rights that amount to a sort of absolute sovereignty over one's own self, one's mind and body, rights that he consistently speaks of as a sort of property right. There follows from this "ownership" of oneself a like right over one's productive labor, and on this is based a right to the product of one's labor. Though Locke never says so in so many words, all these rights include the right to exchange them with others, which would explain why he takes it for granted that one can have a great variety of contractual rights arrived at by mutual consent with other people.[1] Nozick's conception of rights does not seem to have this sort of structure. He does seem to think that we have rights to roughly the same things (person, product, etc.) that Locke does, but throughout ASU Nozick avoids expressing his view of rights in terms of Lockean "self-ownership." He clearly thinks that these are the rights that ordinary common sense applies as it deals with relations between individual human beings: It is wrong to lay hands on another person without implied or express consent, to take away the product of their labor, to violate contracts, and so forth.[2]

It is often said that he simply assumes that people have such rights, and indeed that he assumes without argument that they have the highly constraining set of rights that he thinks they do have. One of the best-known critiques of ASU is a review written by Thomas Nagel when the book first appeared, titled "Libertarianism without Foundations."[3]

Is this a fair criticism? I think it is not, for two reasons.

First, while it is true that ASU argues for political conclusions that many will find very counter-intuitive, the basic argumentative strategy of the book is to appeal to shared common-sense moral intuitions. He turns the moral part of common sense against the political part. If he has correctly identified common-sense morality, and if his argument is a cogent one, this would be an important achievement, even without his giving an independent defense of these moral intuitions. It would present most of his readers with a challenge to which they can only respond by changing their views, either about morality or about the realm of the political. The "no foundations" charge misses the point – or one of the main points – of the entire book.

Second, it actually is not true that he offers no argument for his ethical principles. The most important substantive ethical idea is what he calls "the libertarian constraint." This idea, as he puts it, "prohibits aggression against another" (33). He does not spell it out in detail, but it is clear from many things he does say that what it means is that force can only be justified as an appropriate response to unprovoked force, or as such a response to some other act that is wrongful in the same sort of way as force is wrong, such as fraud. Nozick offers a "formal argument" (identified as such in the index) for this principle. He also calls it an "argument from moral form to moral content" (34). As we will see, it places Nozick's moral foundations much closer to Immanuel Kant than to John Locke. Before we examine it we will need to take a look at the formal point on which it is based.

2. Moral Constraints and Moral Goals

Nozick points out that rights, as we typically think of them, have a feature that is puzzling. A right is a "moral concern" (28) that can be interpreted in more than one way. To put it in terms of an example, suppose that in our community some terrorists capture six innocent people, holding them hostage, and convince us that they will begin executing them, one at a time, unless we hand over to them one other member of the community, someone they were not able to get their hands on so easily, who is also perfectly innocent. Suppose we are certain that if we did this, this one person would be executed, but the other six would be released. If we do comply with their demands, we will save five lives. Suppose, further, that capturing this one person and giving him or her to the terrorists is the only way we can save these lives. Should we? Most people of whom I have asked this question say no – and by a wide margin! Why? One way to put the most likely answer would be to say that we think of this person as having a right to life. But what sort of moral concern is this right to life, exactly?

After all, the six hostages have a right to life as well. If the non-violation of rights is so important, why don't we treat it as a goal (or, as Nozick sometimes puts it, an "end-state") to be maximized? What other sort of moral consideration can a right be? Nozick's answer is that we can treat rights as what he calls "side constraints" or, more simply, "constraints."

But what sort of moral concern is a constraint? Nozick insists that a constraint cannot be explained as a special sort of goal. One way of trying to do this, for instance, would be to treat them as goals that are "lexicographically" ranked above all others, which would mean that these goals are to be achieved fully, with others being pursued insofar as pursuing them is compatible with such complete fulfillment. He points out that this is not how we think of rights, at least not "if there is some society we would choose to inhabit even though in it some rights of ours sometimes are violated, rather than move to a desert island where we could survive alone" (28). This shows that there must be some other goals we would pursue even if the alleged goal of non-rights violation has not been perfectly achieved (yet). Understanding rights as lexicographically superior goals would imply that they are, necessarily, more important than we generally think they are.

In an interesting if rather confusing footnote (29 fn.), Nozick considers another way in which we might try to make constraints out to be a peculiar sort of goal. This approach focuses on a feature of constrained thinking that came dramatically to the foreground in my example of the hostage-takers. One intuitive way to put the reason most of us would not turn that one unfortunate person over to the terrorists, even though this means that six people will die instead of one, is this: In the scenario with the greater number of rights violations, the victims are killed by the terrorists, whereas in the other one *we* are complicit in committing murder. This is a peculiar feature of morally constrained agents. They observe a curiously sharp distinction between their own behavior and that of others. Ideally, an account of moral constraints should be able to explain this fact. Thus:

> One might think ... that each person could distinguish in his goal between *his* violating rights and someone else's doing it. Give the former infinite (negative) weight in his goal, and no amount of stopping others from violating rights can outweigh his violating someone else's rights. In addition to a component of a goal receiving infinite weight, indexical expressions also appear, for example, "*my* doing something."

Nozick leaves us in the dark as to his reasons for rejecting this approach, saying simply: "A careful statement delimiting 'constraint views' would exclude these gimmicky ways of transforming side constraints into the form of an end-state view as sufficient to constitute a view as end-state." It isn't very clear what it means to call this way of understanding constraints "gimmicky," nor exactly why this is a bad thing.

It seems to me that there are reasons to simply reject this account as incorrect, and not merely gimmicky. For one thing, the idea of an infinitely weighted goal seems specious, for reasons that arise from the very nature of goal-directed behavior. Rational individuals invest resources (time, attention, effort, etc.) in pursuit of any given goal, up to the point that the next increment of resources has some use, in pursuit of some other goal, where we value this other use more highly. This seems to be true of all goals. Each has a value that can be specified in terms of acceptable trade-offs with other goals. But this means that though the value of a goal may be very great, it is always finite. An infinitely weighted goal would be one that, if there is ever a choice between spending any amount of a given resource on it versus any other goal, the other goal will simply be sacrificed (except in the unlikely event that the other goal is also infinitely weighted). You might think you place such infinite weight on your life – that is, survival – but you actually do not. There are definite limits to how much you will spend on safety devices, such as smoke detectors, fire extinguishers, seat belts, protective clothing, and so forth. This represents part of your efforts to enhance the probability that you will be alive at any given time in the future. If you look at the food people eat, the modes of transportation they choose (not always the safest, which would typically be walking), and their other habits, you see them constantly taking resources that could have gone to survival-assurance and devoting them to other goals instead, such as comfort, convenience, and entertainment. There are limits to the value they place on mere survival.

Most monotheists believe that God is infinitely good, but since God is not something that is produced by human action, He is not a goal with infinite weight. An infinitely good being and a goal with infinite weight are two quite different things.

But there is a simpler and more conclusive reason for rejecting this account of constraints as incorrect. It is that it is not an account of constraints as such but only, at best, of one possible theory about them. The theory I have in mind is one that Nozick briefly describes at the end of the same footnote:

> The question of whether side constraints are absolute, or whether they may be violated in order to avoid catastrophic moral horror, and if the latter, what the resulting structure might look like, is one I hope largely to avoid. (29 fn.)

If, as I have just supposed, taking constraints to be infinitely weighted goals would mean that one must avoid violating them regardless of cost, that would seem to mean that they are "absolute" in this sense. But I think Nozick is correct in suggesting that there is another view one can take of constraints: that in extreme situations they may be violated to avoid catastrophe.

It is worth pausing to notice that Nozick is carefully avoiding committing himself to a position that he is sometimes accused of holding. Jan Narveson, for instance, has claimed that Nozick's position in ASU is that "if doing x would deprive A of something to which A is entitled by right, then there are *absolutely* no circumstances in which it would be right to do x." This claim is clearly a misinterpretation.[4] Maybe what Narveson is thinking is that a moral consideration that may be violated in extreme circumstances is not really a constraint, but something else. Perhaps it is really just an odd sort of goal. After all, considering costs, and desisting when the cost becomes too high, is the sort of thing that characterizes goal-pursuit. Isn't that what we are doing when we violate a principle to avoid catastrophe? If so, wouldn't that mean the rights are really goals and not constraints?

To see why they nonetheless are indeed constraints and not goals, consider what a constraint is. Though Nozick doesn't define the term in so many words, we can extract a plausible definition from the way he uses it, as in this description of how a combined goal and constraint view would work: "A goal-directed view with constraints would be: among those acts available to you that don't violate constraint C, act so as to maximize goal G" (29). The contribution that the constraint makes here is, simply, to prohibit some acts that could otherwise serve as means to bringing about one's goal. In this comment, he is apparently thinking of a goal-directed view that (like hedonism) asserts a single ultimate goal. However, the characterization can easily be generalized into a definition of side constraints that applies to single- and multiple-goal views: A constraint is a principle that says that, whatever one's goal(s) might be, one may not pursue it/them by the means named by the principle.

Once the distinction between them has been clarified in this way, it is obvious that constraints and goals are completely different sorts of considerations. If we suppose that all human action is goal-directed, we could even say that goals (more precisely, the actions available to pursue them) are exactly what constraints constrain. We can also see why the second view of constraints, in which they may be violated in the face of "catastrophic moral horror," really is a constrained view. A principle that says "you may not use means m_1, m_2, and m_3, unless H [some circumstance involving imminent horror] obtains" still constrains you as long as H does not obtain, in exactly the same way that the "absolute" version of the principle does. The difference is that there are circumstances (i.e., H) in which one principle will constrain the agent, and the other will not.

Perhaps an example will make the point more compelling. Consider the situation presented in the film and novel *Fail-safe*.[5] As a result of a series of strategic and technological misadventures involving radio communications, jamming devices, and computers, a US Air Force bomber receives an order to destroy Moscow with a hydrogen bomb. It succeeds in doing so, and the world faces the imminent possibility of a nuclear holocaust that would destroy civilization as we know it and, possibly, human life itself. To avoid this, and to convince the Soviets that the attack was simply an accident, the American president (unnamed, but played by Henry Fonda in the movie) orders a similar US attack on New York City. In so doing, he violates the right to life of millions of innocent people, including the First Lady and the wife of the general who drops the bomb (and then commits suicide). Obviously, the reasons the president commits this horrific act are goal-based: Preserving civilization and human life are his goals. But, if he regards the right to life as a constraint that applies to him, his behavior up to that moment will be indistinguishable from that of someone who holds the absolutist view. It is only at that precise moment that it is different.

Resources invested in pursuing any given goal will vary over time as the cost of the pursuit changes. If I have a hobby, I will spend more or less time on it as the cost of doing so varies: Perhaps the price of needed equipment rises or falls, or changing circumstances make it less or more compatible with spending time with my family or doing other things that I value, and so on. On the other hand, if I view the property rights of others as constraints on my conduct, I do not reduce my theft-avoidance as the cost of it (or the benefit I could gain by theft, which is the same thing) rises. Though a cleverly executed act of theft would help in the pursuit of many of my goals, I will simply see it as a means that is not available to me.

Viewing constraints as taking means off the table enables us to see why they are sharply different from goals; also, by enabling us to see that non-absolute constraints are still constraints, it helps to show that viewing constraints as infinitely weighted goals is at best an insufficiently inclusive account, since it cannot include non-absolute constraints. In addition, it offers an explanation for the sharp distinction that constrained agents observe between their own conduct and that of others, even appearing to "prefer" six murders committed by others to one committed by themselves. One way to put it would be this: If preferences are relations between goals, this is not a preference. In my story of the

15

hostage-takers, saving the lives of the hostages is a possible goal we would desperately wish we could pursue, but given the way I structured the situation, there are no permissible means to pursuing it that are available to us.

3. Why Side Constraints?

Nozick attempts a reply to the above question in widely separated sections of Chapter 3. One is the section for which the question actually serves as its title (30–33), and the other is "What Are Constraints Based On?" (48–51). I will bring these two parts of his reply closer together than he does. They gain in interest and power if we note the connections between them.

The former one begins with a deep and difficult question about moral constraints:

> Isn't it irrational to accept a side constraint C, rather than a view that directs the minimization of violations of C? ... If nonviolation of C is so important, shouldn't that be the goal? How can a concern for the nonviolation of C lead to the refusal to violate C even when this would prevent other more extensive violations of C? What is the rationale for placing the nonviolation of rights as a side constraint upon action instead of including it solely as a goal of one's actions? (30)

The same issue is raised pointedly by one of Nozick's critics, Marxist philosopher G. A. Cohen, who asks (rhetorically, since he thinks the question cannot really be answered), "if such sacrifice and violation are so horrendous, why should we not be concerned to minimize their occurrence?"[6] As I have in effect pointed out already, most people, when confronted with a case like my example of the hostage-takers, treat the right to life as a constraint and do not take the occurrence-minimizing approach. They choose a course of action in which there are six rights-violating acts rather than only one. However, the question remains as to how it can be rational, on the part of a person who recognizes the horrendousness of such acts, to choose such a course.

Nozick's attempt to resolve this issue is based not so much on an analysis of constraints as on the subject matter to which side constraints apply. Moral constraints make sense because they are about persons, and persons are special. If we were to drop constraints and use the standard of violation-minimization, we would be working a profound change in the moral status of the human individual: "Side constraints reflect the underlying Kantian principle that individuals are ends and not merely means: They may not be sacrificed or used for the achieving of other ends without their consent. Individuals are inviolable" (30–31).

His most sustained argument for this idea, in the second through fourth paragraphs of "Why Side Constraints?," is interesting, but it is also rather confusing. He begins by inviting us to conduct a thought experiment in which we attempt to transform a tool – "a prime example of a means" – into something other than a tool. First, imagine there is "an overrideable constraint" on a certain tool's use. The two examples he gives both involve the constraint's being overridden by a goal: Perhaps the constraint may not be violated unless the benefit from doing so is above a certain level (in which case that benefit becomes a goal that you may use the tool to pursue), or perhaps you may only violate the constraint in order to pursue a certain goal. In that case, you can still use the tool to pursue your goals, even with respect to the conditions laid down by the constraint, but "the object is not *completely* your tool ...." If we move on to add constraints that cannot be overridden, then, with respect to the uses forbidden by the constraints, it is not a tool at all. Rather oddly, he ends this part of the discussion, not with a conclusion, but with a question: "Can one add enough constraints so that an object cannot be used as a tool at all, in *any* respect?" (31).

The non-tool status of this imaginary tool seems intermittent and patchy. That suggests an obvious answer to Nozick's question: "Sure, we can do that. Just prohibit every use to which the tool could possibly be put." But that would not achieve our present task, which is to figure out how constraints can give *persons* the status of non-tools. People want to be of use to one another. A teacher, for instance, wants to be used as a source of knowledge and skill. One of the features that makes Kant's idea of persons as ends in themselves so fascinating is that it seems plausible and even profound at first look, while on closer examination it is not easy to say what it means in practice without saying something overly broad or just plain silly.

However we decide to work it out, it must not involve ruling out all human use of human beings. Notice the wording of Kant's "Formula of the End in Itself," which Nozick quotes (32): "Act in such a way that you always treat humanity, whether in your own person or in the person of any other, never simply as a means, but always at the same time as an end." His wording, "never simply [or merely, *bloss*] as a means," clearly indicates that some use as a means is ruled out by his principle and some is left in. But how should we say which is which?

17

In the third paragraph of the same section, Nozick introduces a concept that might be a plausible basis for this distinction: the concept of choice. "Can behavior toward a person be constrained," he asks, "so that he is not to be used except as he chooses?" Some principle developed along these lines would seem to fit the example of the teacher I mentioned above. The fact that the teachers choose to be used as a source of knowledge seems to explain why it isn't wrong to use them in that way. However, this idea, if taken quite generally, would seem to require that we not make any particular use of an interaction with a person (such as a good that we get from them) in a way that they disapprove of, or disapprove of so much that they would have refrained from interacting with us had they known of it. Nozick seems to worry that such a principle could be excessively burdensome. "Is it morally incumbent on someone to reveal his intended uses of an interaction if he has good reason to believe the other would refuse to interact if he knew?" (32).

I think the answer to this question is "no." Suppose I am about to sell my watch to you for $40. But I intend to purchase a year's subscription to *Playboy* with the proceeds and I know you are something of a prude. Do I have an obligation to violate my own privacy by warning you that I intend to spend the money on pornography? Unless you know me well, you are liable to regard such a disclosure as rather odd behavior on my part. It is possible to have legitimate moral objections to behavior that violates the sort of principle we are considering here, but the plausibility of the objections depends on various factors not mentioned in the principle. For instance, suppose I intend to donate the money to an organization – say, Planned Parenthood, or the National Rifle Association – and I believe you have an unreasonable and intolerant hatred for the organization. I doubt that I have an obligation to warn you of my plans. More importantly, it isn't very plausible to say that, if I don't divulge this information, I am "just using you." The concept of choice must have a role to play in properly explicating Kant's idea (in fact, I think it does) but this notion of revealing intended uses seems to be the wrong way to bring it in.

Nozick's discussion of this subject is rather messy and at times confusing, but it does sketch out a plausible necessary condition for the status of being an end in oneself and not a mere means. If we suppose that the use of aggressive force – for example, armed robbery – is always a purposeful act, then it does necessarily involve using the victim of the aggressive act as a means to achieve some end. Given that force was used, the end was a purpose of the aggressor and not of the victim.[7] If we hand that one person over to the terrorists, we are using him or her to achieve the goal of saving six other lives. To speak of being used as a mere means is a plausible way to capture at least part of what we would find so horrific about this act of aggression, in spite of the undeniably good end for which our victim would be used.

It is sometimes said that Nozick thinks observing side constraints is *sufficient* for treating individuals as ends in themselves.[8] He does not say that. What he says, quoted above, is that side constraints "reflect" the Kantian idea, a word that falls short of committing him to this strong view. Nor *should* he claim that observing constraints is anything more than a necessary condition of treating persons as ends. Aside from the fact that (as we have seen) there probably are other constraints that prohibit using people, it is impossible to give a plausible account of Kant's idea based on constraints alone. After all, the idea is that people are ends and not, simply, that they are non-means. Treating something as an end has to include positively doing something regarding it, not merely refraining from doing something. The moral status of being an end in oneself means more than that others' treatment of you is subject to side constraints: They must also have positive obligations to you of some sort. This was Kant's view. He thought treating humanity as an end includes accepting positive duties toward them. These are what he called "duties of imperfect obligation," which are obligations, not to do any particular act, but to seek certain goals. They include duties of benevolence toward others.[9] This seems plausible enough. It would be bizarre to claim that we regard you as an end in yourself if we knowingly let you die if you are starving.

This raises an interesting issue, which will be obvious to some people. Considering that the political position Nozick takes in his book rules out not only governmental redistribution of wealth based on ideas of distributive justice, such as egalitarianism, but social safety net programs as well, doesn't this notion of positive obligations create a possible opening for his critics? Could they argue that his highly constrained view of the state only reflects half of the Kantian idea he claims to base it on?

Of course they could. What would he say in reply? There is only one place in ASU where he mentions an idea that is more or less equivalent to Kant's notion of a duty of imperfect obligation, and it consists of a single parenthetical sentence. Commenting on what a goal-directed view with constraints added would be like, he says: "Here, the rights of others would constrain your goal-directed behavior. I do not mean to imply that the correct view includes mandatory goals that must be pursued, even within the constraints" (29). This leaves open the possibility that he might reply to this criticism in the most direct way imaginable: by simply denying this entire category of moral principles.

That would not be a very plausible response, for the reason I just gave, that some such principle seems to be necessary for fleshing out the notion of treating persons as ends. More generally, there are any number of traits that are prized as moral virtues, such as generosity and charity, that necessarily involve trying to bring something about, trying to achieve some goal. Generous acts aim to bring about the good of others, charitable ones aim to help those who need help. Never seeking the relevant goal, and thus completely lacking the virtue, is a moral flaw. But that would mean that the goal is indeed "mandatory" in the sense that it is relevant to ethics. I think this one-sentence comment is simply a mistake on Nozick's part.

A more plausible reply to this criticism, still very Nozickean in spirit, would go something like this: Yes, pursuing certain moral goals is part of what it is to treat humanity as an end. But that by itself does not mean we have a duty, or even a right, to pursue them by any particular means. It depends on which means are used. Acts that aim at the well-being of others are subject to moral constraints, like any other goal-directed activities. I ought to help the needy, but I may not do so by robbing a bank or picking pockets in order to donate the proceeds to them. Morality requires me to help the needy, but its constraints prohibit me from doing so by means of the coercive mechanism of the state.

4. The "Formal Argument"

The last paragraph in the "Why Side Constraints?" section is important. It is also a passage that has been misunderstood by one of Nozick's critics: G. A. Cohen, whom I have already quoted in this chapter. It is illuminating to see why this particular interpretation is a misunderstanding. Here is the relevant passage in ASU:

> Side constraints express the inviolability of persons. But why may not one violate persons for the greater social good? Individually, we each sometimes choose to undergo some pain or sacrifice for a greater benefit or to avoid a greater harm: We go to the dentist to avoid worse suffering later; we do some unpleasant work for its results.... In each case, some cost is borne for the sake of the greater overall good. Why not, *similarly*, hold that some persons have to bear some costs that benefit other persons more, for the sake of the overall social good? But there is no social entity with a good that undergoes some sacrifice for its own good. There are only individual people, different individual people, with their own individual lives. Using

one of these people for the benefit of others, uses him and benefits others. Nothing more. What happens is that something is done to him for the sake of others. Talk of an overall social good covers this up. (32–33)

Cohen, in effect, accuses Nozick of committing a fallacy of equivocation. This passage, he says, is "hard to construe," as it is ambiguous as to which of two completely different arguments it gives, and "anyone who is impressed by it has probably failed to spot the ambiguity." It is unclear whether Nozick is opposing argument A, below, or presenting argument B (or both):

A: since persons compose a social entity relevantly akin to the entity a single person is (p), redistribution across persons is morally permissible (q).
B: since it is false that p, it is false that q.[10]

One's efforts to come to grips with this accusation of Cohen's are complicated a bit by his mistaken belief that this argument is about the redistribution of wealth, a subject Nozick doesn't broach until Chapter 7. As you will soon see, the present argument is directly connected with a more complex one, the "formal argument" named in the index of ASU, which is an argument against the use of aggressive force in general. The proposition labeled q in Cohen's attempted reconstruction of the formal argument, therefore, should state that the aggressive use of force is morally permissible. The denial of this revised proposition is what Nozick calls the "libertarian constraint." With that revision, it can be said that something like A is what Nozick means, except that, in virtue of its role in the formal argument, it eventually is meant to result in the revised conclusion of B – though of course without B's idiotic *non sequitur*.

Nozick presents the formal argument itself with deceptive brevity:

Any underlying notion sufficiently powerful to support moral side constraints against the powerful intuitive force of the end-state maximizing view will suffice to derive a libertarian constraint on aggression against another. Anyone who rejects *that particular* side constraint has three alternatives: (1) he must reject *all* side constraints; (2) he must produce a different explanation of why there are moral side constraints rather than simply a goal-directed maximizing structure, an explanation that doesn't itself entail the libertarian side constraint; or (3) he must accept the strongly put root idea about the separateness of individuals and yet claim that initiating aggression against another is compatible with it. (33–34)

I say the brevity of this quote is deceptive because each step in it stirs up a horde of potential issues. These steps can be paraphrased as a series of choices posed to the reader, with the (according to Nozick) more attractive option in each choice getting us progressively closer to his conclusion:

1. Either (a) there are no side constraints or (b) there are side constraints.

If there are side constraints then

2. Either (a) there is a better explanation of why there are side constraints than the thesis about the distinctness of individuals or (b) the thesis is the best explanation of why there are side constraints.

If one accepts that thesis as the best explanation then

3. Either (a) the thesis is compatible with the use of aggressive force against another or (b) it is incompatible with it.

If one accepts 3(b) then, given that one has accepted the thesis about the separateness of individuals, one must accept the libertarian constraint.

It is by no means impossible to escape from this argument before you reach Nozick's conclusion. He makes a point of indicating what the escape routes are: One can try taking any one of the three alternative options in my reconstruction of the argument. But of course he believes there are serious problems involved in taking any of these three escape routes, some of which he comments on in the text. Let's take a look at these options and the means by which one might hope to take them.

There are a number of well-known moral theories that, should you accept them, would in effect be ways of taking one of these options or another. For instance, one could take option 1(a), the denial of moral constraints, by adopting moral nihilism, which holds that all moral phenomena (not merely side constraints) are illusory. Most of us will not find this a very plausible option.[11] Perhaps a more promising way to deny constraints is act-utilitarianism. This is the idea that what makes an action good is that it maximizes the good of everyone who is affected by it, taken together. In this tradition, there are various ways of understanding what this "good" is, that we are supposed to maximize, but in every case it is something that is determined by subjective states of the individual: What is "good" is getting what one wants, or what one prefers, or what gives one pleasure, and so forth. We can generate other ways to take 1(a) by replacing the utilitarian's goal (aggregate subjective well-being) with some other good thing. An example would be to maximize freedom rather than observe side constraints.[12]

Nozick seems to think of act utilitarianism as the principal available way of taking option 1(a). As we will see, two later sections in Chapter 3 – "Constraints and Animals" and "The Experience Machine" – continue the attack on that theory. The target of the thought experiment of the Experience Machine will be the utilitarian's maximand – the value they seek to maximize. The target of the attack so far, on the other hand, is the formal features it shares with any end-state-maximizing theory. As with several classic objections to utilitarianism, the focus here is on two maneuvers that almost any goal-maximizing ethical theory must carry out. Since morality (on this view) is essentially concerned with deciding between the interests of different people, we must first *aggregate* them, combining the good and bad effects we might have on different people into one sum, and then we must *maximize* – choose the alternative course of action that has the best aggregate result. Aggregating prepares us to sacrifice one individual to another by, so to speak, melting them down into one coagulated mass. It makes the individual effectively invisible to the calculating agent. Then, depending on how the good and bad effects are distributed, the maximizing step is liable to *require* us to sacrifice one individual to another. This of course is where Nozick's "no social entity," argument, the one that Cohen found hard to construe, comes in.

Of all the well-known, frequently discussed ideas in ASU, the core of this argument is probably the only one that is completely unoriginal. It is simply John Rawls' main argument against utilitarianism, a fact that Nozick cheerfully acknowledges in a footnote.[13] What *is* original is the way Nozick applies the core Rawlsian idea to his own purposes. First, he applies it not merely to utilitarianism but to goal-maximizing views in general and, second, he eventually uses it to reach a decidedly un-Rawlsian conclusion.

Rawls' argument has more or less been summarized in passages in ASU that I have already discussed. It is based on a particular diagnosis as to what the intuitive appeal of utilitarianism is: that it consists of applying a powerful conception of rationality to the problem of the nature of morality. Rationality, in individual decision-making, is maximizing expected value. The utilitarian simply applies this principle to social choice (choices made on the basis of their effects on the good of more than one person). The Rawlsian point is that the reason this conception of rationality is so plausible in the first case does not apply to the second. The reason it would be irrational of me to fail to "sacrifice" present comfort and ease for the sake of greater future gain is that the latter, the greater future gain, is simply *net* gain. Strictly speaking, this is not a sacrifice at all. If we deal with the interests of two people by aggregating them and sacrificing one of them to the other, there is (so far) no person for whom this is a net gain. It is a pure gain for one and a pure loss for the other. At this point, the burden of proof is on the utilitarian, to show why we nonetheless should treat these two people as something they are not: a single, super-personal entity that enjoys a net gain. Nozick thinks this argument applies equally to all purely end-state-based views.

In Nozick's hands, this argument has the following somewhat complex function. It argues *for* 1(b) (i.e., side constraints) by arguing *against* what is presumed to be the best reason in favor of end-result views. He takes this to be, in addition, an argument *against* 1(a) (the rejection of side constraints) because he assumes that end-result views are the only way to take option 1(a). Actually, we have seen that this assumption is not true. Moral nihilism, if true, would also justify 1(a). Admittedly, this is an alternative he seems to have overlooked. But, as I have said, it is not an especially plausible or appealing doctrine.

In both of the above respects – what he is arguing for and what he is arguing against – Nozick moves beyond the use that Rawls makes of his argument. What they have in common is the Rawlsian diagnosis of the grounds of the powerful initial plausibility of utilitarianism, that it rests upon the underlying plausibility of applying individual rationality to social choice. There is another element to the argument they have in common, though in Nozick's presentation it is suggested more by his tone than by anything he explicitly says. As I have explained it so far, the argument sounds like a rather technical objection to utilitarianism (and other end-state views). There is another aspect of the argument that most people would find to be, intuitively, more clearly ethical in nature. In explaining why he believes utilitarianism would not be chosen by the contractors in his "original position," Rawls says: "Offhand, it hardly seems likely that persons who view themselves as equals, entitled to press their claims on one another, would agree to a principle which may require lesser life prospects for some simply for the sake of a greater sum of advantages enjoyed by others."[14] Rawls' comment here, about suffering lesser prospects simply for the sake of greater advantages for others – like Nozick's saying that using one person for the benefit of another actually only harms the one and benefits the other, "[n]othing more" – suggests that they both think that the theories to which they are objecting violate a sort of moral equality that they see as existing between persons. What could make it just to sacrifice the interests of one person simply and solely to promote the *interests* of another person? Later in Chapter 3, Nozick considers the possibility that there could be beings on a "higher level" for whose sake our interests can rightly be sacrificed. He points out that some people think God is on that level, so that He may rightly "sacrifice people for his own purposes" (46). Divine attributes might be the sort of thing that could make this moral relationship just. Another possible example would be the status that Aristotle attributed to the state (*polis*), as an entity that is "greater and more divine" than the individual.[15] If Aristotle were correct on that point, that might be sufficient to make it just to sacrifice the interests of the individual for no other reason than to serve the interests of such a "divine" being. People used to think that such a relationship holds between sovereign – prince, king, emperor, and so forth – and subject. Perhaps Rawls and Nozick are thinking that in order for obligatory sacrifice to be just, the beneficiary would have to be better than the one sacrificed, and better moreover in the right way. We no longer believe that human agents are related in this way. (Perhaps utilitarianism is a survival of the old ethic of sacrifice, which is grounded in reverence for beings with divine attributes and a hunger for sacrifices, but uprooted from the hierarchical world-view it needs in order to really make sense. Or perhaps it is rooted in the idea that human groups really are divine, like Aristotle's *polis*, just because they are groups.)

Of course, one might accept that there are side constraints and yet attempt to reject the "no social entity" explanation of them altogether. This brings us to 2(a) and (b). Is there a better explanation of constraints than the Rawls/Nozick one? Clearly, there are alternatives. For centuries, a common ethical view was the Divine Command Theory. Applied to constraints, it would imply that constraints are simply laws enacted by God Himself, and they are backed by His unanswerable authority. This would explain why constraints seem so difficult to override. I may not commit robbery, even if I would gain enormously by it, and even if I value my loot more than my victims would. Why not? Because, for whatever reason, God forbids robbery. Kant claimed that we reap a similar advantage if we explain constraints as the laws that are enacted by Pure Practical Reason itself, independently of desires and sensory experience. Needless to say, both these theories bring with them problems of their own.

Another theory that would result in taking 2(a) is rule-utilitarianism. This is the idea that we should use the utilitarian principle, but only to select moral rules: those rules that, if generally followed, would produce better results than alternative rules would produce. Since some of these rules presumably would deny us various means and methods – committing theft, fraud, murder, and so forth – which might advance some goal of ours, the rule-utilitarian clearly accepts side constraints. On the other hand, since they are involved in aggregating and maximizing, rule-utilitarians will not be able to use the "no social entity" explanation of why there are such things as side constraints. There is a problem with rule-utilitarianism, though: By itself, it does not provide an alternative explanation. Rather it commits rule-utilitarians to finding one, if they can.[16] It does, however, indicate that there are theorists who will want to take route 2(a).

Of course, if none of these options are attractive, there is still 3(a), accepting the "no social entity" explanation but denying the libertarian constraint. Who might we expect to take this route? There is one theory whose adherents would clearly do so. Given that Nozick's argument is an extension of Rawls' criticism of utilitarianism, it is clear that he and his many followers (at least those who agree with this criticism) are committed to something like 3(a). Admittedly, Rawls' objection to utilitarianism is just that, and not an explanation of why there are side constraints, but clearly Nozick would be able to raise essentially the same objection to Rawls' position that he would raise against someone who did try to take 3(a): As he sees it, the initiation of coercion exhibits the very feature for which Rawls faults utilitarianism.

In effect, Nozick holds that Rawls' objection to utilitarianism is a slippery slope that leads to libertarianism. The bottom of that slippery slope is a place to which Rawls has no wish to go. Perhaps the most Rawlsian response to this threat would be to rely on a distinction that Rawls uses in other contexts, one that is closely related to Nozick's distinction between goals and constraints. This is the distinction between the right and the good. One might agree that it actually is wrong to use force against someone in order to achieve a greater social *good*, but claim that coercion based on a legitimate principle of justice does not belong in that category at all. Rather than achieving some positive good, one is correcting or preventing something that is wrong – in other words, trying to bring about an arrangement that is right.[17] This principle of justice is quite different from Nozick's, which he presents in Chapter 7 of ASU. Needless to say, we will discuss Nocick's view later.

The formal argument is not a knock-down proof of Nozick's position, nor is it meant to be. It is, however, interesting, original, and worth thinking about. It also represents at least a move in the direction of putting foundations under his ethical position. I now turn to a section of Chapter 3 that moves further in this direction.

5.   What Are Constraints Based On?

For me, the section with the above title is probably the most profound in the book. In it, Nozick attacks one of the toughest issues in ethics: In virtue of precisely what characteristics of persons are there moral constraints on how they may treat each other or be treated?

He lists features that, according to one traditional proposal or another, are supposed to answer this question: (1) sentience and self-consciousness, (2) rationality (the capacity to use abstract concepts), (3) possessing free will, (4) being a moral agent (having the capacity to follow moral principles), and (5) having a soul. With the possible exception of that last item on the list, he faults them all for failing to meet a requirement that he thinks any theory of this sort must meet:

> It would appear that a person's characteristics, by virtue of which others are constrained in their treatment of him, must themselves be valuable characteristics. How else are we to understand why something so valuable emerges from them? (This natural assumption is worth further scrutiny.) (48)

At first sight, the "natural assumption" does not seem intuitively appealing. Why can good things only be explained by other good things? Perhaps he means that the characteristic we seek must be valuable in order to explain why it results in such a *transfer* of value from the rest of us to that person. Respecting the rights of others means forgoing many opportunities to advance one's own goals. This simple fact poses a general problem that any theory of moral constraints must also eventually face, one that he has already raised, in a certain way, earlier in the third chapter of ASU: Why is it rational to accept constraints at all?

As Nozick points out in a later book, *The Nature of Rationality*, during the twentieth century there were great advances in our theoretical understanding of "individual rationality and rational interactions among people" in such technical fields as "decision theory, game theory, probability theory, and theories of statistical inference."[18] I would add microeconomics to this list, and the branch of economics known as "value theory." Generally, the conception of rationality involved in these fields of investigation amounts to seeing it as maximizing (or optimizing or satisficing) the expected value of the results of one's actions. Though they do not rest on single-goal theories like old-fashioned hedonism and classical utilitarianism, they are in effect goal-based, in that they see rationality as a function of the expected value of goals that are achieved by one's actions. This means that, according to the best, most powerful theories of rationality available to us, to knowingly forgo an action that would produce more net value than any alternative action is simply irrational. But if one accepts a side constraint, one will sooner or later be doing precisely that. One would expect that a principle that puts methods and means to achieving goals out of one's reach would eventually mean that one achieves less of them. How can this be rational?

Note that his treatment of the problem of the rationality of constraints earlier in the third chapter of ASU does not help us with this present problem. There he was concerned with the claim of the utilitarian and other theorists with similar views to represent collective rationality in rejecting constraints: They are maximizing collective well-being. Nozick's response, like that of Rawls, was that there is no collective being that enjoys this well-being. Here, the problem is with the individual agent's individual well-being. How can it be rational for *me* to follow moral constraints if this means forgoing greater achievement of what *I* regard as good? I think Nozick's discussion in the current section of ASU can be read as an answer, at least a partial one, to that question.

The problem standing in our way is that constrained behavior seems to mean forgoing value. What he does here is to sketch out an account of something valuable to which constraints have a positive relationship. I would like to suggest that, though he does not deal with the issue of rationality directly and explicitly here, things that he does say can help reduce the urgency of that problem.

The outlines of his view are set out clearly enough. What we need is "an intervening variable M" for which the features in the above list constitute necessary conditions. Actually, in his discussion of this issue, he focuses on (2) through (4) – rationality, free will, and moral agency. He brings the soul (item 5) back into the discussion in a way that gives it a different status from the other features, while sentience (number 1) for some reason drops out of the picture (one could say that it is addressed late, in the section on animals). While being based in some way on these features, M must also have a "perspicuous and convincing" connection to constraints, so that it illuminates constraints and the features on which they allegedly are based (49).

These three features, he says, unite to form another important feature of persons: the capacity to form long-term plans and to guide one's life on the basis of a chosen overall conception of it. The moral importance of this feature, he says, is to be found in the fact that a "person's shaping his life in accordance with some overall plan is his way of giving meaning to his life" (50). He explicitly leaves open the question of whether these two features are identical (i.e., whether meaning simply is having a plan) or whether long-term planning is merely a necessary condition of the creation of meaning. He also leaves open the question of which of the two features is supposed to be M, or whether they both are. He ends by raising questions about how meaning is related to the content of moral constraints. Is it that the behavior that violates a person's rights is incompatible with their having a meaningful life? Or should we construct something like utilitarianism, but with meaningfulness as the maximand instead of happiness? Or does the notion of meaning enter ethics, as he says, "in a different fashion" (50) – apparently meaning some fashion other than determining the content of the moral constraints?

He is sometimes misunderstood on this point.[19] He is not saying we can derive ethical content from the notion of a meaningful life. This, however, leaves the point of this section of ASU somewhat obscure. It seems clear enough that he wants M to explain constraints. But if it doesn't explain their content, just how does it explain them? I suggest that it might shed explanatory light on the rationality of having constraints at all. This possibility becomes a little more apparent if we consider something that Nozick does not seem to notice: There are other candidates for M in the history of ethics. Interestingly, they tend to have certain characteristics in common.

First, recall the criteria for M that Nozick has laid down. There are of course the two I have already mentioned, that the items on the traditional list of features (at least the three that get the focus of his attention) should be necessary for M, and that M should shed some sort of explanatory light on constraints. In addition, he says that due to the fact that M, whatever it is, satisfies the first criterion, it should also help to explain why people have traditionally "concentrated on" these features (49). He also mentions, as an interesting characteristic of his own version of M, that it has the "feel" of something that might help to bridge the gap between "is" and "ought," as it seems to "straddle" the boundary between them. He does not lay this down explicitly as a characteristic that M must have but it makes sense to suppose that it is, given that constraints are "oughts" and the traditional features they are supposed to be based on seem to be pure "ises."

One philosopher who has explicitly argued that there is a certain trait of persons that meets most of Nozick's criteria is Immanuel Kant. This is hardly surprising, as Nozick's ethical views in ASU are, as I have said, in the Kantian tradition. However, Kant's version of M is interestingly different from that of Nozick. Kant's version of M, the all-important characteristic, is that of being a source of the moral law. More precisely,

Kant thought that the moral law springs from pure reason and that each person is an instance of "rational nature." Kant argues, explicitly and profoundly, that rationality, free will, and moral agency (in Nozick's sense) are necessary components of the trait that gives one this special status. In addition, it is at least arguable that Kant's notion of Pure Practical Reason can explain why people think these features are ethically important, and also that it straddles the is/ought divide. As to the light it might shed on constraints, I will get to that in a moment.

Some might wonder at this point if M-traits are, so to speak, "for Kantians only," that they only have any point within the framework of a more or less Kantian moral theory. I would say that their application and relevance is much wider than that. I think one can easily sketch out another example, a theory that is a good deal more naturalistic than those of Nozick and Kant. This view seems to me to be more or less in the spirit of some of the arguments that John Locke gives in favor of property rights.[20] Humans, unlike all other animals, must produce the wherewithal to live. Other animals live by consuming portions of their environment. The deer consumes grass, and the wolf pack consumes the deer. Even the hunter-gatherer way of life, the closest human life comes to the pure consumption way of life of other animals, involves producing weapons, tools, clothing, and shelter. With the advent of agriculture, humans turned to producing their food as well. Radically altering their environment, they constantly respond to unforeseen effects. Rather than respond to the same situations in the same way, or with a finite repertory of behavioral responses, as other animals do, they constantly develop new and better solutions to problems. In other words, they do not merely react to the environment (which is to a large extent their own creation), they have ideas about it and develop new ideas. Because all this effort aims at producing things to be used by human beings in their efforts to survive and flourish, it results in material that is indeed very valuable to humans, sometimes large masses of such material. This attracts the attention of human predators who would live off the productive efforts of others. That of course threatens productivity itself, which requires social cooperation of increasingly complex sorts. But humans have long had a crucial part of the solution to this problem, or this productivity would never have reached this level in the first place: There are norms protecting the productive against predators and enabling the social cooperation that productivity requires. Many of these norms are constraints.

These three versions of M differ in important ways. Kant's version, unlike Nozick's and that of the neo-Lockean I have imagined, carries heavy metaphysical baggage. The neo-Lockean's and Kant's versions of

M have implications as to the content of the constraints, while that of Nozick probably does not. One thing I think they all have in common is the explanatory light they can shed on moral constraints. The sort of illumination I have in mind is of a very particular sort. Notice that each of them attributes a sort of value to persons. The characteristics they attribute to persons – giving meaning to things, being a law-giver, being a creator – are all attributes that traditionally belong to the divine. I would not want to lean on this point too hard, but it does suggest something about the kind of value we are attributing to M-beings. This is not the sort of value that one has as a means to an end. It is not a matter of the uses that the being might serve but rather of what attitudes are appropriate toward it. Traditionally, the attitudes appropriate toward the divine include reverence and worship. The idea of reverencing or worshiping persons, simply as persons, seems crazy (though Auguste Comte did advocate a Religion of Humanity). However, there are other attitudes that might be appropriate to a being that possesses only a mere touch of divinity, such as respect. Respect (*Achtung*) was in fact Kant's word for the attitude he believed was appropriate to beings with his version of M.

What could this have to do with the problem of the rationality of constraints? Notice that there is an aspect of the problem that really is an issue about the appropriateness of attitudes. The general problem about the rationality of constraints rests on the fact that constraints are obstacles to achieving our goals. If you consistently conform to a constraint then, sooner or later, and perhaps very often, there will be some increment of value that you will not achieve, but could have achieved if you had violated the constraint. This is an issue about the rationality of action, and it is the sort of rationality that the value-maximizing conception of rationality is about. But actions are not the only sort of thing that can be rational or irrational. We can question whether it is rational to fear bats, to love people who do not love us in return, or to hope for resurrection and eternal life. These questions are not directly about action. They are about attitudes. In particular, they are about whether a given attitude is appropriate to its object.

The attitude-appropriateness issue, where side constraints are concerned, is based on the fact that, though it is true that side constraints such as individual rights are obstacles to achieving one's goals, that is not how a morally decent person sees them.[21] Suppose that I see you have unknowingly dropped a $50 bill, which I could easily pick up undetected and walk away with. Instead, I hand it to you. I could have spent it on things that I value, but I forgo whatever good I would thereby have reaped because such behavior would violate your rights. Yet if I am a moral person, I do not at that moment perceive your rights as obstacles to my achieving good things.

You might think that this is a truth about constraints and not about M-beings, such as persons. One might object that decent people never see constraints as frustrating obstacles. But that is not true. Imagine that you are driving to work, worried that you might arrive late, and a traffic signal turns yellow, then red just a shade too early for you to slip through the intersection. You might well feel that you have confronted an annoying obstacle to achieving one of your goals. This is so, despite the fact that you recognize that you mustn't cross against a red light – in fact, it is *because* of this very fact, since your recognition of this constraint is precisely the obstacle you face. Yet it is hard to imagine looking at the rights of persons in this way, though, in a sense, they are obstacles of the same sort. Persons and traffic signals are alike in that both represent to us constraints on our conduct, but they are also profoundly different. The various versions of M offer explanations of the difference. Each can be used as a basis for attributing to persons the peculiar sort of value that Kant called "dignity," while denying it to a mere mechanism such as a traffic signal. Individual rights can be seen as imposing costs on us, but human beings, as we see it, are *worth it*; so much so that we do not see these effects as costs at all.

Perhaps the general problem of the rationality of constraints can be solved by connecting the problem about the rationality of constrained action with the other sort of rationality, the rationality of attitude-appropriateness. If one has a certain attitude, considerations can make reasons for action seem plausible though they do not appear from another perspective to be reasons at all. From the perspective of the value-maximizing conception of rationality, constraints do not make sense as reasons for action. From the perspective of respect for persons grounded on some version of M, they do. Perhaps a solid case for the rationality of that attitude can solve, or *dis*solve, the problem of the rationality of constraints.

Nozick's discussion of M opens an area that deserves further exploration.

6. **Constraints and Animals**

Unlike some of the digressions in ASU, the section with the above title (35–42) begins with a perfectly good explanation as to why it is there. Its purpose is to "illuminate the status and implications of moral side constraints" (35). Nozick does so by setting forth a view that he dubs with the very rough but catchy label "utilitarianism for animals, Kantianism for people." Also, as he points out (39–40), this principle supplements Kantianism and other stringently constrained ethical views in a way that makes them more plausible: If such constraints are the whole of one's moral point of view then, since they do not seem to apply to non-human animals (notice that none of the versions of M we considered apply to them), they would seem to leave animals out in the moral cold, so that we may treat them in any way we please. He introduces a third moral status, between persons and mere things, which we may not treat in just any way we wish, though they have no rights.

In addition, I would suggest that this section advances other goals of his as well. In an indirect sort of way, it advances his attack on utilitarianism. In arguing that a modified form of utilitarianism is a high enough standard to suit animals, he enhances the plausibility of his claim that it is not high enough a standard – that is, not constraining enough – to govern our treatment of people. Utilitarianism is, so to speak, unfit for human consumption. At the same time, consideration of what an unconstrained morality, even one as humane as this one, would still permit us to do to animals enhances the plausibility of stringently constrained moralities (for people) such as his.

He introduces the "utilitarianism for animals" position as a sort of conclusion from a case he makes for vegetarianism. As with the "formal argument" for the libertarian constraint, the case he makes takes the form of a challenge directed at the reader. If you cannot successfully respond to the challenge, he believes, you (so far) have no good-enough justification for eating animals. I believe that any omnivore (such as myself) should admit that this challenge is not easy to meet. Here it is:

> Suppose (as I believe the evidence supports) that eating animals is not necessary for health and is not less expensive than alternative equally healthy diets available to people in the United States. The gain, then, from the eating of animals is pleasures of the palate, gustatory delights, varied tastes. I would not claim that these are not truly pleasant, delightful, and interesting. The question is: do they, or rather does the marginal addition in them gained by eating animals rather than only nonanimals, outweigh the moral weight to be given to animals' lives and pain? Given that animals are to count for something, is the extra gain obtained by eating them rather than nonanimal products greater than the moral cost? How might these questions be decided? (36–37)

He invites us to decide this question by considering the following analogy:

> Suppose then that I enjoy swinging a baseball bat. It happens that in front of the only place to swing it stands a cow. Swinging the bat unfortunately would involve smashing the cow's head. But I wouldn't get fun from doing that; the pleasure comes from exercising my muscles, swinging well, and so on. ... Is there some principle that would allow the killing and eating of animals, but would not allow swinging the bat for the extra pleasure it brings? (37)

In effect, he is asking us to fill in the blank in the following principle: *One may kill animals in order to provide _____ for humans.* The challenge is to do this in a way that permits the eating of animals but would not permit swinging the bat.

He assumes, plausibly enough, that this involves finding some increment of good (for humans) that is sufficient to offset the increment of bad, for animals, of holding them in captivity and killing them. Once you accept this, you have committed yourself to treating the moral problem of eating animals purely in terms of cost-effectiveness. That, in fact, is how the utilitarian sees *all* moral problems. Of course, you are not committed to full utilitarianism as a standard for the treatment of animals: You are not committed, positively, to maximizing the good of all the animals that are affected by what you do. But then, as he says, the "utilitarianism for animals" that Nozick is urging on us is really only "negative utilitarianism"; "animals may be used or sacrificed for the benefit of other people or animals *only if* those benefits are greater than the loss inflicted" (39). It does not mandate the maximizing of value; it merely forbids certain net decreases. In addition, the "Kantianism for people" part of the doctrine forbids using or sacrificing human beings for the good of others quite generally.[22]

This position differs profoundly from arguments for vegetarianism that attribute rights to non-human animals.[23] Unlike most such accounts, it might well allow the use of animals in medical research. That is because it does allow us to sacrifice animals for the good of human beings, merely requiring that the expected benefit be sufficient to offset the cost. (It would also prohibit as immoral experiments that do not have sufficiently good expected results.) By the same token, it also allows sacrificing animals for the good of other animals. It might permit people to shoot and kill a certain number of deer on the grounds that if approximately that number are not shot, the deer will deplete their winter food supply, with greater suffering and loss of animal life later on. It makes utilitarian sense to treat them this way, and to think of such a policy as an ethical and humane one, though we would be horrified at the thought of applying it to human beings. Nozick's position seems to have fewer counter-intuitive implications than many other arguments against eating animals.

Yet negative utilitarianism for animals does seem to be flawed, as Nozick acknowledges. In introducing the idea, he describes it as "too minimal" (39). What he doubtless has in mind here is the sort of difficulties he raises at the end of the section (40–42). Perhaps the most interesting of these is the possibility that this idea raises in a new form the difficulty of "utility monsters": "Utilitarian theory is embarrassed by the possibility of utility monsters who get enormously greater gains in utility from any sacrifice of others than these others lose" (41). The problem is not that such beings exist, but that the theory seems to require that, if they did exist, they should get what they want when their interests conflict with those of others – and the fact that they happen to be wired in such a way that they get more utility out of life does not seem to be a very good reason why they should get their way. In relation to animals, humans may for all we know constitute a real world case of a utility monster, with a far greater capacity to enjoy life than cows and chickens and a resulting "right" to impose correspondingly great costs on them. There may well be reasons to place more weight on the interests of humans than on those of other animals (e.g., some acceptable version of M might have this implication), but this does not seem to be one of them.

Nozick's version of utilitarianism for animals is (so far) open to this objection because, as he has formulated it, the standard is quantitative: Animals may be used for the benefit of others only if the benefits are *greater* than the loss inflicted. I would also maintain that this feature of the principle raises the additional problem that is in a way the opposite of the problem of the "utility monsters": In addition to being too hard on animals, it might also be too hard on people. Though he tries to avoid giving animals "the same moral weight as people" (38), this principle seems to do just that. After all, if it prohibits me from deriving utility from my treatment of a chicken if I thereby impose a marginally greater disutility on the chicken, it puts me and the chicken on exactly the same moral footing. This really seems to give the chicken too much.

As I have said, the root of these problems seems to be the purely quantitative approach Nozick's principle takes toward comparing harms and benefits to animals with harms and benefits to people. To be fair, he does seem to suggest that utilitarianism, at least "thoroughgoing utilitarianism" (for animals *and* for people, combined in one group), runs into the excessive lenience problem, and for the same reason that I have just alleged his principle does, when he says that it is committed to ruling that

> we may inflict some suffering on a person to avoid (slightly) greater suffering of an animal. This permissive principle seems to me to be unacceptably strong, even when the purpose is to avoid greater suffering to a person! (41)

If he recognizes that narrowly focusing on quantity causes an undue leveling of the relative positions of animals and people in the case of such "thoroughgoing" utilitarianism, perhaps it would not be a great violation of the spirit of his discussion to modify his principle in some relevant way.

Rather than saying that the benefits to humans should be *greater* than the harm to animals, it should require that they be *sufficient* to justify it. One way to spell out such a revised principle would be to introduce weighting. Rather than considering the mere quantity of a given factor, we can give different weights to different factors. For instance, we might give the interests of humans a greater weight than those of other animals (perhaps because humans have M). This revision is a more or less friendly amendment, given that it is suggested by one of his own comments. But it obviously threatens to undermine the argument against eating animals. If we may weight the pleasures of humans more than those of animals, would it make sense to weight them so heavily that the argument collapses?

Perhaps it would, at least if we combine this revision with another idea about pleasure, which we can borrow from John Stuart Mill. I have in mind Mill's notion of higher and lower pleasures. This is the idea that some pleasures (like solving philosophical problems) are better than others (such as relieving an itch by scratching it), and that this way of being better is independent of the intensity of the sensations involved.[24] I believe this idea, especially if we combine it with the idea of weighting humans more than animals, opens an avenue of resistance to Nozick's argument against humans eating animals. At first, this might sound like an absurd claim, since the pleasures of eating and drinking seem to be paradigms of "lower" pleasures. But if they are indeed low, how low are they? To take an extreme case, is the pleasure of a meal of expertly prepared Peking Duck really comparable to that of swinging a bat? Obviously, it is preferable to it, but that is not my point. Is there a relevant qualitative difference? If there is, that opens the possibility of answering Nozick's filling-the-blank question in a way that permits the eating of Peking Duck but would not permit killing his cow.

Notes

1 See John Locke, *Second Treatise of Government* (Indianapolis, Indiana: Hackett Publishing Company, 1980 [orig. pub. 1690]), Ch. 5, especially sect. 28.

2 This is a point on which I think Nozick would disagree with Michael Huemer. In Huemer's *The Problem of Political Authority: An Examination of the Right to Coerce and the Duty to Obey* (Basingstoke, England: Palgrave MacMillan, 2012), he reaches normative political conclusions roughly similar to Nozick's libertarianism, but regards his argument as superior because while Nozick's is based on the controversial theory of natural rights, his own is based on common-sense moral judgments (*The Problem of Political Authority*, p. 176). Nozick would probably deny this distinction. Natural rights, in the sense that Nozick does assume we have them, are simply rights that are neither gifts of the state nor created by contract. As such, they are precisely the sorts of rights that ordinary common-sense morality assumes.

3 Thomas Nagel, "Libertarianism without Foundations," *The Yale Law Journal*, vol. 85 (1975), pp. 136–149.

4 Jan Narveson, *The Libertarian Idea* (Philadelphia, Pennsylvania: Temple University Press, 1988), p. 54. Oddly enough, Narveson presents passages from ASU that do not fit his absolutist interpretation, including the remark I just quoted from the footnote on pp. 29–30 - and presents them as evidence that Nozick "doesn't really believe" his own doctrine! I have a simpler and more plausible hypothesis: *that this is not his doctrine.*

5 Eugene Burdick and Harvey Wheeler, *Fail-safe* (New York: McGraw-Hill, 1962).

6 G. A. Cohen, *Self-Ownership, Freedom, and Equality* (Cambridge, England: Cambridge University Press, 1995), p. 32.

7 There seem to be exceptions to the claim I am implicitly making here, that the fact that force is used shows that the purpose of the act is a purpose of the agent and not of the victim. Suppose that I see you are about to unknowingly step on to a rickety structure, which would surely result in a fatal fall, and the only way I can save you is to lay hands on you and pull you back. This is clearly a use of force, and yet the purpose, your avoiding a fatal fall, is a goal of yours as well as mine. Probably a fully worked-out theory of aggression should find a way to exclude such cases as not really being cases of aggression at all.

8 For instance: "What Nozick has argued is that respecting individuals' rights is *precisely what it means* to treat them as ends. ... Rights are 'side constraints,' inescapable restrictions on the actions others may take toward the rightsholder that are necessary to protect the rightsholder's autonomy" (emphasis added). John Hasnas, "From Cannibalism to Caesareans: Two Concepts of Fundamental Rights," *Northwestern University Law Review*, vol. 89, no. 3 (1994–1995), pp. 914–915.

9 See Immanuel Kant, *The Metaphysical Principles of Virtue: Part II of the Metaphysics of Morals*, trans. James Ellington (Indianapolis, Indiana: Bobbs-Merrill, 1963), *passim.*

10 Cohen, *Self-Ownership*, p. 33.

11 But not all of us. See J. L. Mackie, *Ethics: Inventing Right and Wrong* (Harmondsworth, England: Penguin, 1977) and Richard Joyce, *The Myth of Morality* (Cambridge, England: Cambridge University Press, 2001).

12 This route is suggested by some of Cohen's criticisms of Nozick. He describes side constraints, apparently meaning *any* side constraints, as "unjustified" (Cohen, *Self-Ownership*, p. 33). He also faults Nozick (p. 33) for endorsing side constraints even when violating them would increase the total sum of freedom enjoyed by everyone, as if this involves some obvious contradiction.

13 He refers us to John Rawls, *A Theory of Justice* (Cambridge, Massachusetts: Harvard University Press, 1971), sects. 5, 6, and 30. These sections are relevant to understanding Nozick's argument here and are very much worth reading in their own right.

14 Rawls, *A Theory of Justice*, p. 14.

15 See Aristotle, *Nicomachean Ethics*, Book I, Ch. 2, 1094b7–10.

16 For a classic argument to the effect that the rule-utilitarianism's commitment to side constraints is actually incompatible with its utilitarianism, see David Lyons, *Forms and Limits of Utilitarianism* (Oxford, England, and New York: Oxford University Press, 1965).

17 In Rawls' theory, the distribution of goods is not regarded as a further good, whose value is to be maximized, but as a matter of right and wrong: "The problem of distribution," he says, "falls under the concept of right as one intuitively understands it...." *A Theory of Justice*, p. 25.

18 Robert Nozick, *The Nature of Rationality* (Princeton, New Jersey: Princeton University Press, 1993), pp. xv–xvi.

19 Jan Narveson attributes to him the idea that a being with feature M "would just obviously accord libertarian rights to all other M-beings." Even if we correct the "would" in this quotation to a more plausible "would thereby be obligated to," it still is not Nozick's position. Narveson also tells us the M stands for "Meaningfulness." Actually, Nozick never tells us what M is short for, if anything. Since its function is to mediate between two other variables, perhaps it stands for "mediation," or "middle." *The Libertarian Idea*, p. 167.

20 Locke, *Second Treatise of Government*, Ch. 5. Though I have no reason to insist on this point, the view I go on to sketch out here might be attributed to the novelist-philosopher Ayn Rand. See her *The Virtue of Selfishness: A New Concept of Egoism* (New York: Signet, 1964), Ch. 1, "The Objectivist Ethics" (esp. pp. 36–37), Ch. 12, "Man's Rights" (esp. pp. 108–115), and Ch. 14, "The Nature of Government" (esp. pp. 126–127). See also her *Capitalism: The Unknown Ideal* (New York: Signet, 1967), Ch. 1, "What Is Capitalism?" (esp. pp. 18–20).

21 I discuss this phenomenon more elaborately in *Character and Culture* (Lanham, Maryland: Rowman and Littlefield, 1997), pp. 171–175.

22 Does utilitarianism for animals fit into the goal/constraint distinction? Goal-based views typically require that one maximize the value of goals achieved, while the view presently under consideration does not include such a requirement. One might make it fit nonetheless in a not-too-gimmicky way, by expanding somewhat one's notion of what a goal-based view is, and then breaking "utilitarianism for animals" down into a goal-based component and a constraint-based one. After all, a view can in principle still be goal-based after the requirement of maximization is dropped. One might aim at achieving value that is great enough, rather than as great as possible, "satisficing" rather than maximizing. What distinguishes a pure goal-based view is that its standard can be explicated entirely in terms of the goodness or badness of results achieved. That is what a satisficing standard does. It says, at least strive to do something *this* good. Nozick's negative utilitarianism for animals is just one more step further removed from maximization. It is concerned with avoiding making things, on balance, worse (in a certain way). However, it is still is, in the same sense, a goal-based view. So far, it can be explicated entirely in terms of the goodness or badness of results achieved. Perhaps the only thing that needs to be added is that the principle constrains you from making things worse (in this way). Thus interpreted, negative utilitarianism for animals is a compound view, consisting of a goal-based element combined with a constraint, and so not a third sort of principle.

23 See Tom Regan, *The Case for Animal Rights* (Berkeley, California: University of California Press, 2004).

24 See John Stuart Mill, *Utilitarianism*, in Marshall Cohen, ed., *The Philosophy of John Stuart Mill: Ethical, Political and Religious* (New York: The Modern Library, 1961 [orig. pub. 1863]), pp. 331–333. It is sometimes said that Mill is being inconsistent here. He holds the doctrine of ethical hedonism, the doctrine that the only thing that makes anything good is pleasure. If that is true, the only thing that can make one pleasure better than another is that it is more pleasant. If there is some quality that a pleasure has other than that of being a pleasure, which makes it better than some other pleasure, then that quality is something, other than pleasure, that can make things good, and hedonism is consequently false. I believe this objection is sound, but it doesn't affect you or me unless we hold the doctrine of hedonism (which in my case, I don't). If not, then, unlike Mill, we have a perfect right to use his idea of qualitatively higher and lower pleasures.

3

The Experience Machine

1. What Is the Argument Here?

The section titled "The Experience Machine" may well be the most frequently reprinted, cited, and discussed four paragraphs in ASU. The author himself returned to their central topic – the thought experiment of the experience machine – for a sustained discussion two more times.[1] Yet they are something of a mystery. For one thing, it is not clear how they are connected with the argument of the rest of the book (the reason Nozick *gives*, at 42, for including it in the book seems rather forced, more a pretext than a reason). For another, though it is clear that he is arguing against a point of view in this section, there is considerable disagreement among commentators as to what exactly the target of his critique is. Is it meant as a criticism of utilitarianism? Or hedonism? And if the target is hedonism, is it ethical hedonism (the only ultimate reason that something is good is that it produces the best available balance of pleasure over pain) or psychological hedonism (as a matter of fact, such a balance of pleasure over pain is the reason we *actually* regard things as good).[2] Perhaps it is psychological egoism (which is like psychological hedonism, except that one's own well-being replaces pleasure over pain). Again, he might be taking aim at what might be called ethical eudaemonism, or the idea that happiness (conceived as a psychological state) is the same thing as welfare – that is, well-being.[3] Or he might be attacking psychological eudaemonism.[4,5]

All of the above interpretations have been stated or assumed by critics and commentators at one point or another.[6] However, most of them are pretty clearly incorrect. One thing that might at least give us pause before

Anarchy, State, and Utopia: An Advanced Guide, First Edition. Lester H. Hunt.
© 2015 John Wiley & Sons, Inc. Published 2015 by John Wiley & Sons, Inc.

accepting most of them is that they rely on concepts – including utilitarianism, hedonism, pleasure, pain, egoism, self-interest, and happiness – that are never mentioned in these four paragraphs. No doubt what these critics and commentators are thinking is that though their concept is not explicitly mentioned in the text, it is necessarily involved in some less direct way in the logic of what Nozick actually does say. We can see that this also is incorrect (though a couple of these ideas do come close to the mark) by taking a close look at the text.

He introduces the thought experiment in the context of a question he has raised at the end of the section on animals: If utilitarianism is not a suitable principle to apply to our treatment of people, is it "at least adequate for animals"? He thinks not, because this would mean that "only animals' felt experiences are relevant." This is what the classic forms of utilitarianism tell us to maximize the value of. Just what this relevance he is talking about here amounts to becomes a little clearer when he drops the question about animals and applies the same question to people: "There are also substantial puzzles," he says, "when we ask what matters other than *people's* experiences" (42). The phrase "what matters" is still not crystal clear, but it does strongly suggest something that he does make clearer later, in his book *The Examined Life*: The question he intends to raise here is "a question of value" – a question of what things are good or the best.[7] Immediately after the question of people's experiences comes the oft-quoted description of the thought experiment:

> Suppose there were an experience machine that would give you any experience you desired. Superduper neuropsychologists could stimulate your brain so that you would think and feel you were writing a great novel, or making a friend, or reading an interesting book.

He then tosses this question at the reader: "Should you plug into this machine for life, preprogramming your life's experiences?"[8]

I think his wording here is in one respect perfectly straightforward. The question he is raising has to do with whether the quality of our experiences, as experiences, is sufficient to make a life a good one, one that is worth living. He takes it for granted that one would not plug into the machine, and he believes that this shows that the answer to his question is "no." Given that pleasure and pain are two of the many experiences we have, it follows that hedonism of some sort is one of the views that stand in the line of fire here.[9] Historically, hedonism is the most common member of the family of views that are under attack here, but there are others. The view that I have called ethical eudaemonism is also part of his target. Nozick's real aim here is to attack what might be called mental state theories of welfare: the view that well-being, or the good life, can be *fully* explicated in terms of the experiences it contains.[10]

Some of the incorrect interpretations might be at least partly Nozick's fault, as they may be influenced by a certain ambiguity in the text itself. When he introduces his question, it is worded in terms of "what matters," but thereafter he repeatedly speaks in terms of what matters *to us*. The former wording suggests he is talking about what is objectively good, while the latter suggests that he is talking about what, as a matter of psychological fact, we regard as good. Similarly, when he first tosses his direct question at the reader, he asks "[s]*hould* you plug into this machine ...?" but later phrases the question as "[*w*]*ould* you plug in?" (emphasis added in both cases). This seems to involve the same ambiguity. Thus it is ambiguous whether his target includes views like ethical hedonism and ethical eudaemonism, or whether it is aimed at the psychological versions of these doctrines. A similar point cannot be made about ethical and psychological egoism.

I can find no convincing way to resolve this ambiguity on the basis of the text of this section. Fortunately, though, we do not need to do so, because Nozick later, in *The Examined Life*, clarified what he meant:

> Notice that I am not saying simply that since we desire connection with actuality the experience machine is defective because it does not give us whatever we desire ... for that would make "getting whatever you desire" the primary standard. Rather, I am saying that the connection to actuality is important whether or not we desire it – that is why we desire it – and the experience machine is inadequate because it doesn't give us *that*.[11]

Clearly, then, he means to be talking about what is objectively good.

So far, the argument seems to work like this: (1) He formulates the thought experiment of the experience machine. He then asks the reader the crucial question: Would you plug in? (2) He assumes that the answer to this will be "no." (3) He takes this assumed fact to imply that we value something beyond mere subjective experiences: We value contact with reality. Then, (4) in a move that I have so far not mentioned, but is adumbrated in the quotations above from *The Examined Life*, he draws some further positive conclusions about what "matters to us" in addition to pure experience. The logic behind steps 2, 3, and 4 is that of an "inference to the best explanation" (see 337 fn. 6): The best explanation for the presumptive "no" answer to the initial question (we would *not* plug in) is that certain other things matter to us – therefore these things (probably) do matter to us. Finally, (5), he takes this to imply that, objectively, these things are necessary for a life's being the best.

He initially discusses three other things that matter to us, in addition to mere experience. First, we want to do certain things. People who are plugged into the machine are doing nothing: It only seems to them that they are doing something. Second, we want to be a certain way.

> Someone who is floating in a tank is an indeterminate blob. There is no answer to the question of what a person is like who has long been in the tank. ... Plugging into the machine is a kind of suicide. (43)

There seems to be more than one assumption behind this comment. He may be supposing, for instance, that traits, traits of personality and character, are essential for determining what sort of person you are, and that these are built up by your own action: Acting is necessary for acquiring such traits. In light of what he has just pointed out – that a person plugged into the machine is not doing anything – this would mean that you cannot acquire such traits in the machine. In that case, he would probably also be assuming that such traits that you have at the time you plug in would gradually decay over time. Note that he is talking here about someone who has *long* been plugged in. This is an important qualification. Without it, he would be committed to saying that there is no answer to the question of what a person who happens to be asleep is like.

The third thing that matters to us is probably the most important, though Nozick does not describe it very clearly:

> Thirdly, plugging into an experience machine limits us to a man-made reality, to a world no deeper or more important than we can construct. There is no *actual* contact with any deeper reality, though the experience of it can be simulated. Many persons desire to leave themselves open to such contact and to a plumbing of deeper significance. (43)

I think his meaning here is obscured somewhat by the fact that he is describing two things simultaneously. One is something that matters to us: contact with reality. The other is a new reason (heretofore not mentioned) why it matters. This seems to have to do with the notion that reality, unlike a dream or an illusory impression, is infinitely dense. There is always more there to discover and observe. The moon had a side that was hidden from us until it was finally observed and mapped in the twentieth century, but there is no other side to a moon in a dream, until and unless the dreamer dreams it up. One reason we desire contact with reality is that we also value the infinite density of reality.

After this passage, this section continues for one longish paragraph, seldom mentioned in the literature, which treats issues raised by the "transformation machine" and the "result machine." They are meant to render plausible his rather tentatively worded conclusion: "Perhaps what we desire is to live (an active verb) ourselves, in contact with reality. (And this, machines cannot do for us)" (44–45) Perhaps one clarifying remark is in order here. Nozick does not say that we would not want to use the result machine. Rather his immediate point here is different from the one he was striving to make in the three paragraphs about the experience machine. The immediate point here is that no one would wish to use the transformation machine to become just the sort of person one wishes to be, *and also* use the experience machine. This is supposed to show that what matters to us is not having the right experiences plus being a certain way. Similarly, his adding the result machine is supposed to show that what matters is not merely having the right experiences plus being a certain way plus having the results we desire brought about in the real world. It is not that the result machine does not give us things that matter to us (it does!). The problem is that it interferes with our getting something else that matters to us: We desire a certain causal connection between ourselves and the world. We want to be the ones who bring about the desired effects.

2. Some Criticisms

What should we think of these arguments? As I have suggested, the literature focuses on the experience machine, more or less ignoring the transformation and result machines. About the experience machine, there is one thing that we should pause to notice at the outset, to avoid misunderstanding. The thought experiment is to consider whether one would plug into the machine *for life*. Readers sometime miss this detail, with the result that the thought experiment becomes much less powerful than it otherwise would be. Suppose, to take the extreme case, that one's experience with the machine is going to last only a short amount of time: Then, within the constraints that are presumably built into the experiment (the episode is certain to be physically harmless, the superduper neuropsychologists can do exactly what they promise, and so forth), there would be little reason *not* to plug in. There would seem to be little difference between machine and a sophisticated amusement park ride, or a pretend sword fight in virtual reality goggles, or a stay in an area in Disneyland where everything you see is an imitation of something else (this is not really the New Orleans French Quarter, that is not really a magnolia tree, and the thing happily twittering in its branches is not a bird but some sort of tiny robot). Certain arguments against hallucinogenic drugs – to the effect that one should never, ever be out of touch with reality – might be applicable here. With the exception of those who find these arguments persuasive (and I can't help wondering if they take steps to avoid dreaming at night) none of us would seem to have any reason, so far, to avoid plugging in under those circumstances. Nietzsche pointed out long ago that humans seem to be quite willing to be subjected to illusory experiences.[12] I would only add that, given the right circumstances, we actually seem to enjoy it. This, however, has no direct relevance to Nozick's point. He wants to devise a test to determine something about what we think is sufficient for a given life's being the best life – and for this nothing short of an entire life in the machine will do.

It is also worth noticing that it is possible to say that one would indeed plug into the machine and – consistent with that – say that one agrees with Nozick about the other three things that "matter to us." The reason is that it can make a big difference how we rank these goods. Perhaps not only do I value the quality of my experience highly (of course!) but beyond that I value it so highly that if the quality were as high as it would be in the experience machine, that would be worth the cost involved in sacrificing things like contact with reality (things that nonetheless do also matter to me). Once again, though, this does no damage to the point that Nozick is trying to make. In fact, against those who hold this combination of values, the thought experiment of the experience machine is unnecessary, since they already agree with his main point. He is trying to reach those who do not think, as a matter of theory, that other things ultimately matter to them in addition to the quality of experience, or who are simply not aware that such things matter to them. Against them, he maintains that (a) they would not plug into the machine and that (b) he has the best explanation for that.

Most criticisms of the experience machine argument take the form of attacking (b) by offering an alternative explanation for one's aversion to plugging in. One family of objections amount to pointing out that there is another good reason to refuse to plug into the machine: concern about the trustworthiness of the machine or its operators. As one commentator puts it, we might reasonably be worried about the possibility of "cata-strophic, unimaginably horrific consequences of malfunction or abuse."[13]

Considered simply as an assertion about what is reasonable, this is obviously true. If someone from the neuropsychology department at my university were to come to me tomorrow and offer to plug me into a machine that allegedly functions exactly as Nozick's experience machine does, I would refuse without any hesitation whatsoever. Indeed, I would not plug in for five minutes, let alone for the rest of my life – and for exactly the reasons these commentators are giving. I would not trust something as fallible as actual, existing human technology to do something like that to my brain. (Frankly, I find the very idea slightly nauseating.) This, however, is completely irrelevant to Nozick's point. This thought experiment is intended to test our values and so, as I have already suggested, we are obviously meant to assume away worries about reliability and trustworthiness. This feature of the experiment came closer to the surface when, in reformulating the experience machine argument in *The Examined Life*, Nozick asked us to suppose that the machine is "provided by friendly and trustworthy beings from another galaxy."[14]

It is possible to revise this sort of objection in a way that it would indeed be relevant to Nozick's point. One might claim that, regardless of what *good* or *reasonable* grounds we might have for not plugging into the machine, it is also true that, as a matter of psychological fact, the *actual* reason we would not plug in is concern about reliability or trust-worthiness. Try as we might to conform to constraints that are meant to set such concerns aside, we are subconsciously moved by them anyway. Thus one's aversion to plugging in tells us nothing about "what matters to us": The real reason is not about values at all.

It seems to me that this revision buys relevance at the expense of plau-sibility. It implies that people simply do not have the powers of imagina-tion that Nozick's thought experiment requires of them. What evidence do we have that this is true? Indeed, such evidence would seem to be impossible to acquire, given that this alleged failure of imagination seems to be undetectable, even by the person who suffers from it.

Another alternative reason for not plugging in that has been put forth by more than one critic is moral in nature. Fred Feldman has pointed out that it might be morally wrong of me to plug in: that is, I might be wrong-ing the many people who I would be abandoning by plugging in.[15] Nozick briefly addresses this sort of concern when he says that "[o]thers can also plug in to have the experiences they want, so there's no need to stay unplugged to serve them" (43). In *The Examined Life* he makes a similar comment about there being no need to stay unplugged "in order to help others."[16] Perhaps the idea is that if some mental state conception of welfare is true, then the experience machine makes available to others far more well-being than I could ever bring to them here in the real world, rendering my obligation to contribute to human well-being obsolete. Hence, if helping others is a reason for not plugging in, mental state conceptions are not true.

Some have pointed out, though, that there is an additional problem involving moral value. Aside from such a generalized obligation to contribute to human well-being we also have specific obligations to specific people: moral commitments to one's spouse, one's children, and so forth.[17] What about that graduate student of mine who is struggling with her dissertation? If I self-indulgently plug in and, as a result, she never finishes her dissertation and never gets her degree, then her wasted effort and ruined plans would be my fault. The fact that she too could plug in to the machine does not get me off this particular hook if she chooses not to do so.

This objection is better than the one about reliability and trust, which ignored what was obviously meant to be one of the constraints built into the thought experiment. I think this one, however, can be handled rather easily by adding another constraint. The purpose of the experience machine scenario is to isolate one question from all others: Does mere quality of experience completely account for our actual, working notion of what well-being is? This objection indicates a way in which, so far, it fails to do that. As I have said, this is a question about value – more exactly, about the value of a life. This objection indicates, in effect, that there is more than one way in which a life can have value. In addition to welfare, there is moral value. One can decide not to live a certain sort of life (e.g., not plug in), not because it fails to yield well-being, but because it is morally flawed. The thought experiment is meant to raise the question of the nature of one of these two ways a life can have value (welfare) whereas, as written, it potentially touches on one's views about both of them (both welfare and moral value). I think this problem can be avoided simply by introducing a constraint into the thought experiment that sets aside concerns about the irrelevant sort of value. For instance, we might ask the reader to assume that in the event that one plugs in, everyone to whom one has special moral obligations would do the same. After all, once one plugs in (remember, this is for life) all obligations that others might have toward one are presumably canceled (except for those owed by the operators of the machines). That would mean then that such obligations could not be violated.

The two objections, or families of objections, we have considered so far really amount to claims that the experience machine scenario fails to isolate Nozick's question about welfare from some other sort of question, either a question of fact (as whether the machine is reliable or its operators trustworthy) or a question of value (such as the question of the moral value of one's plugged-in life). A quite different sort of objection is raised by Elliott Sober and David Wilson:

> The hedonist can maintain that deciding to plug into the machine is so aversive that people almost always make the other choice. When people deliberate about the alternatives, they feel bad when they think of the life they'll lead if they plug into the machine; they feel much better when they consider the life they'll lead in the real world if they decline to plug in. The idea of life attached to the machine is painful, even though such a life would be quite pleasurable; the idea of real life is pleasurable, even though real life often includes pain. ... People who decline the chance to plug in are repelled by the idea of narcissistic escape and find pleasure in the idea of choosing a real life.[18]

The issues raised by this comment are complicated somewhat by the fact that Sober and Wilson seem to assume that Nozick's target is psychological hedonism, whereas I have argued that "hedonism" describes his target too narrowly and that, insofar as it is about hedonism, the ethical variety of hedonism is his ultimate target. However, if psychological hedonism is true, then one of the conclusions that he draws from the thought experiment – that we actually do place intrinsic value on something other than pure experience – is false. More importantly, if psychological hedonism can offer an equally good explanation for not plugging in, one compatible with their theory, then Nozick's own inference to the best explanation would be refuted. One of the best ways to respond to explanation-based arguments like Nozick's is to find an alternative explanation to the one posed in the argument.

That is exactly what Sober and Wilson believe they can do. They interpret the hedonist's explanation in terms of "discount rates." People tend to value things that happen sooner more highly and they place less value (discount) things that happen further in the future. If I am offered a choice between one cup of my favorite soup today and two cups a week from now, I may well take the one cup simply because I can enjoy it now. They point out that a hedonist would refuse to plug in if they had an extremely steep discount rate – so steep as to convert their view into a "hedonism of the present moment."[19] They apparently find the claim that this is how people think – that this is why we do not plug in – to be more or less plausible.

I do not. Admittedly, people do sometimes have extremely steep discount rates. Think of those police videos we have all seen on television, in which a criminal, in obviously hopeless flight from police cars and helicopters, endangers or injures bystanders, damages cars in the street, and eventually completely destroys his own stolen vehicle, thus adding years of prison time to the already-inevitable sentence. What can explain such behavior? One very plausible explanation would attribute to the fleeing criminal a very steep discount rate. For him, staying out of the hands of the cops in the present moment is very important, while he does not care at all about – in other words, discounts completely – the future consequences of what he is doing. However, this does not seem to be the way human beings normally make decisions. The most striking difference between this sort of behavior and the norm is that such extremely steep discount rates seem almost pathologically irrational. Indeed, the extreme discount rate that their hedonist's argument attributes to people who do not plug in seems to involve exactly this sort of irrationality. To let a few seconds of unpleasant decision-making outweigh a lifetime of bliss seems – in terms of the hedonist's values – even crazier than the behavior I just described on the part of the fleeing criminal.

Sober and Wilson's hedonist might point out that she/he is only attributing such a steep discount rate to humans with regard to one thing: present ideas of future states, as compared to those states themselves. Sober and Wilson suggest that we can have different discount rates about different things and at different times.[20] This is true. I can easily imagine preferring one cup of soup now to two a mere two hours from now – if I am hungry. Hunger is a great intensifier of discount rates. It is easy to think of other examples. But there is always some reason why the rate steepens in these cases. It typically has to do with the fact that the period of waiting for the future benefits is worse than waiting periods generally are. That is obviously what is going on in the case of waiting for food when one is hungry. No such explanation seems to be available in the case of ideas of future states. *Why* would we behave like that?

There is actually another way to interpret Sober and Wilson's hedonist argument, one that avoids the implausibility of anomalous and inexplicable discount rates. It involves revising psychological hedonism itself.[21] Rather than saying that people seek pleasant states of affairs and avoid unpleasant ones, one might say that what moves us is pleasant and unpleasant *ideas* of states of affairs. Some of Sober and Wilson's reasoning suggests this approach. Note that when they give examples of good and bad future states of affairs, they mention, not pleasures and pains, but considerations like "a real life" and "narcissistic escape."

On this revised view, the reason I go to the dentist to have a cavity filled is not that I expect my life to have a greater balance of pleasure over pain if I do so. It is that, though my idea of the hour in the dentist's chair is painful, it is less painful than my idea of the long-term consequences of neglecting that tooth (abscessed tooth, blood poisoning, etc.). This rather radically changes the nature of the psychological hedonist's position.[22] It is not a terribly implausible view, but unfortunately it revises hedonism so radically that it is no longer about the issue that Nozick is addressing with the experience machine. After all, if it is revised in this way, hedonism no longer involves viewing mere experiences as sufficient to make a life the best sort of life. In other words, it is no longer a mental state theory of welfare. To be more exact, since we are talking about psychological and not ethical hedonism, it no longer says that we necessarily view the good life in this way. In fact, given that this neo-hedonist's argument claims that what we value is "a real life," it actually agrees with the main point that Nozick is making here. Of course it adds to this that the reason we value reality is that we find the idea of it pleasant. This is an interesting claim, but it is not one that Nozick is discussing here, nor does he have any need to.

The notion that this radically revised sort of hedonism can be used to refute the argument in the experience machine section is based on the deeper error of thinking that Nozick's target is, quite simply, hedonism – that is, that it includes all and only those doctrines that can be called "hedonism." It is not. It is true enough that one doctrine that can be correctly described as "hedonism" is immune to the experience machine objection. But that is no reply to this objection, because hedonism, in this very general sense, is not its target.

The experience machine, so far, is still standing.

There is, however, one problem facing it, and, whether it is a serious problem or not, it is demonstrably real. As I have mentioned already, Nozick assumes that the reader will answer the key question – would you plug in? – the same way he would: with a resounding "no." This is clearly not true of all his readers. I have posed this question to groups of university students many times over the years and there a significant minority – at least 10% – who insist that they would plug in. Among these people, there is a tiny minority whose "yes" turns out, upon cross-examination, to be one that actually does not threaten Nozick's ultimate point. They say that they actually do value things like contact with reality, but that they also (of course!) value quality of experience and that they weight the latter sort of value more heavily than Nozick apparently does. As I suggested earlier, this position is perfectly consistent with Nozick's claim that these other values do matter. However, most of the people who answer "yes" insist that nothing ultimately matters to them but quality of experience.

Perhaps the best response that Nozick might have to these people would be to simply admit that the experience machine thought experiment does not work on them. As I have pointed out, the logic of the experience machine section of ASU is just this: First, the example itself is supposed to elicit a certain intuition. Then, our author goes on to explain this intuition by suggesting some of the other things, besides quality of experience, that matter to "us." I've observed a statistically significant number of "wrong" answers to Nozick's key question. These people behave as if they are not part of this "us." The experience machine argument does not, so to speak, apply to these people. In spite of this, though, it can still apply to the rest of us. However, someone who wants nonetheless to convince this other group of people would have to come up with a different argument – perhaps a different *kind* of argument.[23]

Notes

1 See Robert Nozick, *The Examined Life: Philosophical Meditations* (New York: Simon and Schuster, 1989) pp. 104–108, and "The Pursuit of Happiness," *Forbes Magazine*, October 2, 2000, pp. 255–259. He also mentions it in *Philosophical Explanations* (Cambridge, Massachusetts: Harvard University Press, 1981), p. 595.

2 As we will see below, Elliott Sober and David Sloan Wilson take Nozick's target to be psychological hedonism in their *Unto Others: The Evolution and Psychology of Unselfish Behavior* (Cambridge, Massachusetts: Harvard University Press, 1998), pp. 281–287. Also, in his interesting replies to Sober and Wilson's discussion, John Lemos takes it for granted that their interpretation of the experience machine section is correct. See his "Sober and Wilson and Nozick and the Experience Machine," *Philosophia*, vol. 29 (2002), pp. 401–409, and "Psychological Hedonism, Evolutionary Biology, and the Experience Machine," *Philosophy of the Social Sciences*, vol. 34, no. 4 (December 2004), pp. 506–526.

3 Troy Jollimore believes that the experience machine presents a challenge to two theses essential to eudaemonism: that happiness necessarily has intrinsic value, and that nothing else has any intrinsic value at all. "Meaningless Happiness and Meaningful Suffering," *Southern Journal of Philosophy*, vol. 42 (2004), pp. 333–335.

4 Matthew Silverstein interprets Nozick this way in his "In Defense of Happiness: A Response to the Experience Machine," *Social Theory and Practice*, vol. 26 (2000), pp. 279–300.

5 For elaborate lists of commentators who take these positions, see Fred Feldman, "What We Learn from the Experience Machine," in Ralf M. Bader and John Meadowcroft, eds., *The Cambridge Companion to Nozick's Anarchy, State, and Utopia* (Cambridge, England: Cambridge University Press, 2011), pp. 82–86, fns. 4, 5, 6, 14, and 24.

6 To be fair, they are not all completely wrong. Ethical hedonism and what I have just called ethical eudaemonism are both members of the family of views that he is actually criticizing.

7 Nozick, *The Examined Life*, p. 103.

8 Nozick, *The Examined Life*, p. 103.

9 Unless, that is, Gilbert Ryle was right. He argued, powerfully I think, that pleasure is actually not an internal impression at all, like a twinge or an itch. See his *Dilemmas* (Cambridge, England: Cambridge University Press, 1954), pp. 54–67.

10 This is the interpretation that Jason Kawall uses in "The Experience Machine and Mental State Theories of Well-Being," *Journal of Value Inquiry*, vol. 33 (1999), pp. 381–387.

11 Nozick, *The Examined Life*, pp. 106–107.

12 Friedrich Nietzsche, "On Truth and Lie in an Extra-Moral Sense," in Walter Kaufmann, ed. and trans., *The Portable Nietzsche* (New York: Viking Press, 1953), pp. 42–47.

13 Jeffrey Goldsworthy, "Wellbeing and Value," *Utilitas*, vol. 4 (1992). p. 18.

14 Nozick, *The Examined Life*, p. 105.

15 Feldman, "What We Learn from the Experience Machine," p. 69. See also p. 84 fn. 17.

16 Nozick, *The Examined Life*, p. 105.

17 Feldman, "What We Learn from the Experience Machine," p. 69 and p. 84 fn. 17. Kawall makes the same point, more elaborately, in "The Experience Machine and Mental State Theories of Well-Being," pp. 381–387, but esp. at p. 383.

18 Sober and Wilson, *Unto Others*, p. 285.

19 Sober and Wilson, *Unto Others*, p. 286.

20 Sober and Wilson, *Unto Others*, p. 286.

21 Feldman offers this as a friendly amendment to Sober and Wilson ("What We Learn from the Experience Machine," p. 77–78). He thinks it is a plausible answer to the experience machine argument. As you will see in a moment, I do not.

22 Moritz Schlick held this view and pointed out very lucidly and elegantly how different this sort of psychological hedonism is from the classical sort, in which pleasure plays the role of an end-state that we seek to achieve. See his *Problems of Ethics*, trans. David Rynin (New York: Dover Publications, 1962), *passim*, but especially Chs. 2 and 8.

23 I think it would be a mistake to come down very hard on Nozick for blithely assuming that others will have the same intuitions he has. Philosophers have been doing that for thousands of years. It is only very, very recently that some philosophers have made a serious effort to actually find out, using the methods of modern, scientific psychology, what intuitions people actually do have. See Joshua Knobe and Shaun Nichols, eds., *Experimental Philosophy* (New York: Oxford University Press, 2008).

4

Why State of Nature Theory?

1. Grounding Political Philosophy

The brief chapter with the above title – "Why State of Nature Theory?" – begins Part I of the book, in which Nozick attempts to justify the state. He tells us in broad terms what sort of argument he will use to accomplish this task. Discussions of ASU often ignore this attempt to explain the basic nature of his argument, but they do so at a price. A careful reading can help to clarify aspects of Part I of the book that might otherwise be rather baffling. It can also help to spell out the answer to the question I raised in the first chapter of this book: How could an intuitionist method possibly have radical results?

The question of whether there should be a state is, Nozick tells us, the "fundamental question of political philosophy." It is fundamental in the sense that the very existence of political philosophy depends on it. Anarchist theory, after all, "undercuts the whole subject of *political* philosophy" (4). If the state is not a legitimate institution then there can be no answers to questions in political philosophy. This would seem to raise the question of why one could not then have anarchist theories showing how various state activities are unjust, immoral, or destructive of human well-being. Wouldn't they be theories in political philosophy? Nozick, I believe, would say no, they would not. The reason he would say that will emerge as we look more closely at the way he views his task of justifying the state.

So far, the role that justifying the state plays in political philosophy seems exactly like that often played by attempts to refute skepticism in epistemology. If we suppose that epistemology is the theory of knowledge,

Anarchy, State, and Utopia: An Advanced Guide, First Edition. Lester H. Hunt.

it seems to follow that if, as the skeptic claims, there is no knowledge, then there is nothing for epistemology to be about. The goal served by answering the skeptic is the negative one of removing an obstacle. However, Nozick assures us that the project of answering the anarchist also serves a positive purpose – "an *explanatory* purpose" – that is absent in the project of answering the skeptic. It will serve such a purpose, at any rate, if one does it as he will do it: by using "state of nature theory" (4). What we are trying to explain in that case is "the political realm" itself (6). His project of justifying the state is an example of an interesting wider class of projects: namely, attempts to explain a realm.

The reader confronts several mysteries here, not the least of which is the question of what a "realm" is. Nozick does not tell us, and only gives a few examples, the principal ones being those of the political and the moral. In a footnote (335 fn. 1) he suggests that color and heat are also realms.

Clearly, he is speaking on a very high level of abstraction here. Even though the list of examples is very short – color, heat, the political realm, and the moral realm – they are obviously very far apart, so to speak. I doubt that I can formulate a definition of a realm if it has to cover such a range of widely different phenomena. However, for our purposes, I think it can be useful to restrict this term to a manageable range of cases that raise all the issues Nozick is grappling with here. We will simply have to keep in mind that what Nozick actually means by a "realm" might require a broader, more inclusive definition, which I have not given.

Let us say that, for present purposes, a realm is an array of reasons, reasons either for actions or for beliefs, where a given array can be distinguished from others on the grounds that, in each of them, different *sorts* of ideas are accepted as reasons. In some cases, though not in all, realms can also be distinguished from one another on the basis of the fact that they have distinct subject-matters, and in some cases they can be distinguished on the basis of the fact that they include a smaller subset of reasons – call them "principles" – which govern the use of the other reasons in the realm, so that different realms are based on different principles.[1] For instance, within the realm of religion (or certain sorts of religions) appeals to authority ("... for it is written that ...") are accepted as reasons, both reasons for belief and for action, whereas in the realms of science and philosophy, no such appeal counts as a reason at all. Within the realm of law, on the other hand, one does accept appeals to authority (judges bow to precedent, for instance) but in complex and interesting ways this sort of appeal to authority differs from the ones we find in authority-based religions. When the reasons in one realm are viewed from the point of view of another realm, it can be hard to see why those other alleged reasons count as reasons at all. As everyone knows, some notions that are accepted as valid reasons in religion look like nothing of the sort if seen from the point of view of science. This is one good reason for trying to explain a realm. To explain a realm in the present sense is to explain why the reasons within it are indeed reasons at all.

This is a useful way to think of Nozick's notion of a realm because the problems about the particular realm that concerns him – the political – can be understood as problems about reasons. Consider what officers of the state are doing when they collect taxes. They are not passing a hat and asking for money. They are telling you to pay, and if you fail to give them the amount they demand, they have various ways, all more or less painful, to make you sorry you did not cooperate. Of course, private citizens sometimes act the same way, but when they do, we call them thieves and insist that they be stopped and punished. When ordinary individuals do it, it is called stealing, but when representatives of the state do what, in a perfectly straightforward way, seems to be the very same thing, it is called taxation. The same sort of thing can be said about what the state is doing when it practices military conscription. Here they are forcing people, in some cases very much against their will, to do work that is not merely unpleasant but may very well be fatal to them. If private individuals do such things, these practices are called abduction, kidnapping, or perhaps something worse, and we stop them if we can. Such state practices require an explanation – in particular, it needs to be shown that they are backed by the sorts of reasons that can indicate that an action is justified – that they are *not unjust*. This is true even of the most fundamental functions of the state. States enjoy the privilege of enforcing the basic rules of society with various sorts of coercive measures. If someone who is not an officer of the state attempts to do the same thing, they will be punished if they are caught.

When we ask for an explanation of why a particular policy or practice is justified, many different sorts of answers might be given. Reasons that are *distinctively* political include, for example, "because the king has commanded it," and "because the king has made a law permitting it," and "because a majority of the people have voted for it," and "because the electorate, following the constitutionally mandated procedures for deciding such things, has voted for it." "The political" can be understood as precisely such an array of reasons. Religion, science, morality, and the law are others. Viewed from a vantage outside the political, it is easy to doubt that these distinctively political reasons have the sort of justificatory power that they are supposed to have. Why does the mere fact that someone is the king mean that they have any special rights at all? We might well wish to look for an explanation for the political realm. Why do political reasons count as reasons (if they do)?

2. Explanatory Political Theory

Nozick envisions three broadly different ways of explaining the political:

> (1) to fully explain it in terms of the nonpolitical; (2) to view it as emerging from the nonpolitical but irreducible to it, a mode of organization of non-political factors understandable only in terms of novel political principles; or (3) to view it as a completely autonomous realm. (6)

Of these three, the first describes Nozick's approach. This is what he calls "a fundamental explanation of a realm." The third is, he believes, the least satisfying as a method of producing a successful explanation, in that it does the least to satisfy our desire for an explanation that really explains.

It is also, I think, the one that corresponds to the way that ordinary people have throughout history tended to view the political systems in which they live. The people who thought, for instance, that the king's command makes something right that might otherwise be wrong (an idea in the political realm) thought so because they believed that the king has a special status. The king is in some special way *above* those to whom he issues commands. This was felt to be a sufficient explanation, no additional one being needed. This notion of status, though, seems to be another idea in the political realm. The political is explained in terms of the political. If this sort of explanation is the best that can be given for the requisite key concepts, then the political realm itself will be self-supporting or, as Nozick puts it, "completely autonomous." A similar sort of logic is often at work in the minds of loyal subjects of democratic political systems, the idea being that the judgment of the people has a higher status, is more authoritative than that of a mere individual. *Vox populi, vox dei.* This, too, seems to make the political realm autonomous in relation to other realms.

Throughout the history of the state, people have often thought in ways that are closely related to the third way of explaining the political. Why does Nozick regard it as the least satisfactory of the three? The answer suggested by Nozick's comments in this chapter involves an underlying assumption about the requirements of a good explanation. The idea seems to be that, just as the explanandum phenomenon (the thing to be explained) must not be identical to the explanans phenomenon (the thing on the basis of which one explains it), so the more different they are, the better. He says at one point, regarding explanations of the political realm, that

> the illumination of the explanation will vary directly with the independent glow of the nonpolitical starting point (be it a situation or description) and with the distance, real or apparent, of the starting point from its political result. ... [T]he less close to its result (the less political or statelike it looks), the better. (7)

Is it true that this is one of the features of the ideally illuminating explanation, that the explanans and the explanandum be very different? It would take us rather far afield to try to form any sort reasoned opinion as to whether this assumption is a plausible one or not. Fortunately, as interesting as the question of the nature of the ideal explanation might be in itself, it is not necessary to answer it here. There is a specific reason why the type of explanans and the particular explanandum that Nozick is dealing with ought to be quite different, and different in a specific sort of way. It has to do with the fact that Nozick is dealing here with a particular sort of explanation.

After all, *why* is there a problem about justifying the state? There is a simple and obvious reason why the three state actions that I cited earlier – taxation, conscription, and monopolizing the right to enforce the basic rules of social life – do indeed call for an explanation, and for an explanation of a particular kind. All are things that would be morally wrong if an individual human being did them. Further, the traditionally forthcoming explanation I mentioned, which says that these state actions are not wrong because of the special, lofty status of the human agent that authorizes them or carries them out, seems to conflict with a fundamental principle of many moral theories, which holds that human beings are moral equals, in the sense that they have the same basic rights and obligations. This fundamental principle would seem to mean that no one can have the special sort of status that the king is alleged to have when we suppose that his edicts can transform wrong into right. Similar problems would seem to arise if the individual is subordinated in the same way to those other individuals who are lucky enough to find themselves in the majority in a democratic state. What makes such people special, in relation to everyone else?

What must be explained, then, is why essential state features, characteristics that are necessary to make it a state, are morally permissible. Why is it that they are not morally wrong? The explanation – the explanans set of statements – would have to include moral principles and arguments, ones aimed at showing that the state characteristics involved are compatible with morality. This would mean that the political realm is explained in terms of the moral realm. To the extent that we do this, we are carrying out the first of the three basic ways of explaining the political: "to fully explain it" – that is, to explain features of it that are sufficient to make it political – "in terms of the nonpolitical." This, as we know, is just what Nozick sets out to do.

We can now see, without a deep and elaborate investigation of the nature of the ideal explanation, why Nozick's explanans has to be so different from its explanandum. They must be different in a specific way. One must be moral and the other must be political. This follows from the fact that the reason why the political calls for an explanation is moral in nature. From the point of view of morality, the political seems inherently paradoxical. The explanation must somehow resolve the paradox.

We can also see why anarchist theories about the injustice of the state would not, even if true, be theories in political philosophy. The anarchist argument – at least the sort of anarchist argument that will concern Nozick – is meant to show precisely what Nozick is attempting to refute, that practices and policies that are essential for the existence of a state are morally wrong. The argument consists of attempts to show that moral principles that you and I apply to ourselves and other individuals are necessarily violated by agents of the state. As such, it treats these agents purely as individual human beings, who are subject to moral principles and arguments just as we are. This means that this argument inhabits the moral realm, not the political one. Not only does it deny a distinctive political realm of reasons for action, but it uses only moral reasons in doing so. Thus it is a theory in moral philosophy, and not in political philosophy.

In addition, we have an answer to the question I raised in the first chapter: How can an intuitionist method have radical results? The short answer to that question, which I have already hinted at, is that the intuitionism and the radicalism are mainly focused on different realms. The method is *moral* intuitionism, and the results are *politically* radical. It is in fact partly *because* the moral method is intuitionist that it can yield radical results. It ensures that Nozick will be judging the actions of the agents of the state by ordinary morality, by the moral principles we ordinarily apply to ourselves and to other individual human beings. This is the same starting point from which, according to the anarchist, we can never arrive at a justified state at all.

Though the means by which he will attempt to fully explain the political will be a justifying explanation, the nature of his moral assumptions will not allow him to "explain" the justice of everything states do. The sort of moral starting point he will use both justifies and constrains:

> Moral philosophy sets the background for, and boundaries of, political philosophy. What persons may and may not do to one another limits what they may do through the apparatus of the state, or do to establish such an apparatus. (6)

That his method sets boundaries of this sort is what enables him to use it to achieve two different goals. He intends, in addition to justifying the state, to show which sorts of states and state activities cannot be justified.

It also helps him to avoid a certain problem, what might be called the problem of excessive explanatory power. Some methods of explaining how states are just institutions actually "explain" too much. This seems to be true of the methods that attempt the third of the main ways of explaining the political, the ones that make the political realm completely autonomous. If appeals to the commands of the king are enough to explain why it is unjust to persecute Protestants when the king issues an edict protecting them, then they will also "explain" why it is just to kill them when he revokes his edict and orders them to be massacred. Similarly, the will of the majority will explain why it is just to persecute an unpopular minority when they vote to do so. The method Nozick uses will be much less powerful than this one, and that is actually an advantage over methods like these. Excessive explanatory power, in this context, means "justifying" things that are not just. A political theory with this sort of power makes dealing with the state a game in which all cards are wild, but only for one player.[2]

3. Potential Fundamental Explanations of a Realm

Nozick's "fundamental" explanation of the political will be carried out by means of his own modernized version of "state of nature theory." Such theories represent a particularly vivid way to explain the political in terms of the non-political. A state of nature theory is a *story* in which a political situation, the state, is described as arising from a non-political situation, in which there is no state. In the last four paragraphs of his first chapter, he introduces another feature of the explanation he will offer: It will be a *potential* fundamental explanation of a realm.

Here he is taking a position on a classic issue in traditional state of nature theory. The fact that a state of nature theory is a story immediately raises a question: Does the author of the theory mean that this story is true? John Locke, whose theory on the whole resembles Nozick's more than any other major theory, was quite clear about this. There really was a state of nature in our past, and the native tribes in Virginia are still living in it. Further, Locke clearly believed that some actual states (the legitimate ones) acquire the authority they have over their subjects by means that are in all relevant respects the same as those described in his theory: by the consent of the governed (not explicitly expressed consent, of course, but tacit consent).[3] On this particular issue, Nozick parts company with Locke; he does not mean his state of nature narrative as a historically accurate account of the origins of any actual state. Nonetheless, he thinks that such a narrative can justify the state, including states that actually exist at present, without being true. But how can something that never existed justify something that does? The explanation he gives for this counterintuitive idea is sketchy and incomplete, as his explanations in ASU often are, but it is also very interesting and, I think, worth looking at closely.

In it, he relies on an idea drawn from Carl Hempel, who had served a few years earlier as his dissertation director at Princeton University. The idea he uses is an adapted version Hempel's notion of a "potential explanation." His treatment of it is probably most understandable if one knows something about the idea for which Hempel is best known: his deductive-nomological model of explanation.

In this model, a fully articulated version of the explanans set of statements must include two parts. One is a law-like statement or set of statements. It might, for instance, include a general statement of conditions that result in combustion, such as fuel, heat, and an oxygen source. The other part is a description of certain particular facts about the circumstances of the phenomenon to be explained. These facts must be examples of the conditions which, according to the law-like statements, give rise to the sort of phenomenon we seek to explain. They might say that these circumstances include the presence of fuel, heat, and an oxygen source. The explanandum statement is a description of the phenomenon to be explained: for instance, "there is a fire here." In a proper explanation of this type, it must be possible to state it in the form of a valid argument in which the explanandum statement follows from the others. They logically imply that it is true.

What, then, is a "potential explanation"? Nozick defines this sort of explanation as one that "intuitively (and roughly) is what would be the correct explanation if everything mentioned in it were true and operated" (7). He mentions three ways in which an explanation can fail to be true or operate. It can be "law-defective," meaning that one or more of the law-like statements is false, and it can be "fact-defective," which would mean that one or more of the particular facts about the circumstances of the explanandum phenomenon alleged in the explanation is not the case. In addition to either of these, the explanation can also be "process-defective," in that the explanation presents the phenomenon as arising via a certain process whereas it actually did not do so. It arose from some other process instead. A process-defective explanation is quite good enough for his purposes, Nozick tells us: "[P]rocess-defective fundamental potential explanations (which are neither law-defective nor fact-defective) fit our explanatory bill and purposes almost perfectly" (8). If this is correct it can enable him to avoid the problem about state of nature theories that are historically inaccurate:

> State-of-nature explanations of the political realm are fundamental potential explanations of this realm and pack explanatory punch and illumination, even if incorrect. We learn much by seeing how the state could have arisen, even if it didn't arise that way. (8–9)

His justification of the state can be effective even if it is not true because it is an explanation. Explanations can be effective even if not true.

Obviously, this idea raises some large questions. The most obvious and biggest one is how it is possible for an explanation that is not true to be illuminating nonetheless. There is a way that this daunting question might possibly be avoided. He has just told us that the explanation he will offer is only defective in one way. Perhaps we can find some special reason why explanations that are process-defective without being fact- or law-defective can be illuminating. That might be enough to support Nozick's project and to motivate us to pursue it further.

However, there is another problem that seems to stand in the way of our understanding just how a process-defective explanation is supposed to work. It is not immediately obvious how an explanation can be process-defective without being either fact- or law-defective. After all, the "process" involved seems to be the one that consists of the operation of the particular antecedent conditions described in the explanans.

A Hempelian explanation is clearly a deterministic explanation: These particular antecedent conditions *make* the explanandum event come about. If they actually do exist, why doesn't the process operate?

I think the solution to these two problems – that of why a process-defective explanation can illuminate and that of how it can be process-defective without being defective in the other two ways – are linked. To see how, consider the following example of a historical explanation.

One summer day in 1914, Gavrilo Princip stepped out of a cheap Sarajevo restaurant, where he had just had lunch, onto the sidewalk. That morning he and some other Bosnian separatists had tried to assassinate the Archduke Ferdinand, heir to the throne of Austria-Hungary. The first conspirator to face the archduke's entourage had lost his nerve. The second had thrown a grenade, but it rolled under the wrong car, injuring several guards. The cars had sped away, with none of the other conspirators taking any action. The bomb-thrower had attempted suicide by jumping in a nearby river, but the river was shallow at that point and he was captured by the police. There was a good chance that the arrested conspirator was informing on his colleagues even now.

Suddenly, as Princip looked up the street, he beheld a sight he had never expected to see again. It was the archduke and Princess Sophie, speeding toward him once again in their open car, on their way to visit the wounded guards in the hospital. As the car rolled past Princip, the driver realized he had taken a wrong turn. He applied the brakes and put the car in reverse, rolling past Princip for a second – really a third – time. It was an opportunity never to be repeated. Princip drew his pistol, which was still loaded, and fired point blank into the bodies of Ferdinand and Sophie.

These shots eventually triggered World War I. The war resulted eventually in the Treaty of Versailles, with its punitive provisions. These in turn led to serious disruptions to German society, including the hyperinflation of 1921–1923, which was largely driven by the government's attempts to pay the war reparations required by the treaty, and which more or less destroyed the German middle class. These and other ensuing problems resulted in Hitler's rise to power in 1933. Hitler's policies set Europe on a course that inevitably resulted in World War II, which in turn produced other catastrophic events, including the Holocaust and Stalin's iron grip on Eastern Europe. Thus World War II and its effects can be explained in terms of a certain foolish young man having lunch at a certain restaurant at a certain time, neither earlier nor later.

Suppose the causal connections alleged in this explanation are all real – and surely none of them are entirely implausible – wouldn't this still be a flawed explanation of all these cataclysmic events? One can't imagine it coming from a respectable historian, except as a joke. But what is wrong with it?

That is rather difficult to say, with much precision, but one or two relevant factors seem obvious. One is that the explanation lacks what might be called "explanatory depth." It explains vast world-historical events in terms of an isolated incident. Surely a satisfactory explanation must somehow bring in, either explicitly or by implication, other events. There is another factor that is closely related to this one. Without foreclosing the controversial issue of whether there is such a thing as historical inevitability, we might nonetheless insist that this explanation makes these historical events seem ... well, not inevitable enough. By explaining the course of history on the basis of this one isolated event, it appears to suggest that the history of the twentieth century would have been radically different if Prinzip had skipped eating lunch that day and taken the train back to Bosnia instead. This seems to introduce too much chance into the course of events.

Assuming that the causal connections I have described are real enough, these facts probably are part of a complete explanation. It seems that we should be able to repair this depth- and inevitability-defective explanation by adding something to it. But what should we add? One thing that would help to remedy both of the deficiencies of the Princip's lunch explanation would be to describe various other incidents – political, diplomatic, economic, or criminal acts – that *would have* triggered the war more or less as Princip's shooting Ferdinand had. The more such incidents we describe, and the more plausible we make them sound – that is, the more plausible we make the notion that they would have resulted in war if the assassination had not happened first – the better our explanation would be.

But notice, all these other scenarios, in which other incidents ignited the powder-keg of Europe, are process-defective potential explanations. This immediately suggests a way in which such explanations can be illuminating. They can contribute to showing that the explanandum phenomenon is more inevitable, less dependent on chance, than we would otherwise think. They enable us to say things like, "if that had not caused it, this would have," or perhaps "... any of this wide array of events would have caused it." I am not saying that they would constitute a complete explanation of the war, nor even that they are necessary for explaining it; only that, despite being process-defective, they do, to use Nozick's phrase, pack explanatory punch.

It is also true that some of these alternate scenarios could be process-defective without being either law-defective or fact-defective. It may be that the triggering event in another scenario actually did happen. This would mean that the explanation is not fact-defective. The particular would-be cause did occur. It might also be that all the law-like assumptions that are sufficient to yield the idea that this particular event would result in war are also true, all the assumptions about human nature or about how political and diplomatic animals act (at least in Europe at that time). All these might be true and yet the explanation could be process-defective if the assassination of Ferdinand had already taken place and the war had already started.

An explanation can be process-defective without being defective in either of the other two ways if the particular explanans event has been pre-empted by another triggering event. As Nozick says:

> A potential explanation that explains a phenomenon on the basis of a process P will be defective (even though it is neither law-defective nor fact-defective) if some process Q other than P produced the phenomenon, though P was capable of doing it. Had this other process Q not produced it, P would have. (7–8)

This of course would be enough to make the explanation process-defective.

In the event that it is pre-empted in this way by another cause, process P is, so to speak, relegated to the status of a "backup cause," something that ensures that the result would come about even if the pre-empting causes do not happen. This of course is also what enables them to have the sort of explanatory power I have just described. This, then, is how a state of nature theory that is not true can justify the state. Nozick's version is an explanation. It is designed to explain the justice and, as we will soon see, the desirability of the state. As will emerge in the next chapter, one important strand of this theory is a process-defective potential explanation, and is meant to describe conditions that would give rise to the state if other conditions do not pre-empt them.

4. Law- and Fact-Defective Potential Explanations

The full paragraph at ASU 8, together with the footnote attached to it, makes some rather curious and potentially confusing claims about explanations that are defective in terms of their law-like claims and ones that are defective in terms of their factual assertions. Though Nozick tells us that his explanation will be defective in neither of these ways, it may be worthwhile to comment briefly on these claims of his, if only to clear up any confusion they might cause.

In this passage he tells us several things, not all of which can be easily squared with each other or interpreted in a way that makes them entirely plausible. His main claim here is that potential explanations, at least if they are fundamental explanations, can be illuminating even if they contain false statements that go beyond mere process-defectiveness: "To see how, in principle, a *whole realm* could fundamentally be explained greatly increases our understanding of the realm." First, a good explanation of this sort can be fact-defective: "Fact-defective fundamental potential explanations, if their false initial conditions 'could have been true,' will carry great illumination; even wildly false initial conditions will illuminate, sometimes very greatly." Second, an explanation can be good despite being law-defective: "Law-defective fundamental potential explanations may illuminate the nature of a realm almost as well as the correct explanations, especially if the 'laws' together form an interesting and integrated theory." But surely, the reader might well think, there must be limits to the manner or extent to which an explanation may be good though false – otherwise, we can "explain" simply by making things up. He makes a brief attempt at stating such a limit in the footnote to this paragraph: "It will not increase our understanding of a realm to be told as a potential explanation what we know to be false: that by doing a certain dance, ghosts or witches or goblins made the realm that way" (8).

I see a problem here, with no perfect solution that is readily available. First, why would *knowing* that an explanation is false make a difference as to whether it really delivers explanatory illumination? Does an explanation that is really (not merely thought to be) good suddenly become a bad one because we discover a falsehood that was in it all along? Why? In the scenario I have already imagined, in which we shed light on the historical foundations of World War I by telling stories about events that plausibly *could have* caused it, none of these other events actually did bring it about. This means that these stories can be formulated in such a way that they have false statements in them ("and as a result of this, war was declared"). And yet the fact that the false stories can be told, and *would have* explained the war had certain other things not happened, could itself be illuminating. Indeed, this feature of these stories, that the events involved did not actually happen, but would have produced the explanandum event if they had, seems distinctive of the peculiar way in which they illuminate that event.

And yet there does seem to be a big difference between explaining in terms of these diplomatic events and explaining in terms of dancing goblins, though both can be presented in a form that contains statements we know to be false. What is that difference? Nozick suggests a plausible answer to this question when he says in the paragraph itself (not the footnote), referring to fact-defective fundamental potential explanations, that they "will carry great illumination" if at least the false explanans statements "could have been true." This makes the sort of distinction we are looking for here, since the diplomatic incidents involved are events that could have happened, whereas the goblin dances cannot happen (because there are no goblins).

This is relevant to Nozick's explanation of the state because, contrary to his statement on the matter, the explanation he will offer will be not merely process-defective, but fact-defective as well. That is, it plays its explanatory role by describing events, involving interactions between organizations that provide government-like services to paying clients, that did not actually happen.

It is worth noting, in view of this, that fact-defective potential explanations can be perfectly good explanations. As I have said, some of the alternative scenarios that help explain the relative necessity of World War I could well involve events that did not actually happen. They can fill their role as "backup causes" anyway. They need only be things that *would* have happened, and produced the results to be explained, had certain other events not pre-empted them. As we will see, it can be argued that, to the extent that it is a potential explanation, Nozick's justification of the state is roughly of this sort. An important part of it explains the state in terms of events that would have brought it about (more precisely, would have contributed to bring it about) had they not been pre-empted by other causes.

Finally, there is one more interesting fact that has emerged from my discussion of the argument of Chapter 1. Nozick deals with the classic problem of state of nature theories, of how such a theory can shed light on the political realm even if it describes events that never happened, by casting his theory as an explanation. Throughout his discussion of this idea, he has spoken as though the reason why this explanation can explain is that it is a fundamental potential explanation of a *realm*. The assumption seems to be that there is something about an explanation of a whole realm that makes it special with respect to the matter of truth and falsity. What we have seen here is that, whether this assumption is actually true or not, he does not have to assume that it is in order to carry out his project of justifying the state. Potential explanations, as such, and not only fundamental ones, can be both process-defective and fact-defective and still work as explanations. The example to which I have returned several times, of explaining World War I, is not an explanation of a realm at all. However, it is true that it can still work even if both process- and fact-defective, and the reason for this is precisely that it is a potential explanation. So, regardless of how issues about the unique nature of explanations of realms might be resolved, Nozick's attempt to justify the state, which is cast as a potential explanation that is both process- and fact-defective, may now get under way.[4]

Notes

1 For the role played by the idea of principle in Nozick's later treatment of reasons and rationality, see his *The Nature of Rationality* (Princeton, New Jersey: Princeton University Press, 1993), *passim*, but especially Ch. 1.

2 A range of classic objections to utilitarianism amounts to charging it with the same sort of excessive explanatory power. They take the form of posing a case (the case of the hostage-takers that I described in Chapter 2, above, could be used for this purpose) and pointing out that utilitarianism seems to require us to do something wrong – that it, so to speak, explains why an unjust act would be just. Nozick refers in passing to these sorts of cases (see 28). For a classic statement of this point of view, seeH. J. McCloskey, "A Non-Utilitarian Approach to Punishment," *Inquiry*, vol. 8 (1965), pp. 239–255.

3 John Locke, *Second Treatise of Government* (Indianapolis, Indiana: Hackett Publishing Company, 1980 [orig. pub. 1690]), sect. 119. In the playful philosophical phantasmagoria of Chapter 9, "Demoktesis," Nozick dismisses tacit consent with a wisecrack: "[T]acit consent isn't worth the paper it's not written on" (287). I assume that he means that it is Locke's use of the idea in grounding the legitimacy of the state that is without merit, and not the distinction between tacit and express consent itself. Of course it is possible to consent to something either expressly (e.g., by nodding one's head in answer to a certain question) or tacitly. If I agree to sell you my car, I am expressly consenting to your ownership of my car, and I am tacitly consenting (unless I say otherwise) to supplying you with something that can be used for the purposes for which a car is normally used (something that can be driven, that it will not burst into flames if you try to start its engine, etc.). Tacit consent, however, must be indicated *somehow*. The problem for Locke is whether the behavior he cites (sect. 119) as sufficient to indicate one's consent to the authority of the state – simply remaining within the boundaries of its alleged authority and failing to undergo the expense of moving to another country – really is sufficient. Nozick appears to think that it obviously is not. If that is indeed his view, it seems plausible to me.

4 Perhaps I should comment briefly on his claim, in the same paragraph that I have just been discussing, that law-defective explanations can be good explanations: "Law-defective fundamental potential explanations may illuminate

the nature of a realm almost as well as the correct explanations, especially if the 'laws' together form an interesting and integrated theory." In a general sort of way, it does at first sight not seem very plausible to say that false law-like statements can explain something. Can we explain why there was a fire under the hood of my car by invoking a false theory of combustion, such as the obsolete phlogiston theory? Obviously not. However, we may have here an issue where it does make a big difference whether one is explaining a particular set of facts or an entire realm. Suppose, for instance, someone made a very convincing case for the idea that something like the old doctrine of the divine right of kings would, if true, explain the political realm. That could be very illuminating indeed. For instance, the argument might make it clear to us that the reason divine right would explain why we ought to obey the commands of the sovereign is that the commands of the sovereign have some deep similarity to the commands of God, that the way heads of state figure in our moral thinking is very much like the way God figures in the thinking of the adherents of the main monotheistic religions. The argument would explain the political realm in terms of the realm of religion – and without assuming that the latter realm has any sort of real truth behind it at all! That is, such an explanation would, even if law-defective, shed light on the nature of the political realm. However, interesting as this line of reasoning might be, it is not directly relevant to the main line of argument in ASU, as Nozick will not undertake an explanation of the state that is law-defective.

5

The Invisible Hand and the Justification of the State

1. What Needs to Be Shown?

What sorts of state activities need to be justified, in order to justify the state itself? They would have to be activities that are essential to something's being a state. Clearly, one of the state activities that I discussed as morally problematic in Chapter 4 – namely, conscription – is not essential to a state's being a state. An organization can be a state though it does not force people to fight for it.

There is another characteristic of the state that need not be justified in attempts to justify the state, though for a different reason. States are coercive systems. Their agents are often armed and they both threaten and on occasion inflict violence on people. This feature of the state need not be justified in this context for the simple reason that, so far, its agents might merely be exercising rights that everyone has. We have a right of self-defense, which at times requires one to both threaten and inflict violence. And if we have a right of self-defense, we must also have a right of other-defense, of defending people other than ourselves from attack. Of course, states that punish those who violate the rights of others seem to be doing something rather different from defense in the sense of preventing or deflecting an attack. But both Nozick and his predecessor John Locke assume that, if there were no civil authorities to do so, we would have the right to punish people after the fact who violate the rights of others.[1] If we follow them in making this assumption, that everyone would in the absence of the state have a right to punish, then we need not justify the fact that *it* practices punishment. If we suppose that these rights are transferable from principal to agent, we will have no trouble

Anarchy, State, and Utopia: An Advanced Guide, First Edition. Lester H. Hunt.
© 2015 John Wiley & Sons, Inc. Published 2015 by John Wiley & Sons, Inc.

imagining organizations that are at least somewhat state-like emerging in a state of nature.

A feature of the state that does seem to require a justification is one that I mentioned only briefly in Chapter 4, above. It is suggested by a famous quotation from Max Weber, briefly discussed in ASU (23): that "the state is a human community that claims the monopoly of the legitimate use of physical force in a given geographical area."[2] Nozick easily shows that this will not do as a philosophically serious definition of the state: *Claiming* a monopoly of force is not sufficient to make something a state, and actually *having* such a monopoly is not necessary (23), and so forth. Yet states clearly do seem to be monopolies of *some* sort. Governments promulgate rules and punish those who violate them, and they do not tolerate agencies that try to carry out functions that resemble these too closely. Which functions must it monopolize in order to qualify as a state? And if claiming a monopoly is not sufficient and having no actual competitors is not necessary, what exactly does this monopoly consist in? Further, can *this* feature of the state, whatever it is precisely, be justified as an exercise of rights that individuals have, or would have if there were no civil authorities? As we will see, Nozick's attempts to answer these questions raise thorny questions about what a state is.

2. The Invisible Hand

Nozick's argument for the potential legitimacy of the state has two parts. The first, which I'll call "phase 1," is a "backup cause" explanation of the sort that I discussed above in Chapter 4. It aims to show, among other things, the – to use language that I used there – relative necessity of the state. It means to show that the state is more inevitable than certain arguments against the state would make it seem. In addition, it is also part of the case that he makes that a state can be a just institution: It is not a necessary *evil*. Because of the peculiar nature of some essential state functions, it must at least have a de facto monopoly of these functions, and this is not intrinsically unjust. However, states are not merely de facto monopolies: They actively prohibit other organizations from competing with them. The second part of the argument for the legitimacy of the state, phase 2, aims to show that, in prohibiting competitors, the state (if it does it in the right way) is merely exercising rights that everyone has. The first phase is given in Chapter 2 of ASU, and the second is presented in Chapters 4 through 6. I will focus on the first in the present chapter before moving on to the second in the next.

The first phase is the better known of the two, possibly because of the memorable phrase he associates with it: It takes the form of what he calls an "invisible-hand explanation." Obviously, the phrase "invisible hand" (which for some reason Nozick consistently hyphenates) comes from a famous passage in Adam Smith's *The Wealth of Nations*.[3] Perhaps the best way to get a grip on what this sort of explanation amounts to is to take a look at a quotation from Smith's contemporary, Adam Ferguson: "[N]ations stumble upon establishments, which are indeed the result of human action, but not the execution of any human design."[4] Whenever we find an orderly pattern, *P*, in some part of the world, it is natural to think that either it was brought about as a result of some agent's intention to bring it about, or that it was simply an accident. Nozick's basic idea here, and that of Ferguson as well, is that there is a third possibility. Even if *P* is the result of human action, and even if it exhibits the sort of orderly arrangement that we associate with human intention, there may be some process that systematically brings the pattern about independently of anyone's intention to do so. Nozick calls such a process an "invisible-hand process."

The process by which Nozick's state begins to arise out of a state of nature marks a point on which Nozick's theory is clearly superior to that of his closest philosophical ancestor in these matters, John Locke. Both processes begin with people in a state of nature. Both assume, though Nozick does not use this terminology, that even in a state of nature, humans would still have what Locke calls "natural rights": rights that individual human beings possess, not because the state or some contractual agreement endows them with them, nor because of utilitarian considerations of expediency, but simply because they are human beings. Both also assume that people would know what these rights are but that, nonetheless, violent conflict would break out. At this point, the stories diverge sharply. Locke has the people in the state of nature conceiving of the state as the solution to their current problems, entering a social contract to form one, and then going directly into what he calls "civil society": a society governed by a state.[5] Nozick gives the state of nature more of a run for its money, so to speak.

Locke proceeds as if the state is the only alternative to being completely on your own in your efforts to defend yourself against attack, exact compensation for violations of your rights, and punish wrongdoers. Nozick takes into account the obvious fact that this is not true: People can pool their resources by forming "mutual-protection associations" (MPAs), agreeing that all members will come to the aid of any member whose rights need to be enforced. This can remedy one of the three "inconveniencies" that Locke presents as the main reasons why civil society is desirable: the fact that in a state of nature individuals will often lack the power to effectively enforce their rights.[6] Possessing insufficient power may no longer be a problem. However, Nozick points out that there are still at least four practical problems with this arrangement which would soon become obvious to MPA members: (1) All members are on call at all times, (2) any member can summon the membership to his or her aid, including "cantankerous or paranoid members" (12), (3) they must decide what to do if the conflict that gives rise to a call to action involves a clash between two members of the MPA, and (4) they must decide what to do when the dispute is between a member and a non-member.

Problem 1 can easily be solved by the market. The nuisance of always being on call gives entrepreneurs a motive to offer, for a fee, membership in an MPA in which enforcement functions are carried out by specialists who are paid to do so. This is a straightforward case of division of labor. Presumably, at this point, the internal organization of MPAs begins to sort out into a managerial stratum and people who do various kinds of hands-on work.

As to the third problem – that of disputes between members – there is also a solution that would naturally be arrived at eventually. Given that multiple MPAs are permitted, competition will lead them eventually to solutions that are preferred by their clients. Of the various possible approaches – including nonintervention, various arbitrary selection devices, and deciding conflicting claims on their merits – most people will prefer the last mentioned one, following a procedure that finds out which claimant is actually correct. (Incidentally, this would seem to require them to publish their procedures. Does this mark the earliest inception of a legal system in Nozick's narrative?) Though he does not say so explicitly, this seems to be his solution to the problem of paranoid and cantankerous members. An MPA, especially if they are under the pressure of competing for clients with other MPAs, will not waste resources acting on all complaints.

This is essentially also his solution to the fourth problem. In a dispute between members and non-members, will the MPA always take the side of their own members, just because they are members? Nozick thinks that the MPA will "want to determine in some fashion who is right, if only to avoid constant and costly involvement in each member's quarrels, whether just or unjust" (13).

There is a problem with this comment, which I probably should discuss briefly before moving on with my summary of his argument. To avoid constant involvement with members' disputes regardless of merits, it might be sufficient, simply, to determine whether your client has a facially valid case. This falls short of deciding whether he or she is actually in the right. This opens the argument to the objection that market forces may encourage MPAs to get a reputation for "going to bat" for their clients (provided, perhaps, that they do have cases that are at least arguable), for being biased, in other words, in favor of their clients rather than seriously trying to determine who is right. However, there is a way of reading what he is saying here that makes his argument significantly more plausible. Perhaps among the costs he envisions the MPAs trying to avoid here are dangerous, possibly lethal conflicts with other agencies. The idea might be that agencies that lean too far in favor of their own clients will eventually learn that this is a bad strategy in the long run. One can imagine various ways in which the likelihood of dangerous clashes with other MPAs can be reduced in cases like this – treaties, arbitration arrangements, and so on – but they all involve some sort of commitment to treating their clients' cases, in disputes with non-members, on their merits. This seems to me a more plausible argument than the other one I have just imagined Nozick giving here. However, I hesitate to attribute it to him because, as you will soon see, it seems to conflict with some things he says in the next step in his invisible-hand explanation of the state.

3. The Dominant Protective Association

So far, the process Nozick describes clearly has the main distinguishing features that an invisible-hand process possesses. Individuals, acting out of rational self-interest, are simply trying to solve their own practical problems. No one is trying to create a state. For the most part, they are responding to market forces. They have evolved into business corporations of some sort (perhaps they are consumer cooperatives) and must meet consumer demand in order to have clients and survive. In what comes next, the forces involved have a rather different character. The market is still relevant, but the narrative is driven by the emergence of a distinctively non-market sort of behavior: violent fighting between agencies.

The point of departure is the factor behind what I labeled as problem 4 above: the possibility of conflicts between clients of different agencies. So far, agencies have developed a policy of forming an honest opinion about the merits of their own clients' cases. But that does not mean that the two agencies will agree. People have honest disagreements, especially when their interests clash. What if – as will surely happen eventually – agency A is trying to punish or exact reparation from a client of agency

B, while agency B honestly believes that its client is innocent? Nozick sees three possible outcomes, which we can think of as *Victory*, *Gradient*, and *Federation* (15–17).

The first two assume the agencies will come into violent conflict. In Victory, one agency simply knocks the other out of commission. The clients of the losing agency go over to the winner. (I am not sure why he seems to assume there is no third agency in the area, but this may be a minor problem.) In Gradient, each agency consistently wins battles fought close to its base of operations but wins less and less frequently as it has to go further away. Nozick regards this situation as unstable. Those living in an area dominated by the agency that is not their own will find that their agency cannot offer as much security as the other one would. This gives them a motive to either move closer to their own agency's base or to switch their patronage to the other side. Eventually, this would result in each agency dominating a different geographical area, with some sort of border (perhaps a vague one?) between them.

In Federation, on the other hand, they find a way to avoid potentially catastrophic fighting:

> They agree to set up ... some third judge or court to which they can turn when their respective judgments differ. (Or they might establish rules determining which agency has jurisdiction under which circumstances.) Thus emerges a system of appeals courts and agreed upon rules about jurisdiction and the conflict of laws. Though different agencies operate, there is one unified federal judicial system of which they are all components. (16)

What emerges in each of these narratives is what Nozick calls the "dominant protective association" (hereafter, DPA).

4. What Is the Argument, so far, Supposed to Show?

This completes phase 1 of Nozick's argument for the state. The DPA now has a characteristic that at least resembles the one Weber identified as distinctive of the state: a monopoly of force. Yet, in Nozick's narrative so far, it never was anyone's intention to create a state. Further, nobody is trying to create something that has this particular, monopoly-like feature of the state. It simply emerges as people try to bring other things about. That of course is the main feature that enables it to function as an invisible-hand explanation. As we shall see in the next chapter, his attempt to justify the state is far from over, mainly because the DPA is not a state (yet).

This part of the argument, phase 1 as I have called it, is designed to serve two different functions. One is the "backup cause" aspect of the argument. In it, Nozick attempts to show that one very valuable human activity – namely, the enforcement of rights – can only be carried out in an organized way if it is done monopolistically – and so, to that extent, in more or less the same way states do it. It may be true that existing states are all intentionally constructed but, to the extent that the psychological assumptions on which Nozick's narrative rests are true of actual human beings then, even if it is not intentionally constructed as such, something that is at least state-like would arise anyway.

Of course it is possible for something to be the only feasible way to carry some potentially valuable activity and yet to be unjust. That is where the second function of this argument comes in. Nozick does not emphasize this aspect of the argument as much as he should have for the sake of clarity, but he does comment, rather late in the course of his exposition, that his "story ... [of the emergence of the DPA] assumes that each of the agencies attempts in good faith to act within the limits of Locke's law of nature" (17). Notice that this isn't quite the same thing as saying that they are not violating any rights. If one agency is trying to punish somebody and another agency is using force in an attempt to stop them, they cannot both be right. One of them may well be violating a right, such as the right of the innocent against being punished for things they didn't do, or the right to inflict a just punishment. The idea seems to be that, though at least one of them is making an honest mistake, Nozick's constraining "good faith" assumption specifies that since it is indeed an honest mistake, the agency that makes it deserves no moral blame. Without culpable wrongdoing, one agency ends up with a de facto monopoly. What is perhaps more important, any inadvertent, blameless rights violation is accidentally related to the DPA's monopoly; as far as the invisible-hand process that makes it the DPA is concerned, the agency that becomes the DPA might have always been in the right. In fact, one would hope that it was! Being in the wrong is not essential to its being the dominant agency.

5.   Does the Argument Succeed?

Does the invisible-hand explanation of the state – or, so far, of the DPA – achieve its objectives? Crucial to its doing so is the idea that, at least given certain background assumptions, a DPA would indeed emerge. Would it? I see reason to doubt this.

Nozick gives three reasons he thinks the process he describes has to result in a single dominant agency. It will be helpful to take a close look at them. All have to do with the allegedly unique nature of the service sold by the MPAs (I will number them for the sake of clarity):

[1] The worth of the product purchased, protection from others, is relative: it depends upon how strong the others are. [2] Yet, unlike other goods that are comparatively evaluated, maximal competing protection agencies cannot coexist: the nature of the service brings different agencies not only into competition for customers' patronage, but also into violent conflict with each other. Also, [3] since the worth of the less than maximal product declines disproportionately with the number who purchase the maximal product, customers will not stably settle for the lesser good, and competing companies are caught in a declining spiral. (17)

I think the second reason may be a mistake. It seems to be saying that, because of the nature of the product they sell, competing agencies cannot exist in the same area. This is just another way of saying that the nature of their product makes monopoly inevitable, and cannot be a reason why it is true. It is possible that what he really means here is that competing agencies cannot be "maximal" – meaning, I suppose, as powerful as they can be. This may be true, but it is not clear how it supports his thesis: Why does an agency have to be maximal in order to survive?

More important is the fact that first and third reasons implicitly make an assumption that is explicitly stated in the second one: that the agencies inevitably come into violent conflict with each other. This assumption is actually inconsistent with the third of the three scenarios that Nozick imagines emerging from his invisible-hand process, Federation. In his account of that scenario (16), he explicitly says that one possibility is that agencies will have the foresight to see that fighting would be costly and will take steps to settle differences peacefully. It seems to me that this is more than merely possible: It is required by his assumptions, whereas Victory and Gradient, which assume violent fighting, are inconsistent with them. Here is why.

He tells us (16–17) that the people in his narrative are motivated by rational self-interest. This is probably a necessary assumption, not because it makes his narrative more realistic (it does not – real people are not driven purely by rational self-interest) but because it is needed if his argument is to achieve what it is meant to achieve. Imagine a narrative in which, contrary to the rational self-interest assumption, the reason a single dominant agency emerges is that people have an irrational desire to do whatever others are doing, so that the most popular agency becomes the only one. Or imagine one in which the motivation that drives the emergence of the state is a slavish desire to bow, scrape, and grovel before the maximally powerful. Such narratives would tend to undermine Nozick's ultimate goal, which is to, eventually, make a certain kind of state look like a good thing. Rooting the state in the rational side of human nature might help to achieve this goal, while rooting it in the crazy or foolish side will not.[7]

It seems to me that the Victory and Gradient outcomes are inconsistent with the rational self-interest assumption. After all, fighting between agencies prompted by differing opinions about disputes between clients of different agencies is not likely to result in one agency suddenly and completely destroying the others. Rationally self-interested agents will have time to notice that a policy of simply trying to physically force their view on their competitors is injurious, not merely to the competitors, but to themselves. They might even be foresightful enough to see where such a policy leads and not use it at all. Failing that, they would at least be able to learn from their own painful experiences, or from the fate of agencies that did pursue a policy of force rather than negotiation and arbitration.[8]

Furthermore, to develop a hint I dropped in an earlier section of this chapter, Victory and Gradient conflict with the most charitable interpretation of Nozick's prediction that agencies will make a good-faith effort to decide who is right in conflicts between their clients and the clients of other agencies, based as it was on the idea that only by doing so could they avoid "costly involvement" in the quarrels of their clients (13). As I said when I discussed that prediction, it is most plausible if the costs that it claims the agencies are trying to avoid include violent conflicts with other agencies. If the costs merely consist of wasting time on discussions with one's own quarrelsome and contentious clients, avoiding them would be compatible with a great deal of bias in favor of those clients in conflicts with clients of other agencies. Really trying to avoid bias makes the most sense, as a strategy, if it is part of a wider strategy of resolving conflicts with other agencies in the most peaceful way that is consistent with representing the just interests of one's clients. Such a wider strategy, of course, seems to lead away from Victory and Gradient and toward the scenario of Federation.

So far, my comments on the invisible-hand argument could be taken as a series of "friendly amendments" to it. One can imagine rewriting Nozick's Chapter 2 in light of what I have said. His argument would then be more coherent, and it would also be simpler. The result that would emerge at the end is simply Federation, and not a disjunction of three possible outcomes. Isn't that outcome good enough, from Nozick's point of view?

I don't think it is. The simple reason for this is that in the Federation outcome there is no DPA at all, no entity with a de facto monopoly of power. To put the point another way, I think that Nozick's statement at the end of his description of this outcome – "[t]hough different agencies operate, there is one unified federal judicial system of which they are all components" (16) – is not true. The two agencies, as he describes them, are not "components" in the required sense of the word. They are simply two agencies that have agreed to settle disagreements peacefully and have set up some sort of mechanism to make this possible.

At this point, the difference between what I am saying and Nozick's argument as written might seem merely verbal: Why not describe the result in Federation as a monopoly of force? What is the functional difference between a single agency being dominant, on the one hand, and the agency-plus-agency-plus-mechanism result, on the other?

Consider the difference between a monopoly and an oligopoly. A monopoly is the only producer of a given good, while an oligopoly is multiple producers of a given good, all of whom coordinate their activities so as to fix prices and thus avoid competing. With both monopoly and oligopoly, we have an absence of price competition. However, the agencies in the Federation outcome can still do the one thing that the oligopoly does not do, the thing that makes it functionally equivalent to a monopoly: *They can compete.* Depending on the nature of the conflict-avoidance mechanism they agree on, their clients may well still be able to choose which of the two agencies they wish to deal with. That means that the agencies can still compete for clients by offering similar services at lower prices. They can also compete by trying to offer higher-quality services, or by offering services that other agencies are not offering. Thus the Federation can have the one characteristic that indicates that an arrangement is not monopolistic. By the same token, it is not so far an oligopoly, either.

There is another possibility that might be considered briefly here. It could be either an interpretation of Nozick's text or a friendly amendment. The idea would be that the monopoly of force predicted by his argument is not what I have called the agency-plus-agency-plus-mechanism, but simply the mechanism itself, the arbitrator, rule, court, or whatever the means is that they use to avoid conflict.[9] It seems to be the highest authority, and isn't authority a feature that we identify with states? Doesn't this make it sufficiently state-like to establish the point that Nozick needs to make at this point in the argument?

I don't think so. Whatever this mechanism might be, it does not appear, from Nozick's description of it, to be a monopoly *of force.* The enforcement seems to be carried out by the agencies themselves and, as I have just pointed out, Nozick's invisible-hand argument does not actually predict that they will function in a monopolistic way (i.e., without competing). If the mechanism is a legal system of some sort, then it would appear that there is one legal system in the area that, by agreement, applies to multiple agencies. But a legal system is not a state.[10] A state is a certain means of enforcing laws, and I have just argued that in the Federation outcome, the law is not enforced the way states do it.[11]

There is another group of problems with the invisible-hand argument that is worth discussing, partly because they raise in an interesting way the question of what sort of argument or theory would be sufficient to justify the state. They were raised by David Schmidtz in the course of a discussion of attempts to justify the state. [12] He based them on a useful distinction he draws between two ways of trying to justify an institution, which he calls "teleological" and "emergent": "The teleological approach," he tells us, "seeks to justify institutions in terms of what they accomplish. The emergent approach takes justification to be an emergent property of the process by which institutions arise."[13]

Teleological justifications posit some goal, and evaluate the institution in terms of how much of the goal it achieves, as compared to the alternative arrangements. An example of a teleological justification of the state would be a theory that offers a utilitarian justification of the state. It would justify the state by showing that it achieves more happiness (or some other specified subjective state of people, such as desire-satisfaction) than the various alternative arrangements. Emergent justifications of the state lay down constraints that the emergence of the state must not violate, and then argue that states do not, or at least need not, come about in a way that violates the constraints.[14] A clear case of this sort of theory is John Locke's social contract theory. He specifies some natural rights that function as constraints on the behavior of individuals, and argues that legitimate states get their authority over people in part from the fact that everyone who enjoys the enforcement of their rights by the state thereby consents (tacitly, if not expressly) to being ruled by them. Among other implications, this means handing over one's natural right to punish wrongdoers to the state. Since this is the sort of right that can be transferred by consent, this means that the state gets its right of monopolistic rights enforcement without violating the relevant constraints.

Despite its differences from a social contract theory, Nozick's invisible-hand argument seems to be another emergent justification. Or is it? Notice that Nozick's explanation of the de facto monopoly is process-defective. As far as we know, no existing state emerged from the invisible-hand process that he describes.[15] Schmidtz claims that this means that Nozick's would-be emergent justification of the state's monopoly of force is a "hypothetical consent argument": It attempts to justify the state by referring to consent which the theory describes as possible to give but which is never actually given. The problem with this is that merely hypothetical consent cannot show that no constraint has been violated. If I have in my hands a $20 bill that yesterday was your property, I can justify my holding on to it by pointing out that you voluntarily gave it to me. On the other hand, if I stole it from you, it would do no good to say that, well, you *could have* given it to me and, if you had done so, precisely the same situation would have resulted – that is, my holding on to the money. Only actual consent, such as we have in Locke's theory, can emergently justify.

In fact, Schmidtz claims, it's worse than that: Even if a state-like entity actually does emerge in the way that Nozick describes, it still does not justify that entity. The reason for this lies in the very fact that the process by which the entity emerges is an invisible-hand process. As people do various micro-actions, aimed only at solving their immediate problems, a macro-result emerges, which nobody envisaged: They find themselves under this state-like entity. But that means nobody consented to it. Obviously, this means that it is not justified by their having consented to it.

Thus, Schmidtz maintains, the invisible-hand argument fails twice over. First, it is simply a fictional story, and fictions can't emergently justify anything: Only processes that really happen can do that. Second, even within the fictional world of Nozick's story, where the invisible-hand process does occur, it still does not justify its result.

What should Nozick say to this? I think he could get around the second of these problems – the one about actual, non-hypothetical invisible-hand processes, fairly easily. As I have interpreted it, Nozick's invisible-hand argument is not a "consent argument," in Schmidtz's sense, at all.[16] That is, it is not designed to show that a certain monopoly of force arises, or can arise, in such a way that it has the consent of the people living in the area in which the monopoly is exercised. Consent does play a role, but only in that it is a reason why some of the micro-actions that yield the macro-result are morally innocent. (The other micro-actions are indeed coercive, even violent, but I have argued that they are morally innocent – even if mistaken – for a different reason.)

Some people would probably think that the emergent entity needs to be consented to, or it lacks legitimacy. This might be a reason to prefer social contract theories like Locke's to invisible-hand views. Many micro-actions on the part of many people have changed the macro-situation profoundly. Don't we have a right to a say in decisions that have an important effect on us? As a matter of fact, Nozick argues in Chapter 8 (268–270) – mainly through a series of clever examples that there is no reason to repeat here – that there is no such right.

So the second of Schmidtz's objections is not really a problem for Nozick. What about the first one, the one about merely hypothetical processes? Since it also assumes the consent argument misinterpretation, one might be inclined to think that it, too, falls apart. Unfortunately, though, Schmidtz's objection can easily be extended, so that it is not merely about consent.

Indeed, this can be done very simply. Recall that the point of an emergent justification is to show that a state has come about without violating specified moral constraints. In order to make a reasonable case that some individual or institution has not violated some moral constraint, one must talk about things that actually have happened or actually have not happened. By itself, any hypothetical story – talk of things that merely could happen – is completely irrelevant to that end. In my own interpretation of Nozick's argument I read it as addressing blameworthy wrongdoing, and not constraint violations, but under this interpretation the argument faces the same basic problem. To establish that a given state arose without culpable wrongdoing one must talk about things that actually happened, not things that could happen.

As a matter of fact, this is so obvious, once one has thought of it, that it raises the possibility that showing that a real state can acquire a certain sort of monopoly of force without blameworthy wrongdoing, or for that matter constraint violations, was no part of the point of the invisible-hand argument. If it wasn't, then what *was* his point? Perhaps the invisible-hand argument is really a possibility proof. That is, maybe it is meant to show that the concept of a just state – more exactly, one non-trivial feature of it – is not inherently incoherent or contradictory. That is a rather modest aim, but it is not a trivial one.

In addition to that, I have already argued that the invisible-hand narrative is meant to connect this feature of the state with a desirable function (rights enforcement). It actually is incorrect to say that the invisible-hand process from which the DPA emerges is merely hypothetical, meaning that it is merely something that *could* happen. It is a process that would happen – in certain circumstances, and given certain background assumptions.

It is this aspect of the narrative that enables it to be an argument to the effect that institutions with a certain state-like feature are the only feasible way to carry out the desirable function of rights enforcement.

Oddly enough, though this argument takes the form of a narrative of a state-like entity emerging, this aspect of the argument is not an "emergent justification" in Schmidtz's sense. Since rights enforcement is a desirable goal that (a certain kind of) state achieves, this aspect of the argument actually functions as a novel sort of teleological justification.

Of course, I have argued that steps in the argument that are needed if it is to successfully carry out this function do not work, but I could be wrong about that. Am I?

Notes

1 Warren Quinn cleverly argued that the right to punish follows from the right of self-defense on the grounds that the latter right is not limited to preventing violations of rights but includes a right to inflict harm on another, after the fact, if the other person does commit a violation. See his "The Right to Threaten and the Right to Punish," *Philosophy & Public Affairs* (Fall 1985), vol. 14, no. 4, pp. 327–373. This of course supports the Locke/Nozick position on the right of everyone to punish violations of rights in a state of nature.
2 Max Weber, "Politics as a Vocation," in H. H. Gerth and C. Wright Mills, trans. and ed., *From Max Weber: Essays in Sociology* (New York: Oxford University Press, 1946), p. 78.
3 Nozick quotes the passage at 18.
4 Adam Ferguson, *An Essay on the History of Civil Society*, 5th edn (London: T. Cadell, 1782), Part III, sect. 2.
5 John Locke, *Second Treatise of Government* (Indianapolis, Indiana: Hackett Publishing Company, 1980 [orig. pub. 1690]), *passim*.
6 See Locke, *Second Treatise of Government*, sects. 124–126. The other two inconveniencies lie in the fact that though people know in a general sort of way what rights they have, there is no text spelling this out (so that if people interpret the moral law in a way that is favorable to themselves it will not be easy to show them they are wrong), and in the fact that there is no impartial judge to apply the law. It would be interesting to see whether Nozick's MPAs, as they evolve, can solve these problems as well, without becoming states.
7 The "self-interest" part of "rational self-interest" is probably necessary in order to make the explanation an invisible-hand one. At any rate, it is hard to see how altruism can enter into an explanation of the state without raising the possibility of a deliberate attempt to bring about a socially optimal solution to shared problems – which would seem to be a non-invisible-hand sort of process.

8 I would like to thank Alex Schaefer for first planting this idea, in a somewhat different form, in my head.

9 This seems to be how Roy Childs interpreted the Federation outcome in his anarchist criticism of Nozick: "The Invisible Hand Strikes Back," *Journal of Libertarian Studies*, vol.1, no. 1 (1977), p. 25.

10 This is essentially the answer that that Roy Childs gives to this argument. See note 9, above.

11 The anthropologist E. Adamson Hoebel made a powerful case that all human societies, not just ones that are governed by states, have law in *The Law of Primitive Man: A Study in Comparative Legal Dynamics* (Cambridge, Massachusetts: Harvard University Press, 1961). See pp. 23–25 for some interesting examples of non-monopolistic forms of enforcement. For instance, he tells us there that among the Eskimo, if someone commits more than one murder, then any man may, as a public service, execute the murderer (though only if every adult male in the community – presumably excluding the murderer – approves).

12 David Schmidtz, "Justifying the State," *Ethics*, vol. 101, no. 1 (October 1990), pp. 89–101.

13 Schmidtz, "Justifying the State," p. 90.

14 Schmidtz, "Justifying the State," p. 91.

15 It might also be fact-defective, if no institutions sufficiently similar to Nozick's MPAs have existed. By "sufficiently similar," I mean possessing the features that are sufficient, in Nozick's argument, to set in motion the sort of invisible-hand process that he describes.

16 Gerald Gaus makes essentially the same point in "Explanation, Justification, and Emergence," in Ralf M. Bader and John Meadowcroft, eds., *The Cambridge Companion to Nozick's Anarchy, State, and Utopia* (Cambridge, England: Cambridge University Press, 2011), pp. 132–133. However, he thinks the point solves more problems for Nozick than I do.

6

Risk, Fear, and Procedural Rights

1. The Minimal State, Ultraminimal State, and the Dominant Protective Association

So far, the argument has merely aimed to justify the DPA, which possesses only a rough de facto monopoly of coercive activities including, most notably, punishing and exacting compensation for rights violations. I say "rough" monopoly because there are exceptions to it. For one, it appears to permit individuals to enforce their own rights. The DPA dominates the field in these activities simply because of its relative strength. For this reason, though, the DPA is not a state. The state goes further than this, with a declared de jure monopoly of force: It claims that it may punish and we may not. If the DPA were to declare such a monopoly (or something sufficiently like it) it would become what Nozick calls an "ultraminimal state" (26).[1] But even the ultraminimal state still lacks one feature that states generally have: It does not protect everyone within its territories, but only those who pay for its services. States do not limit the scope of their enforcement activities in this way: They cast their nets much more widely. If the ultraminimal state were to extend its enforcement activities in the way that states do (or do something sufficiently similar) it would become "the minimal state."

Can these features of the state be justified as an exercise of rights that individuals have, or would have if there were no civil authorities? This question takes up the bulk of Chapters 4, 5, and 6 of ASU. It is to this discussion that I will now turn.

During the remainder of the argument, its logical character will change rather abruptly. As Nozick points out at the end (118–119), the argument

Anarchy, State, and Utopia: An Advanced Guide, First Edition. Lester H. Hunt.
© 2015 John Wiley & Sons, Inc. Published 2015 by John Wiley & Sons, Inc.

for the transition from the ultraminimal to the minimal state will not predict that this transition will actually occur. Rather, it will argue that the DPA has moral obligations to particular individuals which, if it carries out these obligations, will mean that it has indeed made the transition to the minimal state. Of course, it may chose not to do so, so this part of the argument does not have the character of a prediction.

Is the explanation he gives nonetheless an invisible-hand explanation? He believes it is because, though it does describe a process that involves people acting intentionally (something that any invisible-hand explanation does), the processes involved do not involve people intending to create a state (118–119). The state still arises as a result of human action without being the execution of any human design. We might say that though he gives an invisible-hand *explanation* of the state, he does not claim that it is the result of an invisible-hand *process*. As long as we keep this distinction in mind, Nozick's claim to have offered an invisible-hand explanation of the state is at least a plausible one.[2]

To see why this claim is important, consider some of the ideas I discussed above, in Chapter 4. Recall that part of his purpose is to explain the "realm" of the political, and to "fully explain it in terms of the non-political" (6): to provide what he calls a "fundamental" explanation of it. While Nozick can't be said to have fully explained the political yet – the explanation is just getting started – the explanation given so far does fill the bill of avoiding any distinctively political ideas in the explanans set of statements. His aim is to depict the emergence of an entity that is state-like, in that it possesses features that are sufficient for us to call it a state, and yet to depict it as arising in the absence of anyone intending to create a state or intending to create an institution that has those features. These features are side-effects of actions that were aimed at non-political ends.

On the other hand, if a theory explains the state as something that is intentionally created, then the idea of the state will have to appear in the explanans set of statements – as the object of someone's intention. That is exactly what a social contract theory like that of John Locke does. In Locke's narrative, the state arises when people in a state of nature agree to enter civil society and submit to being governed by a state. This does seem to be explanatorily less satisfying than Nozick's approach. Notice that in Locke the concept of the state is prior to the state: The state exists because of the idea, and not the other way around. This raises the problem of explaining the idea of the state. Where did it come from? Who was the genius who thought the state up, in a world where no such thing had ever existed, and how did they manage to do that? This problem does not arise in Nozick's account. The state emerges from human actions that are aimed at purposes other than creating it: People observe that it has arisen and give it a name. The idea of the state comes from the state and not the reverse, as Locke's contractual explanation would have it.

2.   General Outlines of the Argument

Nozick's discussion of these questions includes some of the most complex, difficult, and downright confusing material in the book. However, I think I can show that, with some nudging – some charitable interpretation, some tying of loose ends, and perhaps a friendly amendment or two – it is consistent and coherent. As always with Nozick, there are interesting and surprising ideas throughout.

In broad outlines, this discussion, what I have called phase 2 of his full justification of the state, has three parts. One part consists in expanding the definition of the state. In effect, he relaxes the requirement for what is to count as a state. Though Nozick does not emphasize this part of the argument, it is important. One thing that makes it so is that, by the end of this complicated line of reasoning, he will actually not be claiming that the organization that he justifies has the right to prohibit *all* others from punishing and exacting compensation for violations of rights within its territory. Rather, what it does is to decide which of the other potential punishers will be permitted to operate within its territory. It examines the rights-enforcing methods of other agencies to see whether they are sound ones or not. In particular, it passes judgment on the decision-procedures by which they settle questions of justice, deciding whether they fall within the range of permissible procedures. He believes that possessing and exercising this right is sufficient to make this entity an ultraminimal state. The intuitive idea here is that, though this is not exactly a monopoly of force, it is a monopoly of a certain force-related power or capacity. This particular protective association is the only agent to decide who will be allowed to use force and who will not. He thinks this monopoly is sufficient to play the role of what I have called the "de jure monopoly."

On his view, this organization is unique only in that it is in a physically dominant position that makes it, and no other agency in the area, *able* to decide who is a permissible wielder of force and who is too risky. Yet though it alone is in a position to exercise this right, everyone possesses it. Exactly what is this right that everyone possesses? He gives two different answers to this question. In Chapter 5, he says that the dominant protective association may punish anyone who applies to one of its own clients a procedure that it deems unreliable or unfair (101). This is because we all have, in addition to various substantive rights against having various wrongful things done to us, a *procedural* right to the effect that decisions about what will be done to us be made in the right way. Because of the role this right plays in his justification of the state, it is clear that he is thinking of it as a natural right. In addition, according to a line of reasoning that centers mainly in Chapter 4, Nozick holds that the DPA may prohibit agents (either individuals or organizations) from applying procedures to its own members that expose them to excessive levels of *risk* that they will be punished even though they are innocent (88). I will call these two lines of reasoning "the argument from procedural rights" and "the risk argument."

If successful, these two arguments justify the DPA in becoming what he calls (given his relaxing the requirements) the ultraminimal state. What about going the rest of the way and becoming an actual state? This brings us to the third part of phase 2 of the justification of the state. Here, the argument, even in its broad outlines, becomes rather complicated. What follows is my best attempt to make perfect sense of the reasoning we find in the text.

In effect, Nozick treats the argument from risk and the argument from procedural rights as showing that some sort of coercive response to risky procedures is justified. But what response should this be? The answer might seem obvious: One prohibits them! But he helpfully points out (at 75) that there is more than one possible response to actions that violate rights, or what he now begins to call, in a characteristically Nozickean phrase, "boundary crossings":

1. One can prohibit them and punish them if done.
2. One can permit the act but require that the victim be compensated.

Surprisingly, the response that he favors in this case is not on this list, but does come up soon enough. He sets out (at 78–84) a notion that I would put like this:

3. One can prohibit the act but require that the agent who does (or would do) the act be compensated.[3]

One part of the argument is meant to rule out response number 2 as a response to risky methods of rights enforcement. First, he argues that, due to the very nature of compensation, there is no feasible way to compensate for offenses like exposing people to risk of violent assault that would be fair and non-arbitrary (63–65). Second, if compensation is our only response to such risk, there will be harms here for which compensation *cannot* be given. The reason for this is presented in Chapter 4 (65–71) in his discussion of the fear provoked by risk. These arguments rule out the second of the three listed responses to risky activities.

The reason why, of the two remaining listed responses, the third one is the correct one for risky rights enforcement is presented in his discussion of what he calls the Principle of Compensation. There he argues that there is a class of rights violations for which agent compensation is the correct response. These violations are distinguished from others (in part) by the fact that they expose others to the risk of harm but do not inflict actual harm. He argues that prohibitable unreliable decision procedures used by enforcers of rights belong in this category of rights violations: People who are denied protection when such procedures are prohibited by the DPA should be compensated for this loss. The proper compensation, he argues, is to extend the protection of the DPA to them.

This, Nozick believes, is sufficient to satisfy the one remaining feature of the state necessary to make the DPA a state. This is the one that involves the scope of enforcement activities, which Nozick often speaks of as the "protecting everyone" feature. However, as with his claim about the de jure monopoly feature, this one assumes a relaxed version of the requirement. The DPA is now protecting, not everybody, but their willing clients plus people involved in risky enforcement of rights. As we shall see, he recognizes that there can be people who fall into neither of these categories.

3. Dividing the Benefits of Exchange

One of the arguments against permitting boundary crossings on condition that the victim is compensated rests on a distinction between two kinds of compensation: full compensation and market compensation. One thing that might make this distinction initially confusing is that the word "full" seems to suggest that full compensation involves larger amounts of compensation than market compensation does. Actually, it is the other way around. Full compensation makes victims of the rights violations as well off as they were before the event (61), and market compensation does more than that.[4] It gives the victims what they would have gotten if they were able to bargain and sell the right to the boundary crossings to the violators before the fact.

Since similarities and differences between after the fact compensation, on the one hand, and before the fact commercial transactions, on the other, is fundamental to Nozick's discussion of these issues, it should be helpful to take a close look at such transactions – that is, at trade. Suppose I offer to sell you my watch. I would be willing, just barely, to take $50 for it, and of course I would much prefer getting more. Above that price, I prefer any higher price to every lower price. You would be willing, though just barely, to pay as much as $100 for it, but would rather pay a lower price than that. Below that level, you prefer prices insofar as they are low. Obviously, somewhere in the range of $50 through $100 – what is sometimes called the bargaining window – is the price we will agree on. Though any price within that range would make both of us better off than we were before the deal (because any such price is preferred by both of us to no deal at all), bargaining determines how much better off each of us will be. Further, within the bargaining window, every price that is a certain number of dollars better than some other price from your point of view will be worse for me by the same amount. Within this region, bargaining is an instance of what Nozick calls "dividing the benefits of exchange."

So how much should the victim be compensated if we were to have a system that permits boundary crossings provided that the victim be compensated? Nozick rules out full compensation on the grounds that it "is equivalent to a system requiring that all prior agreements about the right to cross a border be reached at the point in the contract curve most favorable to the *buyer* of the right" (63). As he points out, the person in the position of the buyer is a rights violator. This means that, if you were to steal my watch instead of bargaining for it, you only need compensate me by giving me $50 – my worst price![5] Actually, I would argue that, if we define full compensation as he does here, as making one as well off as one was before the boundary crossing (though presumably no better off), it is actually slightly worse than that. If I would be willing (though just barely) to fetch the watch and hand it to you, and then put the $50 in my wallet, I must prefer (though just barely) having the money to having the watch. That means that full compensation would take me to a level marginally worse than the $50 mark.[6] For present purposes, though, it makes no difference which of these two interpretations of full compensation we choose, making victims as well off or making them just marginally better off, as Nozick would obviously say that both are grotesquely unfair to the victim of the boundary crossing.

It seems to me that another objection to market compensation that he raises could be put more strongly than he does. This is the one in which he says that the "best method to discover" the price upon which the boundary crosser and the victim would have agreed on before the fact "is to let the negotiation take place." "Any other procedure," he adds, "would be highly inaccurate" (65). I would point out that, given that we are talking about *discovering* what the market compensation amount is, and not merely estimating it, letting the negotiation take place is the *only* way to accomplish this. The reason is that the amount in question is a fact, not about one person, nor even about two people, but about an interaction between them. It may be relatively easy for me to know what the lowest price I would accept is, and it may be similarly easy for you to know the highest price you would be willing to pay, but neither of us knows enough to predict at what position between these two points our bargaining will end up unless we begin making offers and counter-offers. Neither one of us even knows the actual range of prices in the bargaining window. If either bargainer truthfully reveals their limit price, that person will immediately be stuck with paying/getting that precise amount, or something very close to it. Further, since market compensation, by definition, is the amount that would have arisen from negotiations before the fact, this means that it is actually impossible to achieve after the fact, except by accident, and it may be an unlikely accident at that.

Nozick's case against a market compensation system seems very strong. What about his case against full compensation? Here I think we must make a distinction. If the case he makes is interpreted as a case against full compensation itself, it would seem that it can't possibly be right. After all, the function of compensation in the law is, in the words of one authority, "to right what would otherwise count as wrongful injuries to persons or their property."[7] This is generally interpreted as returning the victim to the *status quo ante*, to the level of wellbeing they enjoyed before their rights were violated.[8] That, of course, is full compensation. The function of compensation in the law is not to enable the victim to, so to speak, make a profit off their injuries (which is what market compensation would do). In civil law, full compensation is what compensation is. Period. Then why does Nozick's case against full compensation seem so plausible?

Well, it *is* plausible, but that is because it is not a case against full compensation *per se*. It is an argument against permitting boundary crossings provided that full compensation is paid. The injustice lies in the boundary crosser *deciding to purchase* the right to do so at a bargain price. His argument is consistent with a system that requires full compensation but also, provided the rights violation meets certain criteria, prohibits and punishes the act.[9]

There is one problem with the argument against permitting compensated crossings, though I think it is a small one. As I have reconstructed it, it seems to go like this. A system of always permitting boundary crossings provided only that the victim is compensated would give either full or market compensation. Full compensation would be unjust and market compensation would (in my amended version) be impossible to carry out (except by accident). Therefore, a system of always permitting boundary crossings provided only that the victim is compensated would be either unjust or impossible (except by accident). The problem is that the first premise, which seems to assume that there are only two kinds of compensation, or only two that are relevant here, is not argued for. Have I misinterpreted the argument? Or is the premise obviously true, so that it needs no justification? Perhaps the best way to think of it is to see it as a task for the reader: If you think that this is a weakness of the argument, try to come up with a significantly different sort of compensation, one that could be used in a victim-compensation-only system, and would not be subject to the sorts of objections he raises here. This would seem to be a very difficult thing to do.

4. Fear and Victim Compensation

There is an extended discussion in Chapter 4 of the fact that people who expose others to risk thereby inspire fear in others. Some of Nozick's subsequent references to this discussion might give a careless reader the impression that he is saying that there is an "argument from fear" here that plays exactly the same sort of role in his justification of the state as the arguments from risk and from procedural rights play. That is, one might suppose that he is saying that the fact that a risky activity inspires fear is, by itself, a reason to coercively prohibit it.[10] I do not think that this is how he means the discussion of fear to be taken. The other two arguments are meant to show that the unreliable or unfair methods used by some agents are, in and of themselves, what Nozick calls "boundary crossings." In other words, they are violations of rights. Rather, the argument from fear is meant to show that, *supposing* that the acts covered by these other two arguments are indeed boundary crossings, the proper response to them is, not to permit them provided that their victims are compensated, but rather to prohibit them. The idea is that, because it is impossible to compensate people for the fear that they would experience as a result of wrongly being exposed to the possibility of harm, such compensation cannot be part of the proper response to it.

He asks us to imagine the following two scenarios (66). X hears that Y, having had an accident and broken his arm, was later compensated with $2,000 (in 1974 dollars – worth considerably more today!). X thinks that this is adequate compensation: It covers the injury. Then Z tells X that, sometime in the next month, Z will break X's arm and then pay him $2,000. X spends the whole month a nervous wreck. He is apparently *not* indifferent to the combination of broken-arm-plus-$2,000. In some way, the $2,000 fails to cover the injury. Is he being inconsistent? Of course not. There is something in the second scenario that was not in the first: the fear engendered by knowing of the injury *in advance*. Further, the fear would not disappear if the *ex ante* compensation were larger. Fear, Nozick points out, is not a "global" emotion; it fastens on parts of packages rather than basing itself upon on-balance assessments (70).

There is a possible response to this, which Nozick puts in the form of a question: "Why couldn't someone who commits an assault compensate his victim not merely for the assault and its effects, but also for the fear the victim felt in awaiting some assault or other?" He replies:

> But under a general system which permits assault provided compensation is paid, a victim's fear is not caused by the particular person who assaulted him. Why then should this assaulter compensate him for it? *And who will compensate all the other apprehensive persons, who didn't happen to get assaulted, for their fear?* (66)

So the objection based on fear is that there is no specific person who inflicts the painful experience of fear and apprehension on people. The apprehension is caused by the possibility of being assaulted by *someone*, but not by any particular person. Compensation cannot be paid because there is no one to pay it.

This line of reasoning, which seems rather simple at first, can become rather baffling as one looks into it more closely. First, compensation is not meant to make injuries disappear. Why, then, is it an objection to compensation that it does not make the fear disappear? Second, inflicting fear on someone, or causing any particular emotion, does not sound like a "boundary crossing" at all. How, then, can it be relevant to the issue of whether we should coercively prohibit someone from doing something?

I think these problems evaporate if one keeps in mind that the argument from fear is an argument for preferring a policy of prohibition to a policy of compensation as a response to actions that are known on *other* grounds to be boundary crossings. He is not assuming that making people feel bad is a boundary crossing. Rather, the idea is that fear and apprehension are side-effects of the compensation-only system, and bad ones. The rhetorical question of his that I've quoted, about compensating Mr. X in the broken arm example after the fact, shows that Nozick realizes that full

93

compensation can in individual cases be a solution to the problem. If the offender who causes X to jump at noises behind him for a month promises and carries out full compensation, this does solve X's problem even though the promise does not make the fear go away: The compensation does make him as well off as he was before. But the second part of the argument, in which he points out that there is no one person or group of persons who causes the fear in a compensation-only system, is meant to show that this case is different: There is no one who can justly be compelled to pay the compensation. The fear is caused by the system itself. It is a cost of the system and consequently a reason to prefer a system that does not have that cost (if both are ways of dealing with boundary crossings).

There is at least one problem with this argument as I have interpreted it. Perhaps it is evidence that my interpretation is wrong. The clever, interesting example of Mr. X and his non-vanishing case of the jitters seems to be a sort of argumentative fifth wheel. It may have profound implications in some other context, but in the context of this argument, it only shows that, if we use a compensation-only system, there will be a sort of evil residue left over that can only be diminished by reducing the frequency of the acts that cause it. But isn't this obvious? The interesting discussion of the non-global nature of fear helps to explain why this is true, but that it is true is (so far) all his argument needs. Of course, it is quite possible that I have misread the "argument from fear," and that the curious case of Mr. X plays in it a crucial role that I have missed.

A somewhat more serious problem, though one that probably can be repaired, is this. As Nozick points out in an earlier section, the threat of having to pay compensation for an injury has some deterrent effect on people who might inflict that injury in the future. If we also require those who are found guilty to pay the "costs of detecting, apprehending, and trying" them, then (as he also points out) the deterrent effect becomes stronger. But, he says, this still might be "insufficient to deter someone from an action" (59). This is true. A compensation-only system shares a potential shortcoming that, as he tells us (60–61), is possessed by retributivist approaches to punishment. If the point of punishment is to give wrongdoers what they deserve – no less *and no more* – that may not be sufficient to bring about the desired level of deterrence. Similarly, full compensation is no more than full compensation – the victim is not supposed to make a profit from the wrong done to him/her. It is true, as he says, that this may be insufficient to deter a particular offender. But this is also true, not only of full compensation, but of all currently existing *criminal* penalties for actions: Otherwise, crime would not exist. The real issue here is about quantity of deterrence: Would compensation-only produce levels of deterrence that would be *unacceptably low*? The claim that it would is plausible on the face of it, but it would be nice to have a persuasive reason for thinking it is. We don't.

Before moving on, I would like to comment on Nozick's remark that fear is a non-global emotion. He is clearly right about that. I would only add that, depending on how you define emotion, it could be said that all emotions are non-global. Emotions, in one sense of the word, are about particular objects. If I am afraid of a bat flitting around my head, my fear has an object: the bat. If I am angry, I am angry at someone. What might be called "moods," such as joy or depression, are different. Joy is not "of" or "about" any particular object (unless the object is the entire world as the joyful person is experiencing it). A mood has causes, but does not have an object in the way that fear does. Emotions and moods have one thing in common, though, that is essential to the point that Nozick is making about fear: Both are experiences of value, of goodness or badness. To fear a bat is to see the bat as bad (i.e., dangerous). To be depressed is to have a sort of generalized feeling of badness or worthlessness, a sense of *why bother?*

If I buy a basket of vegetables at the supermarket with a $5 bill, I do not experience the loss of the $5 as negative. Rather, I experience the entire package – vegetables-minus-$5 – as a positive thing. The value of the $5 bill is experienced only as a part of the package. If I consider the possibility of bartering something to which I am emotionally attached – say, a picture of my wife that was made when I first met her decades ago (suppose that the picture cannot be reproduced, or that I would not be emotionally attached to a mere reproduction) – matters are different. Admittedly, if someone offered me a cool million dollars for it, I would take the million. But I would always feel a twinge about the loss of the picture, even though I obviously value the million, and therefore the entire package, more than I value the picture. The disvalue of losing the picture does not disappear in the greater good of the total package. This case is the obverse of the one that Nozick presents. Instead of getting something bad (a broken arm) and being fully compensated for it, I am losing something good (the picture) and being compensated for the loss. My feelings about that loss are clearly non-global. If you think of some more examples, you should be able to confirm that the non-global nature of fear actually characterizes all emotions (that are about particular objects) – both ones that are experiences of disvalue and ones that are experiences of value.

Even if I am right in saying that Nozick's point about fear standing in the way of on-balance, "big picture," greater-good assessments doesn't contribute to his critique of the compensation-only system, perhaps it does have interesting implications for understanding emotion. Once we have made the inference I have recommended, from fear to emotion in general, I think there is a possible connection with another part of Nozick's argument. This trait that people ordinarily have, of assessing value in terms of part of a package, of failing to think entirely in terms of the greater good, is exactly what the utilitarian would fault them for. A pure utilitarian, someone who really approached value and disvalue in terms of that one doctrine, undiluted and unconstrained by any countervailing way of thinking, would treat people the way I treat the $5 bill, and not the way I treat the picture. Perhaps the fact that most people find the implications of pure utilitarianism counter-intuitive has something to do with the fact that we arrive at assessments of the value of things, to some extent, through our emotions, and not entirely through our intellects.

I can easily imagine a utilitarian taking comfort from this very thought: that we reject utilitarianism, if we do, because we tend to think emotionally. Wouldn't that mean that rejecting utilitarianism is irrational? This only follows if we question-beggingly assume that rational thinking and emotional thinking are mutually exclusive. My own view is that if emotional thinking were simply a bad thing, there would not be so much of it. In fact, if our species were incapable of assessing value and disvalue through emotion, *we* might not exist at all. Our ancestors might have been eaten by dangerous animals they forgot were there because they did not have emotions like fear, terror, and horror to rivet their attention on the hazard that these animals posed. Or perhaps the members of their hunter-gatherer bands might have drifted apart, or failed to cooperate fully, or turned on one another with lethal acts of betrayal, because they did not have non-global emotions like love, loyalty, and respect to bind them together. If one's "instinctive" revulsion at some of the implications of utilitarianism is based on the fact that we think emotionally, that probably means it is connected with an aspect of human nature that is profoundly necessary for our survival.[11]

5. The Risk Argument

Although, as I have put it earlier, the risk argument "centers on" Chapter 4, it is stated most clearly and directly on the first page of Chapter 5. Speaking of the decision procedures used by "independents" – that is, by people who are not affiliated with the DPA – he says:

> If the independent's procedure is very unreliable and imposes high risk on others (perhaps he consults tea leaves) then if he does this frequently, he

may make all fearful, even those not his victims. Anyone, acting in self-defense, may stop him from engaging in his high-risk activity. But surely the independent may be stopped from using a very unreliable procedure even if he is not a constant menace. If it is known that the independent will enforce his own rights by his very unreliable procedure only once every ten years, this will *not* create general fear and apprehension in the society. The ground for prohibiting his widely intermittent use of his procedure is not, therefore, to avoid any widespread uncompensated apprehension and fear which otherwise would exist. (88–89)

Risk itself justifies coercive interference, independently of the sorts of considerations raised by the argument from fear. Everyone has the right to coercively interfere. And if everyone has it, the DPA will have it as well.

The Chapter 4 discussion of prohibiting risky activities raises an issue that, I believe, is of very general interest, reaching well beyond his narrow issue of the moment, which is that of how to justify the state. Nozick says that actions "that risk crossing another's boundaries pose serious problems for a natural rights position." I would add that the reason he gives for this claim actually makes risk a problem for *any* moral position. The reason he gives for its problematic nature is actually not moral but logical. He puts it in the form of a question: "Imposing how slight a probability of a harm that violates someone's rights also violates his rights?" (74). I'll call this *the line-drawing problem*. Risk is the probability that some harm (in this case, a rights violation) will occur. But probability is a continuum, containing infinitely many degrees, ranging (as it is commonly represented) from zero to one, with one representing certainty that the event will happen. What is the degree of probability that a rights violation will occur, which itself constitutes a violation?

Surely, we cannot say that all degrees above zero are violations. On what basis, then, can we draw a line between levels that are acceptable and those that are not? This is an interesting problem, and it is a problem that should be solved no matter what your moral theory might be. Which solution is the right one? Nozick sensibly says that perhaps "the cutoff probability" should be lower for more serious harms (74), but that of course does not answer this question.

He does not try to answer it, at least not in Chapter 4, but he does make an interesting comment on the nature of the possible solutions in a footnote. There, he points out that two "types of theories could be developed." First, a "theory could specify where a line is to be drawn without this position's seeming arbitrary, because though the line comes at a place which is not special along the probability dimension, it is distinguished along the different dimensions considered by the theory." That would be one possible type of theory. Alternatively, he says, "a theory could provide criteria for deciding about the risky actions that do *not* involve drawing a line along the probability ... dimension." He adds, provocatively: "Unfortunately, no satisfactory specific alternative theory of either type has yet been produced" (75 fn.).

It seems that, if we are to place any confidence in the risk argument, there must be some reason to hope that this problem can be solved. To make matters a little worse, I suggest that there is a second problem that stands in the way of solving it. I will call it *the actual-potential problem*. In the Lockean natural rights tradition that Nozick represents, coercion is justified by the fact that it is a response to a boundary crossing. A boundary crossing would seem to be something one actually does. Risk is the likelihood that certain things *might* actually happen. But this seems to be a fundamentally different sort of thing from a boundary crossing. This may be why Nozick says that the phenomenon of risk raises problems, specifically, for "a natural rights position." However, I would argue that this problem can be put in terms that would seem to apply to any moral theory. Intuitively, if we are going to punish you it should be for something you have done, and the same goes for exacting reparation. But if you are exposing me to a risk of a broken arm, this only means that you might break my arm. Precisely because it is something you might do, it is not something you have done. But why doesn't that mean that you can't be punished, or otherwise coerced, on account of it?

As with the line-drawing problem, there seem to be two sorts of possible solutions. We might give some reason why things that have not been done can have the same moral significance as if the agent in question has done them. Or we may find something that the risk-creator actually does (where *creating risk* is not arbitrarily described as "actually doing something"), something that can serve as a basis for justifying the use of force.

It seems to me that the argument from risk requires some hope of a solution to both of these problems, the line-drawing problem and the actual-potential problem. Though the idea that coercion can be justified by risk alone is plausible on the face of it, a theory that uses this idea will gain plausibility if we can assure ourselves that it can be applied in a non-arbitrary way, and one that is consistent with principles that we use in other contexts. In the next section I will argue that, surprisingly enough, Nozick lays out a doctrine in a later chapter of his book which directly implies a solution to both of these problems – including the one that he has pronounced to be so far unsolved. But I will also argue that it solves them in a way that actually *prevents* the risk argument from serving the function of justifying the state.

6. Preemptive Attack

I have said that one reason the risk argument is interesting is that it raises an issue with a much broader application than justifying the state. The broader issue we have looked at just now is the quite general one of the ethics of coercive responses to risky behavior. Actually, the issues his argument raises might be even wider than that. The even-wider issue I have in mind might be called the ethics of basing coercion on future events. It includes not merely the rights and wrongs of responses to risky behavior but, in addition, the ethics of preemptive attack, including preemptive warfare. In a way, forcibly stopping a risky activity *is* a sort of preemptive attack. If all I am doing is driving down University Avenue in Madison, Wisconsin at 100 miles per hour while roaring drunk, I have not hurt anybody – yet. If the police have a perfect right to lead me away in handcuffs – and if anyone in a Lockean state of nature would have the same right – that would be because people don't have to wait until I have hurt someone. Similarly, a country does not necessarily have to wait until its enemy is actually, presently dropping bombs on it before it uses force in self-defense. Both these ideas include an obvious reference to the future.

Nozick discusses the issue of preemptive attack in Chapter 6, and because of the strong connection between the two sorts of issues, what he says there can be applied, with interesting results, to what he says about risk in the risk argument.

Nozick formulates the preemptive attack issue by posing a series of hypothetical cases. The "usual doctrine," he says, holds that "under some circumstances a country X may launch a preemptive attack, or a preventive war, upon another country Y." For instance, X may attack Y if "Y is itself about to launch an immediate attack upon X," or, again, if "Y has announced that it will do so upon reaching a certain level of military readiness, which it expects to do some time soon." On the other hand, X may not "launch a war against Y because Y is getting stronger, and (such is the behavior of nations) might well attack X when it gets stronger still." Why, he asks, does self-defense plausibly justify force in the first cases but not in the last (126)?

Notice that it is possible to formulate the risk issue in exactly the same way. Under certain circumstances, you have a right to preemptively stop my bad driving practices before they have hurt anyone. You may stop me if I am driving 100 miles per hour on a city street while drunk. You may also stop me if I am driving drunk but not speeding. But on the other hand, you may not forcibly stop me from drinking in a bar earlier in the evening, on the grounds that I *might* go out and injure someone because of my diminished mental capacities. Self-defense, or something very much like it, justifies force in the first cases, though not in the last. Why?

With the obvious parallels between these two sorts of issue, it seems natural to try to formulate an answer to the "why" question for one sort of issue and then try to apply that answer, perhaps suitably adapted, to the other. Given that the common structure I have attributed to the two sorts of issue looks very much like the original line-drawing problem, an obvious strategy would be to try to assimilate the preemptive attack problem to the risk problem.

One thing seems to stand in the way of doing so: Nozick gives a simple and, I think, telling argument against basing the distinction between the preemptive attack cases on probability considerations. Take the degree of probability that Y, having grown stronger, will attack X. Now imagine instead the following scenario: "Y is now about to wield a super-device ... that, with *that* degree of probability, will conquer X." Y is committed to trigger the device at the end of one week, and the countdown has begun. Clearly, X may use force in self-defense to prevent this from being done. But if probability were the crucial consideration, this case would have to be treated the same as the third preemptive attack case, which of course it is not (126). So it looks like the preemptive attack problem cannot be assimilated to the risk problem – that is, it is not exactly the same problem.

Or is it? After all, both of Nozick's suggestions for possible sorts of solutions to the line-drawing problem involved basing the line on non-probablistic considerations. Either we can find a level of probability that is special because it is linked to something other than probability, or we define unacceptable risky behavior in terms of something other than probability altogether. Interestingly, when Nozick proposes an answer to the question about preemptive attack, it is a version of the second sort of possible solution to the line-drawing problem about risk.

The difference, he says, between the third preemptive attack case and the other two is not about the probability of future boundary crossings at all. It is about the relation between those possible future events and what the agent *has already done*. The principle that, according to him, distinguishes between them can be adequately paraphrased as follows:

> An act is not wrong in itself and may not be resisted with force if it is harmless without a further decision on the part of the agent to do wrong.[12]

It is arguable that this principle draws the desired line between the three preemptive attack cases. In the first case, the imminent attack, country Y is gearing up for war, the leaders have issued the orders, and they, the leaders, need make no new decisions to violate rights in order for rights to be violated: It now depends on wrongful decisions of others. (Presumably, we are thinking of X's preemptively attacking Y as an attempt to coerce the leader of Y.) In the second case, that of the public announcement of the intention to attack X, the leader of Y is now publicly committing others to carry out their role. The machinery is in motion, and can move toward violating rights without the leader's making any new morally wrong decisions. The same is true of the leader who commits him- or herself to triggering the probablistic weapon that Nozick has imagined. On the other hand, obviously, country Y's continuing to get stronger will not result in harm without new, future decisions to do wrong on the part of the people that country X is contemplating using force against; thus they may not be coercively interfered with, even though their actions do increase the probability of future rights-violating acts against X.

Notice that this principle distinguishes, even more clearly, between my three risk cases. Once I have begun speeding down a city street while drunk, what I am already doing can result in a violation of rights without my deciding to do any other wrong thing. And the same is true if I am not speeding but *am* driving while drunk. On the other hand, if I am quietly getting drunk in a bar, that *can't* violate the rights of others unless I decide to do some (further?) wrong thing (such as drive a car in that condition).

I think this principle is at least as plausible as a response to the ethics of prohibiting risky activities as it is as a solution to that of preemptive attack. As I have said, it clearly solves the line-drawing problem. Just as obviously, it solves the actual-potential problem as well. It bases the right to use force against someone on wrong acts that they have actually done. It also gives plausible answers to the ethical questions we have discussed so far. One shortcoming of the principle as I have paraphrased it is that it makes use of the somewhat obscure phrase, "wrong in itself." This is a phrase that does not appear in his first statement of the principle (127). The first statement says that an act is *not wrong* and so cannot be prohibited if it is harmless without further major decisions to commit wrong. This seems clearly incorrect. The series of events that lead to Y attacking X might begin with the ruler of Y giving a long speech in which he screams that X is an enemy of the true faith and its inhabitants ought to be exterminated. This will not result in Y's harming X unless its rulers do some further wrong thing, and yet giving such a speech obviously *is* wrong. I remedied this problem by replacing "wrong" with "wrong in itself," which he uses in a later (129) paraphrase of the principle. Yet it, as

I say, has the disadvantage of being obscure. (Wrong in itself, as opposed to what?) Actually, I think this problem can easily be remedied by replacing this phrase. After all, the central issue of the discussion of preemptive attack, as in the discussion of prohibiting unreliable procedures in the administration of justice, is not whether a given act is wrong *simpliciter*, but whether it is a boundary crossing and so makes the agent liable to being opposed by force. Thus:

> An act is not a boundary crossing and may not be resisted with force if it is harmless without a further decision on the part of the agent to do wrong

This is both clearer and more focused on the issues at hand than the original statement of the principle.

The fact that this principle applies directly to the problem of prohibiting risky activities, and is as plausible as it is when so applied, means that it *so far* enhances the risk argument for the legitimacy of the state. It will, if we accept it, solve the problem of how we can draw a non-arbitrary line between risks that may be prohibited and ones that may not, and it will solve the actual-potential problem too. So it solves two problems that stood in the way of comfortably accepting risk as constituting sufficient grounds for coercion. However, it solves these problems only by creating a more serious one for Nozick's justification of the state. The reason is that, though the principle does give us reason to think that a non-arbitrary line can be drawn, it does so by drawing that line on the "wrong" side of the risky decision procedures that his DPA is undertaking to prohibit.

Suppose that some such agency is using an unreliable procedure to decide whether to punish me for something I am thought to have done. Suppose further that, because it is unreliable, the decision they would come up with, were they to execute it, would be unjust. Their use of this procedure is harmless unless they make a further decision to do wrong: namely, the unjust decision itself. This is true of any unreliable decision procedure. The unjust punishment, and the decision process that selects it, are distinct and separable. To say that it may be forcibly resisted in self-defense is analogous to saying that country X may preemptively attack country Y at a certain point upstream from the moment when Y's attack on X becomes imminent, and even before Y has committed itself to attacking X: namely, when Y is using unreliable rules of evidence in the cabinet meeting in which it is deciding whether to do these things. Obviously, this is not wrong in a way that gives others a right to violently attack them.[13]

7. Procedural Rights

Though the risk argument, in its present form, does not justify the DPA in prohibiting risky activities of independents, it may be salvageable. There are no doubt other ways of resolving issues like the line-drawing problem, other than the one suggested by Nozick's treatment of preemptive attack. Perhaps there are plausible ones that will support the DPA in prohibiting risky decision procedures. The matter is clearly worthy of further investigation. Nozick's argument from procedural rights seems to me to be less promising.

Admittedly, the idea that in any just legal system everyone will have positive procedural rights is very plausible. You not only have a right, against the legal system, that it not punish you when you are actually innocent, but you also have a right against having your guilt or innocence decided in the wrong way, even if you are guilty. In the legal system of the United States, accused individuals have such a right against being convicted on the basis of evidence collected via unreasonable search and seizure. This is a procedural right. There are weighty reasons for requiring positive law to grant rights of this sort. But the procedural right that Nozick is talking about here is of a fundamentally different sort from this one. It is not a positive right that states ought to grant. Rather it is a right that everyone has, independently of such enactments, and that the DPA is uniquely positioned to exercise because it is the dominant agency. This means it has to be a natural right. The idea of a natural procedural right is a curious one. What, exactly, is this right? Just what is it a right *to*? Nozick's answer seems to be this:

> Every individual ... [has] the right that information sufficient to show that a procedure of justice about to be applied to him is reliable and fair (or no less so than other procedures in use) be made publicly available or made available to him. ... [A] person may resist, in self-defense, if others try to apply to him an unreliable or unfair procedure of justice. (102)

This claim might be plainly untrue, depending on how one interprets it. How one *should* interpret it is not immediately obvious. "Procedure of justice" cannot mean a formal, legal procedure, because the sort of procedure that we are dealing with here may be very informal indeed. Perhaps it could mean something like "any procedure that results in behavior that can be substantively just or unjust." Read in this way, the principle is excessively broad and onerous, and would create a vast array of hitherto unknown rights and obligations. Depending on one's conception of justice, many – perhaps all – of the things that anyone does that have effects on others can be just or unjust. Yet surely I do not generally or typically have an enforceable right to information about how others make decisions that affect me. In many cases, this would mean having rights regarding the thought processes of others, a situation that would clash with very basic intuitions we have about privacy.

Probably, Nozick means to limit "procedure of justice" to procedures in which one is deciding whether to punish someone or exact compensation for some alleged violation of someone's rights. This interpretation makes the principle much more plausible. But notice that what it says, on this interpretation, is that everyone may resist, by force presumably, the application of the decision procedure itself, before it has resulted in any substantive injustice. Why would this be true, if it is? It seems that the only possible answer would have to be that an unreliable procedure would be more likely to result in a violation of rights than a more reliable one – in other words, that it exposes one to higher levels of risk of rights violation. That would mean that the procedural rights argument, insofar as it is plausible, collapses into the risk argument.

There is another problem with this idea of a natural procedural right, one that was pointed out some years ago by Jeffrey Paul.[14] It rests on a certain unusual feature that this idea seems to have. The idea seems to be that if A is contemplating punishing B, not only does B have a first-order right against A, a right not to be punished if innocent, but a second-order right which is about that first-order right: a right that decisions about whether the first-order right is being violated be made by reliable methods. This second right is a "right" in the same sense of the word as the first one: It is enforceable by coercion, and so forth. But doesn't this mean that B has a third-order right that decisions about whether the second-order right is being violated be made by reliable methods? Mustn't there also be a fourth-order right about the third-order one? This process must go on forever. The idea of a natural procedural right implies an infinite series of rights.

Infinite regress arguments like this one can seem unserious and "just clever," but this one does have a serious point. If Paul is right about this, there is a reason why Nozick's idea generates an infinite series of rights. It is that (as interpreted by this objection) this procedural right (a) applies quite generally to rights against users of procedures of justice, and (b) implies that for each of them there is another right, which is also a right against a user of procedures of justice. The infinite regress argument appears to imply that a right that has both these features cannot exist. This peculiar sort of right requires the user of a procedure of justice to do an infinite number of things. To point this out goes beyond mere cleverness for its own sake. Nozick's procedural right can be saved from the regress argument if it can be formulated in such a way that it lacks either (a) or (b).

As a matter of fact, he formulates an idea later in the same section of Chapter 5 in which he sets forth his account of this natural procedural right that might avoid both of the major problems I have posed for that account: both the infinite regress argument and the issue of whether there is anything ethically problematic in what the risky independent is doing, other than what is already addressed by the risk argument. This idea bases the constraint that unreliable independents violate, not on a right possessed by the one to be punished, but on a duty that applies to the would-be punisher.

The principle involved here has to do with the broader problem that he describes as "how to merge epistemic considerations with rights." He thinks it is obvious that it is wrong to undertake to punish a person when one is not in a position to know (that is the epistemic consideration here) that the person is guilty. But how shall we characterize the nature of the wrong being done?

> Shall we say that someone doesn't have a right to do certain things unless he knows certain facts, or shall we say that he does have a right but he does wrong in exercising it unless he knows certain facts? (106)

Believing that he can say everything he wants to say about the issue presently at hand in either of these two ways, he chooses to use the latter formulation. Shortly after that, he proposes "an epistemic principle of boundary crossing":

> If someone knows that doing act A would violate Q's rights unless condition C obtained [e.g., where A is a punishment and C is Q's actual guilt], he may not do A if he has not ascertained that C obtains through being in the best feasible position for ascertaining this. (106–107)

He immediately adds: "Anyone may punish a violator of this prohibition" (107). Of course, if anyone may do this, then the DPA may do it. It may prohibit unreliable procedures.[15]

This principle might accomplish the same result as the procedural rights argument – justifying coercive interference with risky independents – while avoiding both of the problems I have raised for that argument. It is obvious that it side-steps the infinite regress problem, at least if we avoid interpreting it in such a way that candidates for punishment have a right, against would-be punishers, that punishers follow this principle. Under that interpretation, the principle would seem to imply that they also have a right that punishers ascertain that they are following the principle through being in the best feasible position for doing so, etc., etc. – and we are off to infinity again. However, if we avoid talking in terms of such rights, we at least have a hope of avoiding infinite series of them.

The other problem was that of finding something ethically problematic about use of unreliable methods other than exposing others to the risk of undeserved punishment. Here the idea would be that doing something that you know will violate Q's rights if C does not obtain, when (roughly speaking) you don't know that C obtains is morally wrong in itself, even if (maybe through dumb luck) you don't violate those rights. It is irresponsible. This moral wrong is distinct from the heightened risk involved. Perhaps one could argue that the activities of risky independents are wrong because they violate the "epistemic principle," even if those activities do not violate a right. This seems a plausible view, worthy of further consideration.

However, Nozick's argument here requires that one go further than this. It requires one to accept the *idea* that any undertaking to punish someone that violates the epistemic principle – in fact, *any behavior* that violates it – may be deterred by coercion. Such behavior is a punishable offense. This is not obviously true. Not everything that is morally wrong – in fact, not all moral wrong that causes harm to others – is a legitimate ground for punishment. For instance, insulting people is (always/usually/ often) morally wrong and causes hurt feelings and other bad effects, but in the American legal system it is not a punishable offense. In fact, it isn't even a tort: You can't sue someone for insulting you. You can sue for libel and slander, but that is a different matter.[16] Is violating the epistemic principle something that is legitimately punishable?

This doesn't seem a very plausible idea to me. Notice what a strong claim this is. Not only does it mean that violations of the epistemic principle should be treated more harshly than our system treats insults: It requires treating them more harshly than our system treats libel and slander, which are torts (you can be sued) but not crimes (you cannot be punished). It means they should be treated the way we treat criminal assault, though their behavior may, as far as the present argument is concerned, violate no rights at all.

The idea that wrongdoing can justify coercion even in the absence of a violation of rights is not an obviously absurd idea. The idea that Joel Feinberg called "Legal Moralism" – that coercion can be justified on the grounds that it enforces morality as such, even if the forbidden, morally wrong act either does not otherwise do any harm or occurs between consenting adults – is actually fairly widely accepted in one form or another.[17] This is no doubt a good part of the reason why there are laws against prostitution and selling or using certain "recreational" drugs. However, Nozick is obviously not a legal moralist: Such an idea would be utterly inconsistent with the libertarian position that he proclaims on the first page of ASU. This means he cannot think that the wrongness of violating the epistemic principle, by itself, is what justifies suppressing such behavior with threats of punishment. What then, does? To put the issue differently: The argument that is based on the epistemic principle will be more convincing if Nozick – or someone who agrees with his position on this issue – can find a principled reason why this particular sort of wrongdoing can be prohibited and punished, even if it violates no rights, while other forms of non-rights-violating wrongdoing cannot.

8. The Principle of Compensation

The remainder of the argument for the state, as I have said, consists in the rather surprising idea that the risky independents, potential boundary-crossers, be fully compensated for the prohibition to which they are subjected. The compensation – being protected by the DPA – enables it to acquire something that is sufficiently similar to the "protecting everybody" feature of states to enable it to jump the gap that separated the ultraminimal state from the minimal state.

Nozick does recognize the seeming oddity of both prohibiting an act and compensating the agent for having been subjected to the prohibition. Surely, you might think, "either you have a right to forbid it so you needn't compensate, or you don't have a right to forbid and so you should stop" (83). So why fully compensate? Here the argument has two phases: One explains why compensation is due, and the other explains why this compensation should not be market compensation.

The first phase of this argument is one of the most difficult to untangle in ASU. Nozick sees some (though not all) risky activities as presenting us with a sort of moral dilemma (78–79). On the one hand, people who are prohibited from doing some dangerous activity are having their freedom of action curtailed. On the other hand, by doing the action, they are imposing hazards on us: We are unfairly being made to bear the costs of their freedom. However, because the activity is *only* risky, it might well be carried out without anyone being hurt. If we had the ability to tell which agents will eventually harm someone, there would be no problem of prohibiting dangerous activities: We could just prohibit those particular agents. By prohibiting individuals who might turn out to be completely harmless, it seems we are unfairly making them "bear the full burden of our inability" (79). This is just the sort of problem that can be solved by having one party compensate the other.

In what sort of case is compensation called for? Nozick draws a line between the first of the following cases and the other two:

1. Someone drives a car though they suffer from epilepsy (78–79).
2. Involuntary second-party Russian roulette: Someone plays Russian roulette *on another* (79).
3. Someone uses "a risky but efficient … process in manufacturing a product" (79). (More precisely, the case seems to be using such a process sufficiently near places of residence to endanger the residents.)

Nozick believes 2 and 3 may simply be prohibited, with no compensation paid, while in case number 1 the epileptic must be forbidden to drive but must also be compensated. What is the difference?

Initially, he considers formulating the principle that separates the activity in the first case from the other two in terms of nature of the activities themselves: This sort of compensation is due if the prohibited acts are ones that have four characteristics; they (a) are generally done, (b) play an important role in people's lives, (c) cannot be forbidden someone without seriously disadvantaging them, and (d) only *might* do harm to others (81). However, he drops this way of drawing a line between case 1 and cases 2 and 3 because it raises "messy problems about classifying actions" (83). The activity that I have called "involuntary second-party Russian roulette" can also be described as "having fun." Having fun is generally done and does play an important role in people's lives. Depending on how you describe what the person is doing in case 2, he/she is either doing something different from me, as I am entertaining myself with the *New York Times* crossword puzzle, or the same thing. Why is one classification right and the other wrong?

He avoids this issue by sketching his "Principle of Compensation," which relies on the notion of disadvantage rather than that of "doing the same thing." He tells us that "those who are *disadvantaged* by being forbidden to do actions that only *might* harm others must be compensated for these disadvantages foisted upon them in order to provide security for the others" (82–83). This principle is probably broader than the other approach, as it no longer clearly requires that the activity be one that is both generally done and plays an important role in people's lives. However, it does seem to draw the line between his three cases where he wants it, separating the first from the other two. The prohibition burdens the epileptic with a disadvantage in comparison with those who are not forbidden to drive. In the second and third cases, the person is not put at a disadvantage, apparently (the text is not crystal clear about this) because nobody is allowed to do these things. The person who is prevented from using the dangerous manufacturing process (at least, in a residential area) or from playing non-consenting second-party Russian roulette is thereby placed in the same circumstances that everybody else is in.

Before I move on to the rest of Nozick's justification of the state, I would like to pause and consider what we should think of the Principle of Compensation. Once again, I am skeptical. I would feel more confident about accepting it and applying it to risky decision procedures of independents if I could find some other case where it pretty clearly applies. I realize that this is exactly what Nozick is trying to do with the case of the would-be epileptic driver, but that case is itself not very convincing. I cannot find a single state of the US or a single country that handles the issue of epilepsy and driving the way he says they should. In the US epileptics are permitted to drive, but only if they give sufficient evidence that the probability of having an accident-causing seizure is low enough to qualify. In most jurisdictions, the evidence consists in having gone without a seizure for a specified period of time (the length of which varies greatly from state to state). Those who fail to give the required evidence are simply prohibited from driving.[18] As far as I have been able to determine, nobody compensates them.

Nozick's Principle of Compensation actually applies to a wide class of morally problematic cases. The case of the epileptic driver is only one of many. In each of these cases, there is a technological device (or class of devices) that people generally have a right to use, except for certain classes of people who are thought to be excessively dangerous users of the device(s). Motor vehicles are the occasion for a number of such exceptions. People with moderate to advanced multiple sclerosis are sometimes forbidden to drive if their disease makes them prone to have accidents. People with severe cognitive impairments (e.g., Down syndrome) are in effect prohibited from driving by virtue of their inability to pass the required test. In addition, of course, people who repeatedly drive while intoxicated are forbidden to drive. None of these people are compensated. The case of the drunk driver can be accommodated by revising the principle slightly, so that it makes compensation depend on being "unfairly disadvantaged" rather than merely "disadvantaged." (The repeatedly drunk driver, we might say, is a *guilty* dangerous user, so disadvantaging them is not unfair.) The others, however, do seem problematic for the Principle of Compensation.

Another type of device for which we make dangerous user exceptions is firearms. Owning them is recognized as a right, and currently as an individual right, by the Supreme Court,[19] and yet some groups are excepted. Since 1968, it has been illegal in the United States for convicted felons to own guns, and no doubt concern about their being dangerous users is part of the reason for this. Children younger than a certain age are forbidden guns, as, in some jurisdictions, are the mentally disabled and people with a history of mental illness (e.g., people who have been involuntarily committed to a mental institution). None of these people are compensated. One might argue that the drunk driver revision I suggested above would mean that the Principle of Compensation no longer applies to felons. One might also make a case that children and the mentally disabled are actually benefited by the prohibition, because it protects them from injury and death as well as other people – and that this means they are not disadvantaged, so that no compensation is due under Nozick's principle. However, the case of people with a history of mental illness cannot, at least in many cases, be taken care of in either of these ways.

The law does not seem to follow the Principle of Compensation at all.[20] Of course, Nozick is free to say that, if that is so, the law is simply wrong. After all, isn't it unfair that my epileptic neighbor who – unlike the drunk driver and the felon – is dangerous through no fault of her own, is not permitted to drive, while I am? I feel strongly inclined to say: "Of course it is!" But I think it makes a big difference for present purposes wherein the unfairness lies. First, recall that, in the course of discussing the risk argument, Nozick makes it very clear that he thinks that exposing others to a prohibitably high level of risk is actually a rights violation.[21] By prohibiting the epileptic from driving, we are prohibiting her from violating people's rights. It is hard to see how that aspect of what we are doing can be unfair. We are doing our duty (if, that is, the risk argument is right) and compelling her to do hers. Where does the unfairness come from? It comes from the conjunction of two factors: the fact that her being a dangerous driver is due to a natural misfortune, a disease of the central nervous system, for which she bears no moral responsibility *plus* the fact that we have done our duty. If what I just said is right, our contribution to this situation, so far, is not wrongful or blameworthy. If there is indeed unfairness here, it is because nature is unfair: It passes out benefits and burdens, capacities and incapacities, without the slightest regard for equality, just desserts, or anything else that has anything to do with decency or justice. In this way, nature is remorselessly amoral.

There is still one way in which we might be wrong if we fail to compensate the epileptic who is forbidden to drive. We might have a positive duty to take steps to even up the inequalities that are due to nature. There are influential theories that say that we do. When we get to Chapter 7 of ASU we will discuss Nozick's views on these theories. We will see plenty of reason to doubt that Nozick can consistently say that states have a duty to even up inequalities of this sort.

Further, consider the ultimate point of the discussion of the Principle of Compensation: It is to argue that the DPA has an obligation to compensate risky independents by extending protection to them. The case for compensating risky independents seems weaker (i.e., *even* weaker) than the case for compensating the epileptic driver. After all, the independents cannot say that what makes them risky to the rest of us is a brute physical malady for which they bear no responsibility. It is true enough that they don't intend to violate rights, and that they sincerely believe that their decision procedures are reliable. But we say that they are not reliable, and there is no brain disease that caused them to use such methods. It was their idea to do so. It is less clear than it is in the case of the epileptic that they are innocent, and it is accordingly less clear that it is wrong to prohibit them from exposing others to risk without compensating them.[22]

9. Unproductive Exchange and Explaining Why Blackmail Is Wrong

So the risky independents are due an unusual sort of compensation: Instead of compensating the victim of a risky activity after they are injured, we prohibit the activity and give before-the-fact compensation to the agent to whom the ban applies. But why does this agent compensation – as it might be called, in contradistinction from victim compensation – take the form of being offered protection by the DPA? The shortest version of his answer that he gives (84) is that in cases like this it makes sense to place the amount of the compensation at one end of the contract curve (or what I called the bargaining window). Full compensation – but no more than that – should be paid. The logical link between full compensation and protection by the DPA is perhaps obvious: Full compensation means being made as well off as you were before. Where the independents were before being prohibited was that they were protected (albeit by methods deemed by others to be unreliable). So extending protection to them brings them back to where they were.

But why are they due no more than full compensation?[23] It might seem that we have already discussed this issue, when we dealt with the general problem of the treatment of boundary crossings (i.e., why not permit the act but require that the victim be compensated?). But in this case we are talking about people who have not committed an actual boundary crossing. That makes the current problem more acute than the earlier one. I have argued that in the case of victim compensation, giving market compensation is a merely theoretical possibility, because there is no way to know the amount of money for which the victim of an injury would have sold the right to injure him or her, if the bargaining process, which is now impossible, had actually been carried out. In the case of agent compensation, precisely because it is before the fact, the process clearly is possible. We can approach the agents of risky activities, bargain with them, and buy them out. In this case we are concerned with future boundary crossings that the independent might carry out. Bargaining with them is more than a theoretical possibility. Why don't we have an obligation to do it?

The short version of Nozick's answer is that such a buy-out would be what he calls an "unproductive exchange." Needless to say, this adds another layer of complexity to his argument. As a sort of bonus payoff for bearing with him through these complications, he points out that his idea of non-productive exchange can be used to explain why blackmail is wrong and prohibitable. As we shall soon see, this is not as easy as one might think.

He defines unproductive exchange as existing when two conditions are met, which he calls the necessary condition of unproductive exchange and the sufficient condition. Both are important for the argument that follows. The necessary condition is that the exchange makes one of the parties no better off than he/she would be if the other "had n*othing at all* to do with them" (84). To elaborate on an example that Nozick gives (85): Suppose that a historian is writing a history of the university where I teach, and finds, through a series of freedom of information requests that, some years ago, I was quietly disciplined, but not fired, by the university for some rather serious misconduct on my part. Because my behavior might be damaging to the reputation of the university itself (remember, I am making this up!) it took care not to let the whole affair become public knowledge. The historian plans to publish this information in her book. I get wind of this and beg her not to publish the embarrassing information. Seeing that she is reluctant to do so, I offer to pay for her silence. She accepts. Though I am made better off by this transaction than I would have been without it – her silence is worth that much money to me – I am not better off than I would have been if she had never had anything to do with me. (Clearly, planning to write a book that contains humiliating information about me counts as having something to do with me.)

The sufficient condition of non-productive exchange is that it gives to one of the parties relief from "something that would not threaten if not for the possibility of an exchange to get relief from it" (85). Suppose that someone finds the same information that the historian found in the case I have just imagined, and comes to me, threatening to publish the information if I do not pay him off (getting the payment is his only motive for making the threat). Horrified, I pay. Once again, I am better off, in these circumstances and in terms of my own preferences, than I would be if I did not pay (the necessary condition) – but I am buying relief from an evil that would not threaten were it not for this particular way of getting relief from it. In transactions of this sort, if something somehow were to render the transaction impossible, only one of the two parties would be made worse off. (Notice that any transaction that satisfies the sufficient condition will also satisfy the necessary condition, but not the other way around.)

Of course, we have a name for this last transaction: It is blackmail. Blackmail always satisfies the sufficient condition. One thing that makes this notion of unproductive exchange an attractive one is that, as Nozick points out, it can be used to explain why such transactions are wrong and prohibitable. Perhaps I should pause a moment to explain why this is an issue at all. It may not be obvious.

Blackmail, after all, is a commercial transaction, a trade.[24] Consider a transaction in which I sell you my watch for $75. At the end of the transaction, my watch has become your watch, and your money has become my money. What can explain this transformation? Part of the answer is that at the beginning of the transaction the watch was rightfully mine and the money was rightfully yours. If it is not actually my watch, I can't cause it to be rightfully yours in this way. My rights over the watch include a right to transfer those rights to you: I can make you a gift of it. In addition, I can conditionally transfer that right to you: I can agree that, if you give me a certain amount of money, the watch is yours. If you agree to my conditions, we have agreed to a trade.

How is blackmail different from this? In blackmail what is being sold is not a good, like a watch, but a service: the negative service of refraining from publicizing certain information. Certainly, the blackmailer has a right to refrain from publicizing it. Then doesn't he have a right to do so on condition that I meet his terms? So the answer to our question – why is blackmail wrong and prohibitable? – cannot be that the third sort of right that I described above, the right to conditionally grant others a right against oneself, does not exist in the case of remaining silent. It does. So how is blackmail so different from other trades that they are permitted and it may be prohibited?

The clever answer that Nozick in effect offers to this question is to identify blackmail as an instance of a wider class of transactions, all of which he believes are wrong and prohibitable. This class consists of all transactions that satisfy the sufficient condition of unproductive exchange. In a normal trade, as when I sell you my watch, both parties would be made worse off if the transaction were somehow made impossible. This of course is not the case in a blackmail transaction.

Further, in transactions that satisfy the necessary condition, Nozick tells us that the person being paid may not demand any payment greater in value than what they forgo by doing what they are being paid to do. In the case of the historian, since what I am paying her to do is to omit an interesting story about me, she may not charge me more than the expected difference in royalties between the book with the story in it and without it. Apparently, the reason for this, though Nozick never says so in quite so many words, is that if they charge more than this, then this increment of extra value satisfies the sufficient condition: If it were impossible for me to pay her this extra amount, she would (like the blackmailer) be worse off than she otherwise would be, but I would not.

This is why we need not bargain with risky independents and give them market compensation to forgo their risky methods: Typically, one who bargains to sell a service gets more than the value of what the service requires that they forgo. What the DPA must compensate them for is the disadvantage that they suffer from having their risky methods prohibited. Nozick believes that, with one proviso, what compensation requires is that the DPA give to the prohibited independents the cost of their cheapest, least fancy policy. The proviso is that their prohibited activities might have cost them something and the prohibition spares them this cost: Therefore, these costs, if any, are to be subtracted from the amount that they are given.[25] Thus, unless there are some independents who choose to spend this money on something other than a protection policy (which sounds like a very bad idea) the DPA will be protecting people who are prohibited from availing themselves of another source of protection.

10. Assessing the Unproductive Exchange Argument

Has Nozick succeeded in showing that the DPA need not bargain with risky independents and has he succeeded, as a bonus result, in showing why blackmail is wrong in a way that makes it prohibitable?

I see a problem with the discussion of blackmail, one that leads to another one involving the risky independents. As I have interpreted it, it depends on the idea that unproductive exchange, per se, is wrong and prohibitable. There is actually a very large class of transactions that satisfies the sufficient condition and yet clearly may not be coercively prohibited – in fact, Nozick obviously would agree that they may not. The domain of these transactions, as a matter of fact, is bargaining itself. Virtually all cases of bargaining satisfy this condition.[26] Let's go back to my old example, of selling my watch. Suppose you offer to buy my watch for $55. I actually would rather have your $55 than keep my watch: I would be willing, though just barely, to part with it for that amount. However, I think I can do better than that. I make a counter-offer of $95. I am doing something that is essential to the bargaining process: I am holding out, withholding my consent in order to elicit behavior from you that is in my interest. If I had simply said "$55? It's a deal!" it would be a misuse of the word to say that we had "bargained" at all. Obviously, the process of holding out and counter-offering could go on for a while. Suppose, to make the story short, you say: "Let's split the difference – how does 75 bucks sound?" and I agree. You just offered me an increment of wealth – $20 above your last offer – to get me to do something that you want me to do: to stop holding out. But this only buys you relief from something (my continuing to hold out) that would not threaten but for the possibility of getting relief from it in this particular way. If for some reason it were impossible for you to thus offer me increments of money above $55, only one of us would be made worse off (i.e., me). Thus something that is essential to the bargaining process – making more favorable offers to get one's bargaining partner to stop withholding their consent – satisfies the sufficient condition.

There is a simple reason why this is true. If you voluntarily buy my watch, we both benefit from the transaction. We both prefer making the deal to not making the deal. In this respect, we have a harmony of interests. Within the bargaining window, however, we have an absolute contrariety of interests, just as there is between me and my blackmailer. The reason is that, to use a very apt phrase that Nozick has already used in a somewhat different context, in bargaining we are "dividing the benefits of exchange." The exchange as a whole is beneficial to both, and when we bargain we are deciding *how* beneficial it will be to each of us.

There is one large, obvious difference between moves in the bargaining process and blackmail. Bargaining moves represent a dimension, so to speak, of contrariety of interests within an exchange that is characterized by harmony of interests (it is good for both of us). In blackmail, on the other hand, the entire exchange is good for one party and bad for the other. My blackmailer offers me a choice between two things, neither of which I want. Perhaps the idea should be that exchanges that fit the sufficient condition – that is, where the *entire* exchange does so – are wrong and may be coercively prohibited. This principle is worth considering, to be sure, at least if we can come up with a clear and non-arbitrary way of distinguishing between an entire exchange, like making a blackmail payment, and actions that are merely parts or aspects of exchanges, such as the holding out and making a counter-offer by means of which I get $20 more out of you.

However, such a move would threaten to destroy the point Nozick is trying to make here. Remember, the point of all this is to show that the DPA need not buy off the risky independents, giving them market compensation. The reasoning was that anything they get from us beyond what is needed to compensate them for their disadvantages constitutes an unproductive exchange. This seems to be unproductive in precisely the same sense as my holding out and making a counter-offer. So he appears to be committed to applying the notion of unproductivity to parts or aspects of exchanges, not merely entire ones.

Someone who wants the argument about risky independents to work might point out that the conclusion he needs in that argument is actually weaker than the one he reaches in the discussion of blackmail. In the latter discussion he is arguing that this unproductive exchange is wrong and prohibitable. In the discussion of the risky independent he need only say that it is not obligatory: The DPA need not make this payment. My point in that case would be that the only argument he has given to the conclusion that it is not obligatory in the latter case is that it is wrong and prohibitable in the former one. If that argument is no good, then the notion that the DPA need not make this payment is so far unsupported.

Nonetheless, the notion of unproductive exchange is a potentially useful one for moral theory.[27] There are indeed exchanges, and parts of exchanges, that are unproductive in Nozick's sense, and the examples of blackmail and, I would argue, even bargaining itself, suggest that such transactions have a marked tendency to either be wrong or to, so to speak, *go* wrong. The reason for this, moreover, is precisely their unproductivity. When you use clever bargaining strategies, you are not creating value: You are simply moving it around.[28] More precisely, you are attempting to capture value that would otherwise go to your trading partner. Because of this, there are bargaining methods that are, or can be, objectionable on grounds of fairness. Examples would include being very stubborn (e.g., holding out until the last possible moment), failure to disclose pertinent information (e.g., that the house I am selling has termites), using clever bargaining strategies against a partner who is unintelligent or naïve, and exploiting your partner's emotional vulnerabilities (e.g., an irrational fear of disease germs). In all these cases, you are gaining at some other person's expense, and that is just the sort of thing that can easily be unfair.

Notice that I did not say that gaining at the expense of another person is per se wrong: Every successful gambit in a bargaining session involves gaining at someone's expense in precisely the same sense of those words. The point is that it is the sort of thing that can be excessive and consequently unfair.

Finally, there is one more possible way to make Nozick's point here. It is easy to think of laws and regulations that are probably based on the intent to avoid and punish precisely the sort of unfairness I was just discussing. An obvious example would be "price gouging" laws, which make it illegal to raise prices in certain circumstances (e.g., charging $25 for a gallon of gasoline that would ordinarily cost $3.50 in the aftermath of historic Hurricane Sandy).[29] Perhaps someone could cobble together an argument that if the DPA were to buy out the risky independents, thus giving them market compensation, everything the independents charged them beyond what is needed for full compensation would be unfair in this way and hence must not be paid.[30] I do not know whether such an argument could be made convincing. One thing I am fairly sure of is that (to echo a comment I've already made in another context) when we look into Nozick's discussion of fairness-based theories in Chapter 7, below, we will see reason to think that he could not consistently present such an argument himself.

11. Conclusion

I am afraid that my discussion of Nozick's attempt to justify the state has been rather depressing. Though I believe I have learned a great deal in thinking it through, it does not seem to me to succeed in its ultimate aim of justifying the state. If I am right and it does fail, we have seen a plausible possible explanation for this above, in Chapter 4. There we saw that Nozick accepts two limits on his approach to justifying the state. One was that he would limit himself to explaining the political in terms of the non-political. The form this has taken is to explain the political in terms of the moral and, in particular, to explain rights and obligations sufficient to make an institution a state in terms of rights and obligations that would apply to individual human beings in the absence of a state. One result of this is that, as the DPA is formed, "[n]o

117

new rights and powers arise; each right of the association is decomposable without residue into those individual rights held by distinct individuals acting alone in a state of nature" (89). The other limitation is that, unlike the pure utilitarian, he assumes that morality includes the sorts of moral constraints that we ordinarily, intuitively think it does. In particular, he holds that the rights that individuals possess are constraints on the behavior of others. When these two ideas are combined, they yield the result that the constraints that apply to individual human beings also apply to the state.

I suppose one thing we have seen here is how severely limiting these two limitations are. In a way, this provides two rays of hope, perhaps dim ones, for someone who believes that Nozick's attempt fails, but who still wishes to justify the state. One can consider operating outside one or the other of these two limitations. First, you might deny that moral constraints apply to individuals. One family of strategies of this sort is comprised of ones based on utilitarianism. Second, you can deny that the rights of states are reducible to the rights of individuals. One way to do this would be to maintain that the state is a unique, super-personal entity, one that possesses moral super-powers, so to speak, as a result of its unique nature.

Of course, as we saw in Chapter 4, above, these two strategies are far from worry-free. Both these powerful strategies tend to be *too* powerful. They have a worrisome tendency to justify the unjustifiable. In attempting to justify the state, it is possible to accept constraints that are so tight as to doom the attempt to failure, and one may also make them so loose that they become ethically problematic. If my comments on Nozick's attempt are correct, the area between excessive stringency and excessive looseness may be very narrow and difficult to find. Indeed, it may be non-existent. After all, Nozick was some sort of genius, and if he could not land in the zone, that is not a good sign.[31]

Notes

1 Gerald Gaus, in his generally excellent "Explanation, Justification, and Emergence," p. 122, speaks of the institution that emerges from the invisible-hand process in Chapter 2 as "the ultraminimal state." I think this is a mistake, for the reason I have just given. In Ralf M. Bader and John Meadowcroft, eds., *The Cambridge Companion to Nozick's Anarchy, State, and Utopia* (Cambridge, England: Cambridge University Press, 2011).

2 He creates some unnecessary confusion in the Preface when he says: "I argue that a state would arise from anarchy (as represented by Locke's state of

nature) even though no one intended this or tried to bring it, by a process which need not violate anyone's rights" (xi). The phrase "*would* arise," here, implies that the state is the outcome of an invisible-hand process as well as the subject of an invisible-hand explanation. That is simply an inaccurate description of what he does in Chapters 4, 5, and 6.

3 There may be a fourth possibility, which arguably is the one usually taken by civil (as opposed to criminal) law. Any good law dictionary will define a tort as a breach of a legal duty. If you negligently injure someone with your car, it might not be punished as a crime but it is treated as a tort. That means that you are liable to be sued and compelled to compensate your victim. In cases where you are not liable to punishment but are liable to being compelled to compensate, it does not seem true to say that the law *permits* negligent injuries. I am not sure, though, that this makes any difference to Nozick's argument. He might claim that this is not functionally any different from response 2: The law is using language different from his, but it is not actually doing anything that is different.

4 Rather curiously, he later says that full compensation is enough, "but barely so," to make the person "glad, not sorry" that the violation happened (68). This would mean that it makes them marginally *better off* than they were before the event. As we will see in a moment, this makes a difference, though a small one, to his argument.

5 I am assuming for simplicity's sake that the theft has not caused me any other harm beyond the bare fact of not having the watch.

6 On the other hand, the way Nozick characterizes full compensation at 68 (see note 4, above) is consistent with the "contract curve" comment at 63: It interprets full compensation as making the victim marginally better off than they were before.

7 Robert E. Goodin, "Theories of Compensation," *Oxford Journal of Legal Studies*, vol. 9, no. 1 (Spring, 1989), p. 56.

8 Goodin, "Theories of Compensation," p. 59.

9 Also notice that in a system of tort law the acts for which only compensation is required (i.e., they are not punished) are for the most part negligent acts. The actionable effects of negligence are involuntary (the drunk driver was not *trying* to crash into the other car!), which means that a compensation-only response to them does not have the character of permitting unilateral bargain rate purchases.

10 For instance, at 88–89, he says: "If it is known that the independent will enforce his own rights by his very unreliable procedure only once in every ten years, this will *not* create general fear and apprehension in society. The grounds for prohibiting his widely intermittent use of his procedure is not, therefore, to avoid any widespread uncompensated apprehension and fear which otherwise would exist." To say that preventing people from inflicting fear is not the reason for prohibiting an activity in this case might be taken to suggest that it is the reason, a sufficient reason by itself, in other cases. But that is something that he never does say.

11 Here I am open to an obvious objection: "Emotion has great value for human life and survival, it's true, but emotional thinking, assessing value and disvalue via emotion, is irrational, unnecessary, and bad." To fully reply to this would take us too far afield in what was already something of a digression. I will have to content myself with a very brief comment: An emotion *is* an assessment of value or disvalue. If I experience fear when an angry dog lunges at me, that means (among other things) that I assess the dog as dangerous to me and hence as bad. To experience emotion without assessing value via emotion is an impossibility. I treat these issues at greater length in *Character and Culture* (Lanham, Maryland: Rowman and Littlefield, 1997), pp. 119–135.

12 I have altered Nozick's wording in several ways to eliminate features that would distract from the present discussion, but not, *I think*, in ways that significantly alter his meaning. I will discuss one such change in the text below. There are others. Here is what he actually says in the passage I am paraphrasing: "Perhaps the principle is something like this: an act is not wrong and so cannot be prohibited if it is harmless without further major decisions to commit wrong ..." (127). I have changed "cannot be prohibited" to "may not be resisted with force" to make it more immediately clear how it is related to our discussion, which is about using force. It is clear from Nozick's discussion that the action that is ruled out by this principle is the use of force, that this is what "prohibiting" means here. Also, the principle as he states it here is ambiguous as to whether the further decision to do wrong referred to in the principle is a decision on the part of the agent against whom we are considering applying force, or whether it can be a decision on the part of someone else. I have disambiguated the principle in line with an explicit statement he makes at 129: "This principle does *not* claim that no one may be held responsible or be punished for attempting to get others to do wrong because to succeed the attempt requires the decision of *others* to do wrong. For the principle focuses on whether the thrust toward wrong already has been made and is now out of *that person's* hands." Thus, what he means does seem to be what I have him say in the text, above.

13 Nozick does notice that what he is saying about preemptive attack is logically relevant to the risk argument, but the only connection he notes is one that supports a certain feature of the earlier argument. This was his attempt to resist the possibility that the risk argument "proves too much," that it would not only justify the dominant protective agency in passing judgment on the methods used by other agencies and prohibiting those who use procedures that are unreliable or unfair, but would also do something he says it does not do: namely, justify it in prohibiting people from forming or joining other protective associations at all. He says that his treatment of the preemptive attack principle shows that his "argument provides no rationale for [such] actions and cannot be used to defend them" (129). His point seems to be that merely joining another protective association is an act that is not itself a boundary crossing considered in itself and is harmless in the absence of a

subsequent decision on their part to do wrong. My point is that the same is true of agencies that do use unreliable decision procedures, insofar as they are *only* using the procedures and not coming to unjust decisions or acting on them.

14 Jeffrey Paul, "The Withering of the Minimal State," in Jeffrey Paul, ed., *Reading Nozick: Essays on Anarchy, State, and Utopia* (Totowa, New Jersey: Rowman and Littlefield, 1981), pp. 72–73.

15 How, exactly, is this principle related to the argument based on procedural rights? Here I think the text is more confusing than it needs to be. The first thing he says about the matter is this: "On this view [i.e., the epistemic argument], what a person may do is *not* limited only by the rights of others. An unreliable punisher violates no right of the guilty person; but still he may not punish him" (107). The second sentence seems to say that the epistemic argument implies that those who might be punished *do not* have a right against the punisher, that unreliable methods not be used against them. What he should be saying here is that this argument does *not*, by itself, imply that they *do* have such a right. Later in the same paragraph, he says: "On this view, many procedural rights stem not from rights of the person acted upon, but rather from moral considerations about the person or persons doing the acting" (107). This seems to say that the epistemic argument does imply that the, so to speak, punishee does have a right against the punisher. What he should say, given what he most likely means here, is that the constraint that follows from the punishee's procedural rights – that one may not use unreliable methods – also follows from considerations about the duties of the punisher. As I say in the text immediately following this point, these are two alternative routes to the same practical result.

16 This is connected to the issue Nozick raises about how we should describe behavior that violates the epistemic principle, whether we should say one doesn't have a right to do so, or whether we should say one does have a right but does wrong in exercising it in this way. In a footnote (341 fn. 10), he briefly flirts with the idea that the difference between these positions is merely verbal, without clearly and explicitly embracing it. We can now see that the difference between them is not merely verbal at all. Throughout ASU, "right," as in "has a right/has no right," is consistently used in such a way that claims about rights immediately (i.e., without additional premises or reasoning) justify coercion. Rights may be enforced coercively, and if you have no right to do something then you may be coercively prevented from doing it. On the other hand, claims about being a wrongdoer do not immediately have such implications. So the position he flirts with in that footnote is wrong. On the other hand, the claim he makes in the text – that he can say everything *he* wants to say using either of these two ways of talking – is correct, but only because he holds the substantive moral view that this particular sort of wrongdoing may indeed be coercively forbidden, and not because these two ways of talking mean the same thing.

17 For an early formulation of the principle of Legal Moralism, see Joel Feinberg, *Social Philosophy* (Englewood Cliffs, New Jersey: Prentice-Hall, 1973), pp. 36–41.
18 Allan Krumholz, MD, "Driving Issues in Epilepsy: Past, Present, and Future," published on the web site of the American Epilepsy Society: http://www.ncbi. nlm.nih.gov/pmc/articles/PMC2673400/
19 See *District of Columbia v. Heller*, 128 S. Ct. 2783; 171 L. Ed. 2d 637; *McDonald v. City of Chicago*, 130 S. Ct. 3020, 561 US 3025, 177 L. Ed. 2D 894.
20 It might be worth mentioning that it can be argued that the law also fails to treat the third case – the dangerous manufacturing process – in the way Nozick assumes it should. He gives no details about the nature of the hazards posed by this process, but it sounds like it falls within a category that the law variously calls "abnormally dangerous" or "ultra-hazardous" activities. The idea is that there are activities that have economic value, that produce or transport goods, which cannot be carried out safely. The landmark case here is the British one of *Rylands v. Fletcher*, L. R. 3 H. L. 330 (1868), which concerned a dam and reservoir built by a farmer which leaked and damaged a neighbor's property. What the law does, since Rylands, is to permit these activities but to apply the rule of strict liability to them: that is, if the activity harms person or property and the responsible party is sued for compensation, the plaintiff does not have to show that this party was negligent. Other examples of activities treated this way in the law include blasting, drilling for oil, transporting gasoline in tanker trucks, and crop-dusting. Interestingly, this seems to be the only sort of case in which the law clearly takes the second of the three responses to boundary crossings – in which the activity is permitted, on condition that any victims be compensated. (See note 3, above.)
21 For instance, he introduces the line-drawing problem (74) by asking: "Imposing how slight a probability of a harm that violates someone's rights also violates his rights?"
22 For a very different account of the Principle of Compensation discussion, see Eric Mack, "Nozickean Arguments for the More-than-Minimal State," in Ralf M. Bader and John Meadowcroft, eds., *The Cambridge Companion to Nozick's Anarchy, State, and Utopia* (Cambridge, England: Cambridge University Press, 2011), pp. 100–103. On one point Mack's interpretation seems clearly wrong to me. He attributes to Nozick the following argument: "[T]he dominant agency's prohibition of these risky actions is not itself feared. Hence, the right of the independent … may permissibly be infringed as long as due compensation accompanies this arrangement" (p. 102). The second statement only follows from the first if we assume that it is true of unfeared rights violations in general. Since people don't experience fear of offenses against their property (unless the loss suffered would be ruinous), this would mean that one could permissibly help oneself to the property of others, provided only that one fully compensates them for it afterward. This is a position that Nozick explicitly rejects (at 64), and quite rightly so.

23 Though this is indeed how Nozick characterizes the issue he has set up by the end of the discussion of the principle of compensation, I think it this mischaracterizes the conclusion of the argument he has just given. Full compensation, as I have just said, makes you as well off as *you* were before. The kind of compensation we have just been discussing erases the difference in wellbeing between you and *other* people that would otherwise be caused by prohibiting your hazardous activity. He is actually talking about a third sort of compensation, which differs from both full and market compensation. Perhaps we should call it "fairness compensation." However, this will not make any difference as far as the present issue is concerned, at least if we assume that where the prohibited independents were before the prohibition (i.e., protected) is the same as where others are after it. In that case the measure (extending protection to them) that erases one of the two disparities will also erase the other. (I suspect that formulating the issue in terms of this third sort of compensation is simply a mistake, and that his discussion of this matter would be more coherent if made out in terms of full compensation.)

24 The following comments can be read as a more elaborate spelling out of a way of thinking about the issue that is expressed in a comment by Murray Rothbard that Nozick quotes at 86 fn.: "Blackmail would not be illegal in a free society. For blackmail is the receipt of money in exchange for not publicizing certain information about the other person. No violence to person or property is involved."

25 Notice that I have just formulated this line of reasoning in terms of full compensation, and not in terms of what I call "fairness compensation" in note 23, above.

26 In the following argument, I am following the lead of Eric Mack in his "Unproductivity: The Unintended Consequences," in *Reading Nozick: Essays on Anarchy, State, and Utopia*, pp. 113–114. (See note 14, above.) I am formulating it rather differently than he does, however. He says the transactions involved here are part of "all typical free market exchanges" (p. 178), though it is clear that the phenomenon he has in mind is bargaining and not markets. If one thinks of markets as economists often do, as something that sets prices via certain impersonal forces (mainly, price competition among suppliers of goods and services) then bargaining and markets are mutually exclusive. In our culture, the only things we bargain about are typically unique objects, such as my used watch, which are things that do not have market prices attached to them. This might sound like a very petty point to be making, but it actually does make a difference regarding something I will be saying in a moment.

27 Here I am parting ways with Eric Mack, who seems to think the idea is spurious. See note 26, above.

28 On the other hand, trade itself does create value. If you buy my watch from me, I value the money I get more than the watch I give up, and vice versa in your case. The watch and the money have been moved to more highly valued uses.

29 See David Futrelle, "Post Sandy Price Gouging: Economically Sound, Ethically Dubious," *Time Magazine*, November 2, 2012. This essay was only published on *Time*'s web site at http://business.time.com/2012/11/02/post-sandy-price-gouging-economically-sound-ethically-dubious/ The act I just described in the text was apparently treated as a crime throughout the area devastated by this storm.

30 Once again, I am framing the issue in terms of full, not fairness compensation. See note 23, above.

31 Here is another ray of hope for would-be justifiers of the state: Eric Mack, in his "Nozickean Arguments for the More-than-Minimal State" (see note 22, above), puts forth a justification of state powers that is clearly meant to stay within the safety zone. One interesting feature of Mack's would-be justification is that it is meant to justify taxation (if only for very limited purposes). As we will soon see, Nozick believes that taxation is not justifiable.

7

Has the Dominant Protective Association Become a State?

1. What Does the Argument Prove, if Successful?

Ignoring the concerns about Nozick's justification of the state that I have expressed in Chapters 5 and 6, what does the argument show if I am wrong and it actually is successful? What is the conclusion for which he argues? Obviously, it is that the dominant protective association, with the functions he assigns to it, is justified. From this he takes it to follow that states can be just institutions. Does this last inference go through? In other words, is the DPA, as it has developed by the end of Chapter 5 of ASU, a state?

One thing is clear. It is easy to make this organization sound un-state-like. It appears to be a business corporation, like an insurance company, which sells a range of available services to those who choose to purchase them. Recall that it evolved out of "mutual-protection associations" (12), which consisted of the people being protected by the association. Presumably, as it grew and developed, any property held by the organization was owned by the members. Subsequent changes it has gone through – including division of labor, arrival at monopoly or semi-monopoly status, and extending protection to risky independents – have done nothing to change that. This would seem to mean that it is actually a consumer-owned cooperative, as indeed are some American insurance companies. (That is what the "mutual" in Mutual of Omaha means.) It is, as they say in the insurance industry, "policy-owned": It is owned by those who purchase its policies.

One immediate consequence of this is that the DPA consists entirely of private property and its owners. The intuitive distinction between public and private, which people habitually apply to existing states, seems to

Anarchy, State, and Utopia: An Advanced Guide, First Edition. Lester H. Hunt.
© 2015 John Wiley & Sons, Inc. Published 2015 by John Wiley & Sons, Inc.

have no application to the DPA. It does not claim to represent the public in general, but only its clients and, as we will see in a moment, it is likely that not everyone in its territory is its client. Of course, it does claim the right to defend its clients against everyone in the area, but that is a very different matter from representing everyone.

Another concept that does not seem to apply to the DPA is citizenship. The question of what, precisely, citizenship is, is a deep and fascinating question, but I don't think we need to investigate it in order to know that it is distinct from being a paying customer, and that of course is the relationship that binds each of the members of the DPA to it.

Another typically crucial political concept that does not seem to apply to the DPA is authority. It does not claim authority over anybody. Authority, in the sense I mean here, is what one has when one's telling somebody to do something is, by itself, a reason to do it. When you were six years old, and your mother said "go to bed now," you probably took that as a reason to go to bed now. If your little brother or sister said the same thing to you, it was not a reason to go to bed now. That is the difference between someone with authority and someone without it. (Authority is sometimes confused with force, whereas the two are actually near-opposites. Genuine authority, if and when it exists, gives you reasons for acting that are independent of threats to back them up. Force is a physical relationship while authority is a moral one.) Authority in this sense is something that the DPA does not claim to have. It punishes people for violating, not its own edicts, directives, or rules, but the *rights* of its clients, and it treats these rights as existing independently of its own policies. If it punishes me, that is because I did something wrong in itself, not because I disobeyed its commands.

This represents a rather radical departure from traditional justifications of the state. Typically, political philosophers take states to be institutions that by nature, perhaps by definition, expect to be obeyed and they have accordingly treated the task of proving such a duty of obedience as an essential element of justifying the state. This was clearly true of Locke, who was at pains to justify what he called "the legislative, or supreme authority" of a just state, though he also thought it very important to argue that such legislative authority, in a just state, is limited to the task of codifying in clear terms the rights that all people have under the law of nature.[1] In the essay by David Hume that I discussed in Chapter 1, "Of the Original Contract," Hume makes it quite clear that in his view justifying state authority comprises the *entire* task of justifying the state itself. Despite the great differences between their political theories (Hume places no such limit on such authority as Locke does), both these philosophers seem to think that an institution that did not demand to be obeyed would not be a state. Yet the DPA seems to make no such demand. Rather, it punishes people for doing things that they should not do, independently of being told that they may not do them. It does not claim a special status for itself, so that its voice has a moral weight that is not possessed by anyone else in its domain.

If I am right about this, there is another conclusion that follows from it. The states that we know of, other than the very simplest ones, are hierarchies. Subjects of the state are ruled by bosses who in turn are subject to the authority of bosses above them. The ultimate authority in a state, the one that recognizes no higher earthly authority, is the sovereign, and the state or condition of being the sovereign is of course called "sovereignty." States as we know them claim to be hierarchies with the sovereign at the top and its subjects at the bottom. In an absolute monarchy, the sovereign is the monarch; in a democracy it is (at least in theory) the people. Is the DPA characterized by sovereignty? Not if it does not claim to have authority.

There are two other features that are typical of states that do not characterize the DPA which deserve to be mentioned. Indeed, it is rather important that the DPA does not possess these features. These are two of the state activities I identified as ethically problematic in Chapter 4, above: conscription and taxation. Both these activities violate the "libertarian constraint" that Nozick set out in Chapter 3 of ASU. Both use force against people who are not doing something morally comparable to using unprovoked force (or other morally similar activity, such as fraud) themselves. Someone who is refraining from serving in the military is not, simply in virtue of that fact, breaking into other people's houses, taking money from them under false pretenses, or doing anything else that is similarly violative of the rights of others. Serving in the military may be, especially in times of national emergency, an admirable thing to do, and it may be better, other things being equal, than not doing so, but failing to do it is not a boundary crossing. Similar things are true of someone who is not giving money to the government. Consequently, forcing people to serve in the military or to give money to the government are acts of aggression and prohibited by the libertarian constraint.

In case it is not obvious that the DPA does not collect taxes, I would just point out that charging a fee for services, which is something that the DPA does do, is quite a different thing from collecting taxes. In a fee for services, getting the service is conditional upon paying the fee. If you don't pay the fee, you don't get the service. Of course, the provider can still give the service away for free, but the point remains that if you don't pay the fee you are not *entitled* to get the service. This implies a second feature of fees for services. Paying the fee is voluntary. If you are willing to do without the service, you needn't pay the fee. Taxation lacks both of these features. There are no government services that are conditional upon my paying my taxes, and furthermore I do not have the option of not paying.

The fees paid to the DPA are voluntary. If you do not want the DPA to enforce your rights, you needn't pay it anything. In that case, of course, it will not treat aggressive attacks on your person or property as crimes to be investigated and punished. If you don't mind that then, provided that the manner in which you enforce your rights does not expose others to undue risk, that is your right. (Perhaps you will purchase a policy from a – non-risky – competing agency.)

As I remarked at the beginning of Chapter 5, the fact that a given institution does not do either of these two activities does not clearly mean that the institution is not a state. Indeed, you might say that this fact is an essential part of the solution that Nozick would offer to the problem that I raised about these activities in Chapter 4: namely, the problem of how we might explain how states can have a right to do these things while individual human beings do not, and would not even in a state of nature. Part of his solution is to take the position that states themselves have no right to do these things. His view is that to force people to fight for you, and to take people's property by force and without their consent, are simply unjust activities. The rest of the solution would be to show that there is no need to justify such activities in justifying the state. This is accomplished, I am sure he would say, by doing what he thinks he has done by the end of Chapter 5 of ASU: drawing a portrait of a convincingly state-like institution that does neither one of these unjust things.

This of course brings us back to the original question of the present chapter. Is this institution a state? The features of the DPA that have come to light in the course of my discussion so far make me very skeptical. I think it is helpful here to recall the intellectual path that brought Nozick to the position that he takes in ASU. When he was a graduate student, classmate Bruce Goldberg introduced him to the feisty, talkative, and brilliant libertarian economist Murray Rothbard. Rothbard was what is sometimes called a market anarchist. He believed that the only just society is one in which rights are enforced by competing protection agencies, like the ones at the beginning of Nozick's invisible-hand narrative. At that time, Nozick regarded himself as a socialist. He was, or had recently been, a member of Students for a Democratic Society, a prominent left-wing group. He must have found Rothbard's views preposterous, but he also seemed to find them interesting. They had at least one intense discussion (how marvelous it would have been to overhear it!). Nozick became interested enough in Rothbard's libertarian ideas to wish to devise a crushing refutation of them. As he worked on this, however, his own views changed until he became a libertarian himself. Of course he did not become an anarchist like Rothbard but what is sometimes called a minarchist: an advocate of the state, but of a minimal state. That at any rate is how he characterized the position presented in ASU. His project is to emerge out of Rothbardian anarchism but to go no further than the minimal state.

Whether he realized it or not, the system that is actually embodied in the text of ASU is really much, much more like that of Rothbard than it is like any state existing in our world. Nozick's emergence from Rothbardian anarchism does not go very far. At the end of Chapter 5, despite the transformations the DPA has undergone, it is still one of Rothbard's protective agencies. It does some things that Rothbard's agencies are not supposed to do (a fact that I will be looking into in more detail shortly) but its fundamental nature is much the same. I have argued that the outcome of the invisible-hand process that is most consistent with its background assumptions is Federation, and not Victory or Gradient, and that as described by Nozick this loose structure would contain agencies that could, and presumably would, compete with each other. Being business corporations, they do not do a number of things that it seems states always do, such as collect taxes or demand obedience and claim sovereignty.[2]

One strategy to get a grip on the question of whether the DPA is really a state would be to make a list of features that seem to always be possessed by states as we know them and make a parallel list of features the DPA has acquired by the end of Chapter 5 of ASU. The next step would be to weight or rank the features of the state in terms of how essential to being a state they are. Perhaps claiming authority is more essential than taxation, which is more essential than claiming single-ultimate-authority sovereignty, and so forth. We could then see how close the DPA is to Rothbardian agencies and how close it is to actual states in terms of both the more and less essential characteristics. We might find that it is so much closer to one end of this continuum than to the other that we need not go into the question of where to draw the line between institutions that are states and ones that are not. This would be an interesting project to carry out, partly because it would force one to sort out the structure of one's own concept of what a state is. My own suspicion, as I've suggested, is that Nozick's minimal state would end up a close neighbor of the Rothbardian agency, but it would carry us too far afield to carry out this project here.

There might be a sort of shortcut to getting a grip on this question, however. At the end of Chapter 2 of ASU (24), Nozick identifies exactly two features of states that would be sufficient to carry the DPA from the status of a Rothbardian agency to that of a minimal state. The first is that states announce that they will punish others who use force without their express permission (where this permission may be given in some generalized way, as by issuing a regulation of some sort). This feature, as you recall, is meant to satisfy the criterion that Weber attempted to capture with his imprecise talk of a "monopoly of force." It would bring the DPA, according to Nozick, to the status of an "ultraminimal state." The second is that a state "protects everyone" in its domain, and not merely its clients, as the DPA does at the end of Chapter 2. If the DPA justly acquires both characteristics it will have justly become a minimal state. Let's take a close look at what these two features, insofar as the DPA justly acquires them in Nozick's theory, and see whether they seem enough to make it a state.

2. The Monopoly of Force

Nozick's attempts to show that the DPA satisfies – that is, comes close enough to satisfying – this criterion of statehood involves some potentially radical departures from traditional conceptions of the state. One is that he deems it sufficient that the DPA's "express permission" is published in the form of an announcement that it will prevent competitors and alternative protectors of rights from using unsafe decision procedures. This, as we have seen, is not the same as prohibiting competitors and alternatives altogether. Another departure is less obvious but Nozick is honest enough to point it out. In fact, he subjects it to some concentrated attention. This has to do with the fact that the right that is exercised by the DPA is a right possessed by all. Wherein lies its monopoly then? It resides in the fact that it is the only one that can exercise it (more exactly, that it is almost the only one, and the only one that can exercise it very much). It is only a de facto monopoly, not a de jure one.

The DPA is, roughly speaking (a qualification I will omit for brevity in the rest of this section), the only human agent that is able to enforce individual rights. What gives this agent the right to *be the one* who carries out this important function? Possessing such a right, the right to be the one, is what "legitimacy" would be, as Nozick uses that term (134).

Nozick's surprising answer to this question is: nothing. In an interesting aside that might shed light on what this question actually means, he points out that the notion of a right to "be the one" who gets to perform a function involved in the maintenance of public order is not utterly alien to the sort of natural rights and state of nature theory that he represents. Though he, like Locke before him, thinks that all would have a right to punish any infractions in a state of nature, he thinks the same is not true of the right to exact reparation. Suppose that you know that someone has robbed me of $50, and that you also know where the money is and how to get it. Do you have a right to do so, and return it to me? What if I have forgiven the thief and am so impressed with his contriteness, and so moved by his poverty, that I want him to have the money? Clearly, you need to consult with me before acting, and may only act with my consent. The general rule here, according to Nozick, is that the only people who have a right to exact compensation for a wrong are the victim of the wrong and those who are authorized by the victims.

At first Nozick appears to be taking this distinction between punishing and exacting compensation as intuitively obvious, but he eventually does offer a *reason* why they would be different in this way: "[U]nlike compensation, punishment is not owed to the victim ... and so it is not something he has any special authority over" [137]. The fact that compensation is owed to the victim means that this is one of those obligations that is simply the other side of a right. That the perpetrator owes compensation to the victim is simply the fact that the victim has a right to it. If you assume individuals can unilaterally relinquish or transfer their own rights, and that no one else can do this, this would immediately imply that the victim of a rights violation, and only the victim, can declare whether the violator (still) owes them compensation or not. This in turn implies a need for would-be exactors of compensation to seek the consent of the victim before acting, and this is the "authority" that Nozick is talking about here. On the other hand, the victim does not have the right to declare that the wrongdoer shall not be *punished*, which means that the wrongdoer's being punished is not a right that the victim possesses as an individual.

The act of authorizing someone else to act in one's behalf is the clearest way one can acquire the right to "be the one" to exercise a right. The notion that one can indeed create rights – more precisely, transfer them – in this way is extremely intuitively appealing. This is why Locke's theory of governmental legitimacy uses this very idea. I suggested as much, somewhat elliptically, when I earlier characterized the relationship between Lockean citizens and their state as a relationship between agent and principal (Chapter 5, Section 1). I can create such a relationship by giving my consent (e.g., by signing a power of attorney) to another person to exercise certain of my rights in my behalf (e.g., to withdraw money from my bank account or manage my investment portfolio). Within the limits set by this transfer of rights, the actions of the agent count as if they were done by the principal. This in Locke's view is how states acquire legitimacy: Citizens participate in a social contract, consenting (at least tacitly) to the existence of a state, where the state is conceived as a central authority exercising in their behalf the rights of all the citizens to punish violations of rights. That is, they are consenting to the state's being the one who does this. Though Nozick's theory is not a social contract theory, it is committed to this same general notion of transferring rights by consent: The DPA is the agent representing its clients, the principals, in the matter of punishing and exacting compensation. However, no one is consenting to the DPA's being the *one and only agent* that does this. They are simply consenting to its exercising some of their own rights. This is one reason why his theory is not a social contract theory of the state. It is also why Nozick's state, as he calls it, does not claim to have the sort of legitimacy – the right to be the one – that Locke believes his state has.

It would be difficult to prove this definitively, because actual states do not use this terminology, but it does seem that, like Locke's state, they claim to have what Nozick calls legitimacy. The most obvious signs of this are behavior rather than words. All states proceed as if not only do they have a right to make rules and force others to follow them but also as if, in addition, this right is absolutely unique. No other agency in the realm could conceivably have it. As if to support this seeming claim to moral uniqueness they surround themselves with all sorts of signs and symbols – from pompous ceremonies and legislative halls with intimidating architecture to eye-popping monuments and memorials – which make them look and feel uniquely impressive.

In failing to claim legitimacy, the DPA falls far short of making the sort of claim to moral uniqueness that actual states do seem to make. Does it fall so far short that it should not be called a state at all? I think I should delay attacking this question until I have said a few words about the nature of the issue of defining the state. Before that, though, I need to address the other main feature of the state that Nozick adds to the Chapter 2 DPA, the one that is supposed to transform the ultraminimal state into the minimal state.

3. Protecting Everyone

As to this alleged feature of states, there is a conceptual problem that must be cleared up before we can go further. It is clearly not true that states protect everyone in their domains and, more importantly for our purposes, failing to do so does not mean that they are not really states. Richard Wright, in his autobiographical *Black Boy (American Hunger)*, describes his childhood in the Deep South, where mob violence and lynching of African Americans went virtually unpunished. It is a vivid picture of a system in which lawless mobs serve as a virtual arm of the state, creating an atmosphere of terror in which the victims of oppression dare not resist.[3] Clearly the governments involved were not protecting everybody. And yet these institutions obviously were genuine states. Eric Mack makes a similar point by reminding us that states have been known to "slaughter their own subjects."[4] As we look dispassionately back at the approximately 6,000 years of the history of states, we can surely say that few functions seem more state-like than campaigns of expropriation, and even terror and murder, against portions of their own subject populations – generally for the benefit of another portion of the same population (especially the officers of the state itself).

Of course, Nozick is aware of all this. So when he says that one of the crucial "necessary conditions" for being a state is that it "protect[s] the rights of everyone in its territory" (113) this must be a misstatement of what he really means. What would be a better way of stating the actual state feature that he is trying to capture here? It might be acceptable as a friendly amendment to his theory if we could figure out what the real difference is between the DPA at the end of Chapter 2, on the one hand, and states as we know them, on the other, with respect to the extent of its protective services.

It seems to me that there is a real and profound difference here, and it is related to the difference between taxation and services for a fee. The difference has to be put negatively (in terms of what someone is *not* doing) rather than positively (in terms of what someone *is* doing). The Chapter 2 DPA will *not* protect people unless those people pay it to do so. Protection is conditional upon payment. On the other hand, a state's protection is *not* conditional in this way. It isn't that the state by definition protects everybody, but that, if it doesn't protect a given individual, it's not because the individual didn't pay it to. There are two negations here, one applying to states and the other to the DPA. Each one seems distinctive, essential to making this institution the sort of institution it is. The question then is, at the end of Chapter 5 of ASU, how similar has the DPA become to the state with respect to this Chapter 2 difference? To what extent has the difference been overcome?

Here the answer almost seems to be obvious. I have already said that the Chapter 5 DPA is in the business of selling protective services for a fee. With respect to the real difference between the Chapter 2 DPA and the state that the phrase "protecting everyone" is meant to capture, the DPA is still profoundly different from the state. Yet the situation is a little more complicated than this.

Let's take a look at who is and is not protected by the DPA at the end of Chapter 5. We can begin by examining who would not be protected.

Nozick remarks at one point (110) that the DPA would not intervene in "disputes where all concerned parties chose to opt out of the state's apparatus." Opting out would seem to mean neither contributing money to the institution nor calling upon its help when one's rights are violated. Such opters-out, then, would be a class of people who would not be protected.

How will these people deal with the problem of protecting their rights? In the passage from which I have just quoted, he speaks of "one independent … about to use *his* procedure of justice upon another" (109, emphasis added). This suggests that he is imagining them to be do-it-yourselfers, in matters of rights protection. Presumably, if some of these independents are known to use reliable procedures of justice, they would be allowed to remain independent.

In addition, Nozick remarks that other protective agencies "can come into the market and attempt to wean customers away" from the DPA (109). That is, the DPA will have no right to coercively stop clients from switching their custom to competing agencies. That would mean that some independents, in the sense that they are independent of the dominant agency, can be clients of another agency rather than contenting themselves with the status of do-it-yourselfers, provided of course that the other agency is a reliable one. Like the reliable do-it-yourselfers, these people would not be protected by the DPA either, even if they are living within its sphere of control.

On the other hand, who *would* be protected by the DPA?

First, and most obviously, there are those who voluntarily pay for their services because they want them.

Then there are the risky independents who, in line with a distinction I've made above, I am treating as falling into two categories: clients of agencies who use insufficiently reliable procedures of justice, and known-to-be-risky do-it-yourselfers. Apparently, both groups are compensated for not being allowed to use their unreliable methods by being covered by the protection of the DPA. More precisely, they are compensated for the "disadvantage" imposed by the prohibition, which Nozick conceives as the difference between the agency's least fancy policy and the monetary cost, if any, of their prohibited activities. In the event that they spend this money on a policy with the DPA (which Nozick seems to regard as very likely) then the DPA will protect them.

134

This, as I understand it, has an interesting further consequence. He considers the category of prohibited independents whose prohibited activities have no monetary cost but do cost something in terms of time, energy, and so forth. These appear to be do-it-yourselfers. This category splits into two sorts of cases. First, he says, if the independent "has other financial resources he can use without disadvantaging himself," then paying him the above difference will suffice as to compensation. There is another sort of case to be considered:

> But *if* the independent has no such other financial resources, a protective agency may *not* pay him an amount *less* than the cost of its least expensive protective policy, and so leave him only the alternatives of being defenseless against the wrongs of its clients or having to work in the cash market to earn sufficient funds to total the premium on a policy. For this financially pressed prohibited individual, the agency must make up the difference between the *monetary* costs to him of the prohibited[5] activity and the amount necessary to purchase an overcoming or counterbalancing of the disadvantage imposed. (112)

Clearly, since the monetary costs of the prohibited activities of a "financially pressed" individual are likely to be zero, this seems to mean that they will be covered and protected for free. It seems to me that the DPA is likely to regard as unreliable all do-it-yourselfers who are such simply because they cannot afford to be otherwise. In that event, the poor, in general, will be covered for free.

This might seem an odd position for Nozick to take given that, as we will see when we discuss Chapter 7, he is opposed to the redistribution of wealth. However, the reason for this particular policy is not redistributionist; that is, it is not meant to correct the distribution of good things, as when some people have "too much more" than others. Rather, it is based on the rights and wrongs of disarming a segment of the population and leaving them exposed to the depredations of criminals.

This, then, is who is and is not protected by the DPA at the end of Chapter 5. In general, opters-out will be unprotected. In particular, reliable do-it-yourselfers and clients of reliable competing protective agencies will be unprotected by the DPA. In addition, if among the unreliable opters-out there are any brave souls who spend their compensation money on something other than protection because they are willing to be completely unprotected, they too will be unprotected by the DPA. Who *will* be protected? The DPA's entirely voluntary clients will be, of course. In addition, prohibited unreliable do-it-yourselfers and clients of unreliable protective agencies will be covered, and subsidized to one degree or another, if they choose to avail themselves of the DPA's services. In addition, (probably, most of) the poor will be covered for free.

So where are we as far as the "protecting everyone" feature of the state is concerned? I think it makes a big difference whether we approach this question in terms of Nozick's original characterization of this feature or whether we do it in terms of my "friendly amendment" version of it. Though my revision was "friendly" in the sense that it made the characterization more plausible, it actually causes trouble for Nozick's attempt to make a case that the Chapter 5 DPA is state-like with respect to this feature.

He insists that although the DPA does not interfere with people who choose "to opt out of the state's apparatus" (except of course for disputes with its own clients), this "does not show that the dominant protection association is not a state" (110). Interestingly, the practice that our author is envisioning here seems to be fundamentally the same as one that Henry David Thoreau puts forth as a practical proposal in the conclusion of his essay "Civil Disobedience":

> I please myself with imagining a State at last which can afford to be just to all men, and to treat the individual with respect as a neighbor; which even would not think it inconsistent with its own repose if a few were to live aloof from it, not meddling with it, nor embraced by it, who fulfilled all the duties of neighbors and fellow men. A State which bore this kind of fruit, and suffered it to drop off as fast as it ripened, would prepare the way for a still more perfect and glorious State, which I have also imagined, but not yet anywhere seen.[6]

I suppose that the point Nozick is making, and that Thoreau is simply assuming, is plausible enough: that this practice would not be inconsistent with an institution's being a state (though it may be worthwhile wondering, as Thoreau does elsewhere in his essay, why no state actually ever does allow opting out).[7]

Yet a problem remains regarding the issue of whether the Chapter 5 DPA is a state. It has to do with the fact that, under the influence of his own misleading formulation of the issue in terms of "protecting everyone," Nozick seems to be thinking of the question in quantitative terms. He points out that the DPA's protection will extend to certain groups beyond its purely voluntary clients. Is it protecting *enough* people to be a state, yet? It is as if the question is this: Where, in Thoreau's imagined withering-away process, does this institution cease to be a state because there are too few left who have not opted out? And where along that spectrum is the DPA at the end of Chapter 5?

If we accept my friendly amendment, we see that this is not the right question. This feature of the state is not a matter of the quantity protected, but of the principled way in which protection is related to payment. Is payment a condition of being protected, as it is in a commercial transaction, or is protection disconnected from payment, unconditional – as it is in the practice of states? It looks as if, strictly speaking, protection is still conditional on payment. After all, the risky independents will only be protected if they do decide to spend their compensation money on the DPA's services. Nozick might reply that there is something here that is *close enough* to the sort of unconditionality that we have in the case of the state. He could point out that there is a complicated state of affairs here that is independent of the risky independent's consent to pay. First, they are prohibited from availing themselves of their former sources of protection. This doesn't have their consent at all. Second, they are compensated for this. Whether they asked for it or not, it is theirs. Finally, Nozick thinks that circumstances make it *likely* that most of these people will be protected by the DPA. None of this complex set of factors is dependent on their paying for payment. In fact, it is independent of their will altogether. And it results in a state of affairs which is similar to that which would result in genuine, full unconditionality. Doesn't this bring the DPA close enough to this feature of the state?

Once again, I think the answer is no. What we see here is simply a case of giving a commercial product away, for free. The motive for this act is to enhance the product – safety, security from injustice – for one's paying customers. There is indeed a sort of unconditionality in both cases. Protection, or something related to it, fails to be conditional upon something. In one case (the state) protection fails to be conditional upon paying for it, while in the other (the DPA) certain factors that, taken together, are supposedly likely to result in protection fail to be conditional upon whether one wants coverage by this institution or not. The former sort of unconditionality implies that the nexus between the supplier of the service and the recipient is not commercial – in other words, is not a trade relationship. The latter does not have that sort of significance at all. It is, in fact, a commercial strategy.

4. Defining the State

It seems impossible to rationally decide whether someone has succeeded in justifying the state – especially if the results are as different from the most familiar examples of the state as the Chapter 5 DPA is – without somehow tangling with the question of what a state is. Nozick's astute critique of Max Weber's famous attempt to define the state (discussed briefly above in Chapter 5, Section 1) is enough to suggest, at least to me, that producing a formal definition – a set of conditions that are both necessary and sufficient for something's being a state – is not easy to do. Nozick refrains from attempting such a definition, which may well be a wise move in itself, but he does spend several pages engaging the issue of what a state is (115–118).

The core of the discussion there is a rather long quote, the longest in ASU, from anthropologist Lawrence Krader's book *Formation of the State*.[8] In it, Krader is attempting to identify some features that states have in common and distinguish them from other, non-state forms of what he calls "government" – that is, means of executing and enforcing the basic rules of a society. The feature that Nozick emphasizes is what might be called the "continuously existing stable institution" feature. Krader points out that in a truly stateless society – such as the San (or "Bushmen"), the Inuit, and the Australian Aborigines – any central authority that might protect people against wrongdoing is "nonexistent, weak, or sporadic." In these societies, according to Krader, wrongdoing is suppressed by "total group participation." Such societies rather resemble Nozick's early protective associations, in which everyone is on call at all times. Other societies, Krader points out elsewhere in his book, show *some* specialization in the matter of the maintenance of order, though they fall short of forming a state. The Crow, for instance, had different "associations" that had certain military or policing functions. Every year, one of them, appointed by the chief, would enforce the rules of the buffalo hunt, the ones that enable the hunting party to coordinate and cooperate with optimal results for the group. They were empowered to punish infractions with summary punishment in the field (e.g., smashing the malefactor's weapons).[9] However, when there were no issues for the association to deal with, it did not exist as such. Its members in that case do the same things any other young adult male does.

Nozick claims that, in stark contrast to this, the DPA does have "enduring administrative structures, with full-time specialized personnel." These, he says, make the DPA "diverge greatly – in the direction of a state – from what anthropologists call a stateless society" (117). This is true of what I have just called "truly stateless societies," such as the Inuit. However, it is not true of societies that have some state-like elements and yet are not states, such as the Crow. As Krader points out elsewhere, the Crow did have one enduring institution: the position of the chief. However, "[t]he office of the chief on the Plains was limited and ill-defined; it was a social role in the acting-out of which the principal took no initiative but carried out the decisions of the council." On the other hand, the tribal council was "neither a permanent nor regularly constituted institution."[10] Evidently, the chief could not claim, like the ancient Russian prince Krader describes at the end of Nozick's long quotation, to be the sole authorizer of violence: "If harm was done by one subject to another," Krader says, "without the prince's express permission, this was a wrong, and the wrong doer was punished. Moreover, the prince's power could only be explicitly delegated." In his view, this last point, the need for explicitness (rather than a vague, tacit understanding) in authorization seems to be a particularly important requirement as a distinctive feature of the state (cited on 116–117).

Krader seems to regard both these features – the continuously existing stable institution feature and the sole authorizer of force feature – as necessary ones if something is to count as a state. Crow government fails to qualify as a state because all the state-like elements in it are either impermanent or insufficiently authoritative. What about Nozick's DPA? While it does differ from Crow government in that it possesses the first feature, permanence, it seems to lack the second, what we might describe as sufficient authority. Indeed, he quickly admits that it makes no claim "to be the sole authorizer of violence" (117). Much less does it claim that its explicit authorization is necessary for violence to be permissible.

His response to this sort of objection is not surprising from what we have seen him say earlier. He admits that the final form of the DPA does not meet "the Weberian necessary condition" of being a state, the "monopoly feature" as I have been calling it, but says it does meet a condition for statehood which he calls "a slight weakening" of this one, and insists that the case for weakening it is "very strong" and that "doing so … is wholly desirable and appropriate" (117–118). Now that we have briefly looked at the nature of the state as an anthropologist like Krader sees it, this weakening does not seem so slight. Nozick concludes by saying that, to acknowledge this weakening, he would sometimes refer to the organization he has justified as "a statelike entity" and not simply as "a state" (118). Here he seems to acknowledge (if only briefly – he doesn't keep the pledge about calling it a state-like entity) that this issue of whether the DPA is really a state is not entirely closed by his discussion of it.

As I have said, the only way to get to some sort of rational resolution of this issue is to deal in some decisive way with the problem of defining the state. That would clearly take us too far afield but before moving on to the issues in Part II of ASU, I would like to offer a few comments on the nature of this problem. They are offered only as possible guidelines for further reflection and research.

5. How the State Functions

Unless we think that it is possible to define the state by posing a set of necessary and sufficient conditions that capture the ordinary language meaning of the word (and good luck with that!) we need to ask what it would be like to create a definition that is not simply our own arbitrary invention.

One thing that has emerged from our discussion here that might be useful is that some, perhaps all, of the features that make something a state can be conceived as points along a continuum. Thus the monopoly of force feature can range all the way from a mere de facto monopoly of the ability to prohibit enforcement methods it deems unsafe to a fully de jure monopoly on the right to prohibit all uses of force that the state does not explicitly authorize. We have seen that Nozick thought of the protecting others feature more or less this way: that is, as a matter of degree. In addition, we can think of state claims to possess authority (in the sense used in Section 1, above) in this way as well. According to one anthropologist, some states allow their subjects to occupy an "intermediate position" of "semi-subordination," between completely accepting or completely rejecting state sovereignty.[11] He does not say just how this works, but one can think of various dimensions within which an authority-claim can be more or less intensive. It can be directed at more or fewer subgroups in the population, it can be more or less clear that it exists, or more or less clear that there are penalties for disobedience (which can be more or less stringent), and it can be applied to more or fewer potential actions and areas of one's life.

To the extent that one sees state features as capable of this sort of continuous variation, it makes sense to think of the concept of the state as possessing a *core* and a *periphery*: There are cases that clearly correspond to the concept to the maximal degree, and there are others that deviate from this core in various ways, but still can properly be regarded as states.[12] If that is right, then the basic question raised by any reasonable effort to define the state is: Which features that seem typical of states lie close to the core? I think that in order to answer such a question we need to make some sort of substantive judgments about states themselves. Though it is true enough that we use whatever conception we have of the state in constructing a theory of the thing that the conception is about, still it cannot be the case that first we define the state and then we theorize about it. The two elements – the definition and the theory – must evolve together.

A number of features of states have shown up in our discussion so far that seem to be either universal or extremely typical. In addition to (a) the monopoly of force feature, (b) the protecting others feature and (c) claiming authority, there are the very strong tendencies on the part of these institutions to (d) claim sovereignty (ultimate, undivided authority) for itself or the most important part of itself, (e) claim legitimacy, and (f) collect its income in significant part by means of taxation (a charge levied coercively in the form of an unconditional obligation). Also worthy of mention, perhaps, is the fact that, like various other institutions, they (g) always display a marked division of labor between those who participate in the institution.

To these seven features I would like to add three more. States are markedly different from a hunter-gatherer band in that (h) they are associated with social stratification of one form or another. In a modern bureaucratic state, society is regulated by rules written by legislators and, more often, by bureaucrats. Plain people are often permitted to cast votes for or against the legislators (though not, of course, for or against the bureaucrats) but play no direct role in writing most of the rules. As far as the rules are concerned, their direct role is mainly to obey. That is a modern sort of stratification. In addition and closely related to this, there is the fact that (i) with the advent of the state come *offices* which in a certain way are more important than the person who occupies them. In states, rights, duties, and above all authority attach to the position that one occupies, usually in a clear hierarchical organization and not to the individual who occupies it. Finally, (j) states are able deliberately to make rules. A chieftain in a pre-state form of social organization does not have this authority. Rather, the leader's relationship to the rules is almost the reverse of the one we find in state government. Whatever authority or power they have is defined by the rules, rules that the chieftain did not make, rules that evolved over time as a result of the practices of the group.

The last feature I would like to mention is often brought up by anthropologists but has long been more or less ignored by political philosophers. It is the fact that (k) throughout most of their long history so far, states have been very closely associated with religion. Indeed, there have been rudimentary proto-states in which the "king" has *only* magical functions (e.g., making it rain).[13] More importantly, in early states we often see sovereigns who claim to be gods, or to be descended from a god. More recently the sovereign was said to be in some way appointed by a god (the "divine right of kings"). No doubt this association with religion had a number of different functions but one predictable result would be that one comes to transfer to the state some of the mystique one associates with the gods. This historical feature of states seems quaint and obsolete today, when so few states make claims like this, but a case might be made that it is still relevant and worth considering. For instance, a case might be made that people still do associate something of the mystique of the gods with the states to which they are subjected.[14] Also, one might argue that a truly secular state is an inherently unstable institution because it cannot command the respect it demands and needs.[15] Then again, one could try to make a case that the fact that people have found the church–state connection so natural reveals something interesting and important about the state itself.

Which of these features belong in the core of the concept of the state and which are out on its periphery? It seems to me that such questions cannot be answered without some notion of how the state actually functions or, more generally, the impact it has, or systematically tends to have, on human wellbeing or illbeing. What are some of the salient state impacts that might be relevant here? I will briefly list several, partly for the sake of illustration, and partly to suggest possible avenues of further research.

First, states have always been *extraction devices*. Obviously, they extract money from people, but there is more to this extraction function than that. For a while during the American Civil War, the Confederacy levied in-kind taxes on agricultural products (in effect, simply confiscating part of the crop) and as far as we know, this may well be the oldest form of taxation, levied by the earliest states. In addition, that which is extracted need not be a thing at all. A state that forces a section of the population to work in a state of bondage, as serfs or slaves, is extracting labor. Perhaps the best statement of this state function is that it extracts *value*. It extracts value from those who produce it. At this point, there is a rather obvious connection between this list, of state functions, and the list of typical state features: To the extent that value-extraction is what we think states are really about, feature (f), taxation, moves far into the foreground. Though there are many other ways a state can extract value (e.g., through a rule that compels you to use something that is rightfully yours in a way that is favorable to my interests but not to yours, or to sell it to me on terms that are more favorable to me than you otherwise would) the most conspicuous is simply to tax it away.[16]

The second function is one that anthropologists often mention, though philosophers tend to ignore it. It is that, as Krader puts it, "[c]onscious membership in society and in a social stratum is ... developed by the formation of the state."[17] Once your entire linguistic or cultural group is ruled by one agent with the powers that a state has, it becomes more intuitively appealing and emotionally gripping to see yourself as a member of that group, and not merely of a certain family, clan, or village. Now, Krader points out, nationalism becomes possible: The benefits that the state confers on those favored by it enhance the belief that this group is unique and valuable. This feature might seem of marginal importance, but for the fact that this new type of group acquires genuine power via, among other things, the next two state functions.

The third function is that of supporting group expansion.[18] Non-state societies, if they are successful and thrive, must split into parts. For instance, a hunter-gatherer band may find that the group has grown too big to be supported by the game animals and other resources that remain in the area. At that point, a portion of the extended family band may move on in search of better opportunities. When this happens, the new group is functionally identical to the group it is leaving. In both groups there will be people who can hunt game, people who defend against enemies, people who settle disputes, and so on. States do not work this way at all. Because of the peculiar way in which it employs the division of labor, subgroups that split off from it do not function as complete societies on their own. The farmers who move over the next hill in search of better soil and forage will still rely for the maintenance of social order on the original group and therefore will still be members of it. The first states were something profoundly new in the world: a society that can expand without fission. As they expand, they can assimilate other, weaker groups and extract value, and consequently greater and greater power, from them. There is a certain limit to the power that a non-state group can acquire. With the advent of the state, there are no longer any such limits on power.

This power is further enhanced by the fourth function, which is that states greatly facilitate coordination and cooperation among the socially approved wielders of force. As economists would say, it economizes on transaction costs. In stateless societies as described by anthropologists, if someone who is performing the function of a judge, or policeman, or warrior needs the cooperation of someone else in one of those fields, they must persuade that person to cooperate with them (hence the great tradition of Native American oratory). This is one of the places where, in the state-based society, offices become important. If one occupies the relevant sort of office, one can be entitled to obedience or cooperation simply because of one's title. To the extent that the state is well-constituted and running smoothly, there will be little need to cajole or manipulate essential people into cooperating.

Lacking permanent offices, which endure through time while individuals come and go, is one of the things that make it difficult for the stateless societies to act concertedly, *as groups*, and make it more or less impossible for such a group to pursue very long-term group goals across generations. This makes an enormous difference for the group's ability to conduct war. Many people have commented on the burden born by American Indian warriors in defending their way of life against the encroaching Europeans during the nineteenth century. Though often superbly skilled in tactics, horsemanship, and the use of weapons, they did not seem to pursue long-range strategies and even had great difficulty achieving cooperation between different tribes in the face of an obvious common threat.

Here there is an interesting issue that is too complicated for an endnote but probably too important to be omitted. It is not clear whether we should say that the state enhances the group's capacity to wage war, or whether we should say that it is with the advent of the state that war itself becomes possible. Anthropologist Elman R. Service takes the latter approach. Reversing the old "conquest theory of the state" – which holds that the first states were formed when a sedentary, agricultural people were conquered by a more mobile warrior culture (which became the state)[19] – Service held that war does not make states; rather, states make war.[20] More recently, Keith F. Otterbein has argued persuasively for a more complex thesis.[21] In his view, the first states did indeed bring war-fare into a world of agriculturalists who had known only peace for per-haps thousands of years. However, before the agricultural revolution, when the hunter cultures were at their height, warfare was widespread and at times very destructive. On Otterbein's account, though, the nature of the fighting in the two sorts of war was quite different. The older, paleolithic, sort of warfare was associated with ambushes and lines (war-riors standing in a line and hurling projectiles at an opposing line) while the newer, late-neolithic, sort was associated with battles and sieges.[22] It seems to me that the difference between Service and Otterbein on this issue is largely a matter of how one defines war. Otterbein is impressed by the fact, which he carefully documents, that the older sort of fighting can be as lethal to individuals and as destructive of cultures and peoples as the state-based sort. Service, on the other hand, points out that paleolithic raids, "no matter how deadly ... seem to result in an equilibrium of vio-lence rather than a 'just peace'. ... War is, on the other hand, a contest having as its aim a peace in which the balance of power is shifted."[23] Service defines war in terms of its function, while Otterbein is more impressed with its sheer physical effects, which are simply the effects of mass violence.[24] He gives an impressive account of the long-standing conflict between the Iroquois and the Huron, which was so devastating to the Huron. Service, though, would fasten upon a distinction that Otterbein

144

conveys as he characterizes the precise nature of that devastation: "No political incorporation occurred," Otterbein tells us; rather, "the Hurons were annihilated."[25] In case the implications of this distinction are not obvious, consider what the thousands of Northern Cheyenne and Lakota who annihilated General Custer and his men at Little Bighorn did immediately afterward: They *went home.* In the same circumstances the Romans would have immediately set about building permanent fortifications, a bath house, and other facilities needed for a very, very long stay. Societies like those of the Cheyenne and Lakota cannot do that. I would say that if you believe, as I do, that human institutions ought to be defined in terms of their function (e.g., conquest, changing the balance of power, etc.), and not in terms of its most conspicuous physical effects (e.g., wholesale death and destruction), then Service has the edge on this issue. Without relying on this point, though, I think I can say that, since its beginnings, an important function of the state has been to facilitate the practice of warfare and to exploit it for distinctively state-dependent purposes, such as territorial expansion, the assimilation of other communities, and the systematic extraction of value.

Finally, as the fifth, sixth, and seventh state functions I will list the three that Locke identifies in his *Second Treatise.* As we saw in the first section of this chapter, he pointed out that the state affords us an opportunity to make the basic rules of society. In addition, it enables us to turn disputes over to "a known and indifferent judge," which will further help us to avoid violence and feuding. Finally, by pooling the power of many people, it ensures that the punisher will wield sufficient force to ensure that the rules are indeed enforced – something that will fail to happen if people are left to fend for themselves (this, as you may recall, is the only alternative to the state that Locke recognizes).[26]

Which characteristics of the state should be closest to the core of our conception of it? To a considerable extent, this will be influenced by our views about which of the functions of the state – from the eight I have just discussed or perhaps others that I have omitted – are the most important. To take an analogical case, the definition of the word "table" will need to include some reference to the fact that people use tables to support objects, such as plates and dinnerware. It is because of this factor that it should also include some reference to the fact that tables, necessarily, have prominent horizontal surfaces. Similarly, the functions of the state, state functions such as the eight I have discussed and/or others, should play a prominent role in our definition of what a state is. Our views on this matter should heavily influence which of the (a)-through-(j) sorts of features enter into our definition. One thing that has become obvious in our discussions of the functions of the state is that the people who systematically tend to benefit from its activities – the fact that an institution has a function after all means that it benefits someone – may in some cases be only one portion of the state's subject population, and they might very well be gaining at the expense of others. This brings out another point that may be less obvious. We should not rule out in advance the possibility that the best account of what a state is will indicate that it is not merely morally problematic but that it is by nature to some extent an unjust institution. From this point any number of possible lines of inquiry diverge. One possible destination would be to conclude that, if Nozick has succeeded in justifying something, it is an institution that is not a state but which actually in some respect is morally superior to the state.

6. Is the DPA's Failure to Claim Legitimacy a Deficiency?

Does the DPA need the legitimacy that it fails to claim for itself? I would like to make a case that dealing with this question adequately would involve dealing with just the sort of issues that are raised by attempting to define the state.

Samuel Freeman makes some comments that suggest why someone might think that having a mere de facto monopoly is not enough:

> What exists to maintain the effectiveness and stability of libertarian political power other than its de facto monopoly? Do people have reason to respect this power, or do they comply with its judgments, orders, and decrees simply out of fear? If political power is based simply on a natural monopoly, then in what sense can it be seen as the exercise of political authority as opposed to simply the employment of brute force? That some private body monopolizes political power is no reason to respect it (although it might be reason to fear it). There is then likely to be no general recognition of the moral or legal authority of the private state in libertarian society. But without the public's sense of its authority, libertarian political power lacks one of the most effective means for enforcing rules and judicial judgments, namely, the sense of allegiance and political obligation to authority. Moreover, the exercise of effective judicial power depends on such concepts as jurisdiction over parties and particular grievances and disputes, as well as the validity of judicial judgments based in an authorized body of laws. The mere exercising of judicial powers and making and enforcing judgments would seem to be insufficient to give rise to these normative concepts.[27]

Freeman seems to be saying that if the monopoly here is merely de facto – if, that is, the DPA does not claim to have a right to be the monopolist – then it cannot logically claim to possess authority but merely brute force instead. I think my brief discussion of the nature of authority above, in the first section of this chapter, suggests at least a partial answer to this charge. If "authority" is meant in the sense that I was using it there – in which one's telling someone to do something is in itself, even apart from the threat of force to back up the command, a reason for doing it – then this part of Freeman's argument rests on a false dichotomy. It is true (as I pointed out in the first section of this chapter) that power that rests on authority (in this sense of the word) does not rest on mere brute force. However, failure to claim authority only implies reliance on naked force, without further argument, if there is no third alternative. In the Lockean natural rights tradition, there is. Force can be used to enforce a shared understanding of the basic rules that enable us to live together in peace. It can be based, in other words, on what Locke calls the law of nature. This is the same basis that do-it-yourself justice would have in the state of nature, and it is clearly different both from authority (which no one would have in the state of nature) and from mere brute force.

The point, then, about the DPA's power being based on brute force does not follow yet, without further argument. Further argument is indeed possible, though, and it can touch on some very important issues. As Freeman points out elsewhere in his essay, there are important matters that are left indeterminate in the natural law. It may be obvious that we may not violate the property rights of others, but it may not be so obvious what is one's own property and what is not. The example he mentions is riparian rights, the property rights one acquires to water by owning land adjacent to its source.[28] If I own land that includes part of the bank of a river, it seems plausible to say that I have a right to use water from the river, but it will not always be obvious to everyone how much I may use (e.g., by damming the river). How can the DPA settle matters like this without claiming the right to make rules that others must follow just because orders coming from this source have a moral status that no other voice in the community can have? Wouldn't this mean claiming more than a mere de facto monopoly?

As a matter of fact, the indeterminacy of the law of nature is a subject that Nozick does discuss. Though he does not discuss it in the context of whether the DPA needs to claim authority, or anything more than a de facto monopoly of force, I think what he does say about it suggests a possible response to the problem that Freeman presents. The example of indeterminacy that he gives is from criminal law and not, like Freeman's, from property law, but the fundamental point is the same. Natural law, Nozick points out, may not by itself resolve disagreements about how much punishment a given offense might deserve (141). He introduces this point as the basis for an additional possible sort of support for his own argument – that is, for his defense of the state. At this point in his argument, he says, his reasoning has rested on the familiar phenomenon of human factual uncertainty and ignorance. Here he is referring to the sort of human fallibility that gives rise to the problem that was exposed in the risk argument: Sometimes we are convinced that someone's weighing of the evidence as to whether another person committed a given offense is faulty. Now he is indicating a whole new dimension of possible disagreement: Even if we agree on the facts, we can disagree on matters of moral principle. He points out, tellingly, that even within the Lockean natural rights tradition there are strong disagreements on issues such as "intellectual property rights." Can novelists, for instance, legitimately have property rights in novels that they produce – not copies of the novels, but the novels themselves? Some neo-Lockeans think that such rights are unjust government-created monopolies, while others think that they rest on the same foundations that support all property rights: They protect the results of productive effort (344 fn. 15).

The argument that Nozick suggests at this point is interestingly different from the risk argument. The risk argument was about whether the DPA would be within its rights if it were to prohibit some individuals from relying on certain self-protection methods and offering to extend its own protection to them. The present one is about whether it is rational for individuals to accept the DPA's de facto capacity to make rules and apply them to those same individuals. His answer to both questions is "yes." In the case of the latter issue, the reasoning turns upon the relative value of peace, on the one hand, and having things one's own way, on the other: "Disagreements about what is to be enforced, argue reluctant archists, provide yet another reason (in addition to lack of factual knowledge) for the apparatus of the state …. People who prefer peace to the enforcement of their view of right will unite together in *one* state." Of course, being Nozick, he cannot resist tossing in a startling little snapper in the last sentence in this discussion: "But of course, if people genuinely do hold this preference, their protective agencies will not do battle either." (141–142).

This last comment seriously undermines this line of reasoning as an argument for a monopolistic state. The possibility that the protective agencies will not do battle undermines the likelihood of two of the three possible early outcomes of the invisible-hand process in Chapter 2 (victory and gradient), and I have already argued that the third outcome (federation, which is the outcome of agencies' agreeing to not do battle) need not be a single, monopolistic organization. That would mean that, if people do genuinely prefer peace to having their own way, a preference that Nozick finds reasonable, the crucial invisible-hand process will not come to fruition, will not produce a DPA.

Nonetheless, however much damage this line of reasoning might do to Nozick's justification of the state, it might serve as the basis of an ade quate response to Freeman on the issue of the alleged need of the state to claim authority. In the context of the natural rights tradition that both Locke and Nozick work in, a case can be made that the preference for peace over having one's own way is a good reason for accepting the laws produced by the DPA, provided at least that these laws represent an attempt to codify, clarify, and specify those rights, a process that for brevity I will call "interpreting natural rights." The argument might go roughly like this. Given the insufficient specificity and clarity of natural rights themselves, there must be an interpretation of those rights, spelling out what they mean in detail. There can be only one such interpretation in a given area (this is an intended implication of the invisible-hand explanation).[29] Since having an interpretation is necessary, and since having only one is a necessary condition of having any at all, this is a very good reason for me to accept the one that is in force, even if it is does not (indeed, is extremely unlikely to) spell matters out in the way that I would if I had the power to do so. This reason, though, only applies in full force to the extent that the legal system really *is* an "interpretation" of the rules necessary for human beings to live together and cooperate in peace. To the extent that the system does something else – for instance, loots the rightful property of one section of the population in order to enrich another – this reason does not apply.

Notice that this reason is not based on any special property of the law-generating agency, such as would give its voice a moral weight that cannot be possessed by any other agent in its realm. It is based on the needs of the people to whom the system applies, and on moral principles that apply to all. You might say that it attributes to the DPA *virtual* authority, in that it is a reason for acting *as if* it had (within a strictly limited sphere) the authority attributed to the state by a traditional political theory such as that of Locke.

This sort of virtual authority arises in the context of the very narrow sort of state that Nozick envisions. What about the sort of extraminimal state supported by Nozick's left-liberal critics, such as Prof. Freeman? Notice that Lockean natural rights, as Nozick understands them, are constraints on one's action. They tell us (at least if properly clarified and specified) what things we may not do to our fellow human beings. To the extent that a state's functions extend beyond interpreting and enforcing such constraints, the rightness of its actions must be supported by goal type considerations: promoting scientific research, supporting the arts, helping the needy, making the distribution of wealth more fair, and so on. If such a state is acting within its rights, that is because pursuing or achieving this goal makes it so. This applies to state coercion: If the state pursues a given goal by placing requirements on people and using coercion to make them conform to these requirements, where it is not simply enforcing moral constraints that apply to them independently of the goal they are pursuing, such coercion can only be justified on the basis of the worthiness of the goal involved. The goal, however, is not by itself enough to justify them. These requirements, after all, cannot themselves be viewed as mere interpretations, in the above sense, of basic moral requirements. Even if I have a natural moral obligation (i.e., an obligation that is independent of the state's commands) to pursue all of the state's goals myself, there is an infinitude of ways to pursue any one goal, and I do not naturally have an obligation to employ any one of them. For any particular means of pursuing a worthy goal, I will always be within my rights to pursue the goal by some other means.

The state does not merely promote knowledge, art, and so forth. It can only do so by doing things like deciding which kinds of art it will pursue, and by what means. It must coerce me to cooperate in supporting and cooperating with very specific measures to promote its goals. Yet there is no way that I have anything like a natural moral obligation to cooperate in carrying out these specific measures. Even if I have an obligation to promote the arts, this does not mean that I have an obligation to support any particular genre or any particular artist. Yet states can only pursue such goals by compelling individuals to do precisely such particular things. If I do have an obligation to do such particular things, it is an obligation that the state creates. How does it do that? Does it create this obligation, as Freeman might say, by means of the exercise of brute force? In order to avoid this alternative, it seems one must show that the state has some special status that makes its say-so a reason to do what it says. Perhaps it is wiser than the individuals who are subject to its rules, or perhaps it is special because, unlike any individual, it represents "the voice of the people," and the voice of the people, like the voice of God, brings authority with it by its very nature. Perhaps we all entered into a social contract to give it such authority over us. Whatever the reason might be, it seems that a state that goes beyond the modest functions of Nozick's DPA *must* claim to have authority.

On the other hand, as I have suggested, a case can be made that his DPA need not make this claim, that its failure to do so is not a deficiency in terms of its own standards and goals.

Notes

1 John Locke, *Second Treatise of Government* (Indianapolis, Indiana: Hackett Publishing, 1980 [orig. pub. 1690]), sects. 124 and 136. See also sect. 129.
2 Eric Mack mentions a number of other features that we associate with states which the DPA does not have: a constitution, a legislature, political parties, and elections. Of course, these features are not essential to something's being a state – indeed, throughout most of human history states have had none of these features – but the reason the DPA does not have them is, as Mack seems to suggest, that the DPA is really a business corporation, and businesses do not have these things. Eric Mack, "Nozickean Arguments for the More-than-Minimal State," in *The Cambridge Companion to Nozick's Anarchy, State, and Utopia* (Cambridge, England: Cambridge University Press, 2011), p. 104.
3 Richard Wright, *Black Boy (American Hunger)*, can be found in an excellent edition: Arnold Rampersad, ed., *Later Works* (New York: Literary Classics of the United States, 1991 [orig. pub. 1945]), pp. 5–246.
4 Mack, "Nozickean Arguments for the More-than-Minimal State," p. 114 fn. 1.
5 The text here actually says "unprohibited" but the logic of the passage requires "prohibited." I assume that this is a typographical error.
6 Henry David Thoreau, "Civil Disobedience," in Elizabeth Witherell, ed., *Thoreau: Essays and Poems* (New York: Library of America, 2001), p. 224.
7 What he says is actually closer to wondering at the fact that states don't even seem to recognize the possibility of opting out: "One would think, that a deliberate and practical denial of its authority was the only offense never contemplated by its government; else, why has it not assigned its definite, its suitable and proportionate, penalty?" Thoreau, "Civil Disobedience," p. 211.
8 Lawrence Krader, *Formation of the State* (Englewood Cliffs, New Jersey: Prentice-Hall, 1968), pp 21–22.
9 Krader, *Formation of the State*, pp. 40–42.
10 Krader, *Formation of the State*, p. 35.
11 Ronald Cohen, "Introduction," in Ronald Cohen and Elman R. Service, eds., *Origins of the State: The Anthropology of Political Evolution* (Philadelphia, Pennsylvania: Institute for the Study of Human Issues, 1978), p. 3. Here Cohen is explicitly disagreeing with Krader, who insists that it is a necessary condition of states that, once their monopoly of force is established, it requires that everyone "must accept the state or reject it": "There is no middle ground." Krader, *Formation of the State*, p. 27.
12 This will have to do as an answer to an objection that I am sure Michael Huemer would have raised by now. As I noted in Chapter 2, note 2, his book

The Problem of Political Authority reaches political conclusions roughly similar to those that Nozick reaches, but with some important differences in the way he argues for those conclusions. The most basic one, other than the (perhaps merely apparent) one I mentioned there is that, unlike Nozick, Huemer devotes no space to discussing what a state actually is. He has said (personal communication, April 2014) that he believes such a discussion would be a waste of time at best. He believes (if I have a firm grasp of his position here) that such discussions assume that it is possible to define the relevant concept by producing necessary and sufficient conditions for their referents. He believes that this is in fact never possible, unless we are dealing with a technical concept invented by theoreticians (e.g., mathematicians). I think this impossibility claim of his is probably correct, at least as it applies to ordinary-language concepts that are philosophically interesting, such as "morality," "causation," "God," religion, or "the state." However, the approach toward definition that I am taking here does not aim at necessary and sufficient conditions, but at distinguishing between core, periphery, and features that lie beyond the periphery. Michael Huemer, *The Problem of Political Authority: An Examination of the Right to Coerce and the Duty to Obey* (Basingstoke, England: Palgrave MacMillan, 2012).

13 For an interesting example, see Krader's account of the Dinka and the Shilluk of the upper Nile Valley in *Formation of the State*, pp. 35–38.

14 Herbert Spencer adopts and develops this position in his *The Man versus the State* (Caldwell, Idaho: Caxton, 1940 [orig. pub. 1892), Ch. 6, "The Great Political Superstition."

15 Friedrich Nietzsche advances this view in his *Human, All Too Human: A Book for Free Spirits* (Cambridge, England: Cambridge University Press, 1996 [orig. pub. 1878]), sect. 472. Seen in the context of the entire history of the state, secular states are still a fairly recent phenomenon. It is perhaps too early to say that Nietzsche is wrong about this. In fact, if we consider the bitter hatred and contempt that modern political parties often have for those currently in power (when power is held by their opponents), it looks like he might yet be proven right.

16 For an economic, legal, and ethical discussion of another tool for extracting value, see Richard Epstein, *Takings: Private Property and the Power of Eminent Domain* (Cambridge, Massachusetts: Harvard University Press, 1985).

17 Krader, *Formation of the State*, p. 27.

18 Here I must admit I am simply following Ronald Cohen, *Origins of the State*, p. 4.

19 The locus classicus for this theory is Franz Oppenheimer, *The State: Its History and Development Viewed Sociologically* (Indianapolis, Indiana: Bobbs Merrill, 1914 [orig. pub. 1907]). Radical libertarians often like this theory, perhaps because it makes the state seem morally tainted. This fondness, a sort of reverse sentimentality, raises thorny questions about why the origins of the first states approximately 8,000 years ago would affect the moral status of states today. Exactly what is the connection between what

happened so long ago and the moral status of the state today? It seems to me that, if you want to make the moral status of states look dubious, Service's inversion of the Oppenheimerian thesis is more promising. If it is true that the original states brought war into a world that was previously innocent of it, this might tell us something about the nature of the state itself, something morally unattractive that might still be true of it today.

20 Elman R. Service, *The Origins of the State and Civilization* (New York: W. W. Norton, 1975), pp. 270–273.

21 Keith F. Otterbein, *How War Began* (College Station, Texas: Texas A & M University Press, 2004), especially Ch. 1.

22 Otterbein, *How War Began*, p. 18.

23 Service, *The Origins of the State and Civilization*, p. 271. Service's last comment, which seems to have the form of a definition of war, is actually a quotation from another anthropologist, Paul Bohanan.

24 I interpret the quotation from Bohanan (see note 22, above) as Service's definition of war. Otterbein seems to define it simply as a sort of intergroup (as opposed to interindividual) conflict: namely, *violent* intergroup conflict. See Otterbein, *How War Began*, pp. 84–85.

25 Otterbein, *How War Began*, pp. 208–213.

26 See the passages cited in note 1, above. See also Locke, *Second Treatise of Government*, sects. 125–127 and 130.

27 Samuel Freeman, "Illiberal Libertarians," *Philosophy and Public Affairs*, vol. 30, no. 2 (Spring 2001), p.144.

28 Freeman, "Illiberal Libertarians," pp. 139–140 fn. 69.

29 I have called this conclusion into question, but that is not relevant to the present issue, which is whether Nozick has an answer to Freeman's objection to the DPA's failure to claim a more than de facto monopoly.

8

Distributive Justice

1. Some Terminology and Basic Concepts

Though he makes the term "distributive justice" the title of Chapter 7, Nozick begins the chapter by expressing a degree of skepticism about it. This term, he says, "is not a neutral one." "Distribution" after all is an ambiguous word. The fact that I have $10 while you have $20 and Jones has $30 could be called a distribution. In this sense, a distribution is simply the structure or pattern that holds between different people's shares of something. On the other hand, there is "distribution" as in: "In the aftermath of the latest natural disaster, many people saw flaws in the local relief agency's distribution system." A distribution can be the act of an agent, and by extension the structure or pattern that results from it. The phrase "distributive justice" can suggest distribution in the latter sense. "Into this process of distributing some error may have crept. So it is an open question, at least, whether *re*distribution should take place ..." (149).

His more neutral way of characterizing the present issue describes it as the problem of justice in holdings. "Holding" here refers to the mere, brute fact of possessing something, with no moral judgment or causal history implied or assumed. So the issue he grapples with in Chapter 7 concerns multi-part states of affairs like this one: my holding $10 plus your holding $20 plus Jones holding $30. What can make things like *that* just?

This way of putting it brings us a little closer to clarity, but at the same time it creates an ambiguity, one that is never resolved in ASU. Is Nozick trying to put forth a theory of distributive justice, or is he rejecting distributive justice altogether in favor of something else? The locution of

Anarchy, State, and Utopia: An Advanced Guide, First Edition. Lester H. Hunt.

"justice in holdings" enables him to avoid committing himself on this question. The question is not a merely verbal one. The traditional phrase, distributive justice, refers to a subject that a very long line of philosophers, going at least as far back as Plato, have theorized about. Their theories are bewilderingly various but, as we will see, they do have something in common that justifies applying one term to them. Nozick's view, however, differs from *all* of them. This raises the distinct possibility that he and the traditional theorists are simply are not talking about the same thing. This is good news, in a way, because it means that they can both – Nozick and the distributive justice tradition or some part of it – be right. After all, two theories can only directly contradict each other to the extent that they say something about the same thing. I will eventually argue for the view that they are indeed about different things and that in some non-trivial way they are both right. However, I will also suggest that the truth in the distributive justice tradition is rather different from what its proponents typically think it is.

Before we look into Chapter 7, it will be helpful to examine two distinctions or pairs of concepts. Neither figures prominently in the text of ASU – though one is featured in a footnote (343 fn. 10) – however, both, I think, lurk enormously behind it.

One thing that all conceptions of justice have in common is that they are all in some way about "what you have coming to you." All are about ways in which it can be fitting or right that you should have a certain thing or that a certain thing be done to you (or that you not have the thing or it not be done to you). This is true of each of the three traditional categories of justice: retributive justice (which is about which punishments fit which crimes), rectificatory justice (which is about compensating people for wrongs done to them) and – distributive justice. A few years before Nozick began writing ASU, the philosopher Joel Feinberg made a distinction between two sorts of reasons why a person might have something coming to them, which he called "entitlement" and "desert."[1] No doubt, there are many other sorts of reasons, but these two seem peculiarly relevant to distributive justice. Suppose I give a student an A in my course because I think she did excellent work. I think she deserved an A. Suppose that, due to some computer glitch or recording error, this does not appear on her transcript. An injustice has been done: She is entitled to three units of A that she did not get.

Deserving an A and being entitled to it are two different things. A person deserves something, Feinberg tells us, in virtue of "some possessed characteristic or prior activity."[2] More precisely, this characteristic or activity – which in this case is the student's excellent work – must indicate that the person satisfies "certain conditions of worthiness."[3] She deserves an A because her work is worthy of that grade. On the other hand, she is entitled to the A because I gave it to her. Though Feinberg does not explicitly define entitlement, the examples he gives all seem to be rights that arise from a social process of some sort (e.g., a presidential election, which assigns the rights which taken together constitute the office of the president) or from institutional rules and regulations that assign rights. The rules of my institution authorize me to assign grades in this course, which is why the student is entitled to an A. Notice that, because desert and entitlement are based on different things, they can go their separate ways. You can be entitled to something you do not deserve, and you can deserve something to which you are not entitled. As we shall see, at this point the distinction between entitlement and desert, along with other related distinctions, becomes very interesting.

Nozick's "entitlement theory of justice in holdings" will take the idea of entitlement in a direction that Feinberg would not have dreamed of, but it will prove helpful in grasping the implications of Nozick's theory to keep in mind Feinberg's original contrast between entitlement and desert. It might also eventually help us in forming a rational opinion about whether we should accept the theory, reject it, or amend it in some way.

The other distinction, in addition to the one between entitlement and desert, that I think it would be helpful to consider at this point is that between justice and fairness. Actually, the relationship between these two concepts lacks the precision we generally associate with the word "distinction," as both of them are extremely vague. Both, however, are ideas we use all the time. I have already said a little something about what "justice" generally means. What, insofar as it is possible explain it clearly, does "fairness" mean? Fairness, it seems to me, can always be analyzed as a kind of equality. This is true even though fairness often requires us to treat people very differently. Was it fair to give my student an A while others got lower grades? In doing so, I was guided by the idea that it would be unfair to her to give her the same grade as someone who accomplished less. The definitions of different levels of achievement are applied to everyone equally: If you do something that the rule defines as A work, you get an A, otherwise not. If someone doesn't do this, they shouldn't blame the rule. The uneven outcome is due to the uneven behavior. After all, if I give an A to everyone the result in a way would be very unequal if the students display widely differing levels of achievement: Some would achieve the grade after doing and achieving very much while others would get the same result by doing and achieving very little. Getting a good outcome with comparatively very little input is a bonus I am bestowing on some and denying to others. That is not equality.

A good way to get an intuitive grasp of the difference between justice and fairness is to reflect on a story that is often told of Sidney Morgenbesser, one of Nozick's philosophy professors when he was an undergraduate at Columbia University. The story is told in various versions and goes something like this: During the Vietnam era, Morgenbesser took part in a student demonstration and in the ensuing chaos was beaten by the police. Later, being interviewed for jury duty, he was asked if he felt he was ever treated unfairly or unjustly by an officer of the law. He said, "Unjustly yes, unfairly no." Asked what he meant by that, he said "An officer hit me on the head with his nightstick, which was unjust. But they were doing it to everybody – so it wasn't unfair." (I hope no explanation of the anecdote is necessary.)[4]

Some of the deepest issues in theories of distributive justice have to do with the relationship between justice and fairness. John Rawls famously derived justice from fairness. His theory of "justice as fairness" holds that the principles of justice are those principles that would be chosen in circumstances that cannot possibly produce unfair results, in part because the parties to the agreement begin in a position of complete equality. Alternatively, one might think that fairness is a subset within the wider field of justice. One could argue that this in effect is what the distributive justice tradition does. Most, perhaps all, of the traditional principles of distributive justice can be understood as forms of fairness. Consider egalitarianism, for instance. If there really is a valid objection to some people having a lot while others have little, it is that it is unfair. On the other hand, retributive and rectificatory justice don't seem to be, fundamentally, matters of fairness. The thief who steals your wallet is not merely being unfair to you. And the people who put the thief in jail are not doing so in order to be fair (to whom?). If someone negligently destroys your property and refuses to pay for it, that isn't unfair – it is just plain wrong. That payment is yours by right. Justice in such cases does not seem to be purely a matter of fairness. However, distributive justice, as it is usually understood, is precisely that.

It also, in the traditional accounts, is often a matter of desert: The distribution of holdings can only be just if people get what they deserve. Nothing else would be fair. Much of the radicalism of Nozick's approach lies in the fact that, in his account, justice in holdings has nothing to do with either fairness or desert. For holdings to be just, there is no need for them to be fair. There is also, as far as justice is concerned, no need that people get what they deserve.

2. The Entitlement View

In his initial statement of it, Nozick's own conception of justice in hold-ings, the "entitlement theory," is simplicity itself:

1. A person who acquires a holding in accordance with the principle of justice in acquisition is entitled to that holding.
2. A person who acquires a holding in accordance with the principle of justice in transfer, from someone else entitled to that holding, is enti-tled to that holding.
3. No one is entitled to a holding, except by repeated applications of 1 and 2.

Finally, a distribution is just if, and only if, everyone is entitled to the holdings they possess under the distribution.

One glaring, even somewhat shocking feature of this account, is that it is obviously incomplete. The principle of justice in acquisition and the principle of justice in transfer – what do these principles say? He never tells us! And the reason for that, I think, is simple: For his purposes, it makes no difference what these principles say. If the entitlement view, even in this sketchy form, is true, if *some* satisfactory version of these principles can be given then all competing accounts of justice in holdings are false.

Remember, at this point in the book he believes he has justified a certain sort of state: one that enforces Lockean rights, but does no more than that. Now he is turning to the task of resisting what he sees as the most formidable sort of argument for a state that is more extensive than that: the sort that claims that the correct principles of distributive justice can justify the state in using coercion against people who are not violating the libertarian constraint. He believes that if the entitlement view – any version of it – is true, then all such arguments fail. He believes that fully spelling out the entitlement view, interesting as that would be, is not needed for accomplishing his present purpose, which is simply to resist the more-than-minimal state.

Nonetheless, though he does not spell out the view in any detail, I am sure it will help us to weigh and assess the things he does say about it if we briefly consider what some of these details would be or might be. One way to get a grasp of entitlement is to think of it in terms of what I call "entitle-ment processes." An entitlement process, let us say, is a procedure, carried out by human action, all or part of the point of which is to assign rights. (I am not sure whether this is a definition or merely a necessary condition of being an entitlement process, but I don't think that matters here.) Nozick does indicate (at 157) a number of examples of what he regards as legitimate entitlement processes: being paid for one's labor in a competitive economy, winning at gambling, sharing one's mate's income, giving and receiving gifts, cashing in an investment, making things, and finding things. Because the topic under discussion here is justice in holdings, his examples are limited to processes that assign property rights, but as I have defined them, there can be other sorts of entitlement process, because there are rights that are not property rights. Possible examples include: weddings, assigning grades, judging contests, and democratic elections. Notice that if you believe in democracy you do hold an entitlement view of at least one sort of right: namely, the right to wield political power. If democracy means anything, it means that rights to political power are to be based on entitlement and *not* on desert. The person who has a right to occupy the office is the one who won the election, even if (as will usually be the case) that person was not the most deserving possible candidate. (The most deserving person was probably not even a candidate!) Participants in a military coup, who are removing a democratically elected president with someone they find preferable, might consistently believe in a desert view of political power, but a (small "d") democrat cannot. A democrat would say that what the coup-plotters are doing is terribly wrong, even if the replacement president is (in Feinberg's sense) more deserving.

3. A Taxonomy of Principles

Nozick sets the entitlement view against the background of the competing sorts of theories in several interesting if rambling pages (153–156). His discussion there takes the form of a sort of taxonomy of principles of distributive justice, one that is almost as confusing as it is enlightening. Here is how I make sense of it.

The entitlement view, he tells us, is a *historical* principle: "[W]hether a distribution is just depends on how it came about" (153). Are there other historical principles, in addition to entitlement? Is there something all the other principles have in common? I will argue that there is something wrong with Nozick's treatment of both these questions, but that these problems can easily be fixed. As a matter of fact, the "fix" makes his account of these principles somewhat simpler than it appears on the page. Please bear with me.

The first category of theories that are alternative to entitlement is *current time-slice principles*. Rather oddly, he initially says that on this sort of view all that matters as far as justice is concerned is "who has what." I say oddly because, as the reader soon realizes, *who* has what is the main thing that does *not* matter on a current time-slice view. On this sort of view, what matters for justice is (at most) the magnitude of shares of the thing distributed and the relations between the shares. Egalitarianism is such a view, because it only cares about a certain relationship between the shares: that they are the same. Utilitarianism is another one, because it only looks at the magnitudes: If we know how much utility is produced by a distribution, and have the same information about the possible distributions that are alternatives to it, then according to the utilitarian we know enough. According to time-slice views,[5] nothing is lost as far as justice is concerned if the people involved trade places, as long as the relevant features of the distribution remain the same. Distributions are just or unjust in and of themselves: There is no need to compare them to something that is not a distribution.

Notice that Rawls' "difference principle" is also a time-slice principle. That is the principle that social and economic inequalities must be reasonably expected to be to the advantage of the least well-off group of people. One thing this idea has in common with utilitarianism is that, ultimately, the thing that both principles distribute is utility: What matters from the point of view of justice, for both, is the value that someone derives from a distribution. One way it differs from both utilitarianism, which only looks at quantities of the good being distributed, and egalitarianism, which only looks at structural features, is that it looks at both. It attends only to the advantage of the *least* well off, which is a structural consideration, and what it does about them is to *increase* their wellbeing, which is a quantitative consideration. One thing it has in common with both principles is that it makes no difference who occupies any position in society, nor whether people change places, provided that the distribution itself remains the same. As Rawlsian economic planners introduce new inequalities over time, they continually improve the lot of the least well-off, but notice that it may not be the same worst-off people whose lot they are improving each time. The currently worst-off individuals may have been better off under an earlier institutional arrangement, but their decline in fortunes is made just, under the difference principle, by the fact that they are still better off than the previously worst-off group of people were. What makes this distribution just is the relationship between it and other distributions, and nothing else.

Of course, throughout history, many theorists and ordinary people have thought that to determine whether a given setup is distributively just there is a need to compare a distribution to something that is not a distribution. Aristotle took it as obvious. "All are agreed," he said, "that justice in distributions must be based on desert (*kat' axion*) of some sort."[6] Theories like his are examples of what Nozick calls *patterned principles*, or ones that require that "a distribution is to vary along with some natural dimension, weighted sum of natural dimensions, or lexicographic ordering of natural dimensions" (156). It is clear enough from the examples he gives that what he means by this rather intimidating formulation is that a holding is justified by some fact about the person who holds it. Thus any principle based on what Feinberg calls desert (which would require that the holder satisfy a certain condition of worthiness) would be a patterned one. Patterned principles are ones that can be formulated by saying "to each according to his ...." There are as many patterned principles as there are ways of filling in that blank: to each according to his moral merit ... productive contribution to society ... degree of effort put forth ... skillfulness ... unmet needs ..., and on it goes.

When Nozick says that these principles should "vary along with" the relevant feature of the person, he seems to mean something fairly specific. In his brief discussion of the patterned principle that calls for "distribution according to moral merit," he says that what it requires is that "no person should have a greater share than anyone whose moral merit is greater" (156). So a Nozickean patterned principle is perfectly realized if two rankings – one giving the order of everyone's shares (e.g., from highest to lowest) and the other giving the order of everyone's possession of the relevant feature (in this case from most meritorious to least) – are the same. This is worth noticing because it means that his patterned principles only require that we be able to rank possession of the feature – say, that one has more and another less – and not that we actually be able to measure it. (Some versions of patterned principles, as formulated by people who endorse them, do require this.)[7]

Is there, among the categories he discusses, a single term for all non-entitlement principles? A likely candidate would seem to be *end-result* or *end-state principle*s. These are all those principles that hold that the justice of a situation is independent of how it came about: They are un-historical. Nozick stops short of saying that these principles, collectively, are *the* alternative to the entitlement view. The reason for this seems to be that he thinks there is at least one principle that is patterned, and therefore is not an entitlement view, but is historical. This is the principle, which I've already mentioned, of distribution according to moral merit.

I would say that he is simply mistaken on this point. What he seems to be thinking is that your moral merit is a fact about your past, your moral history, so to speak. But this is not, so far, a fact about the history *of the holding*: It is not how the holding came about. As far as this principle of moral merit is concerned, my holdings are just if they are commensurate with my moral merit. It could have been given to me by the Commissar of Distribution, or it could have fallen on me like manna from heaven. Such things do not affect the justice of my holdings, under this principle. That means it is un-historical or, in other words, an end-state principle, pure and simple.

As a matter of fact, it seems impossible that there could be a plausible historical principle of justice in holdings that is not an entitlement principle. First, notice that by "justice in acquisition" he must mean justice in original acquisition: that is, this principle must be about acquiring legitimate title to something that was previously unowned. (If it was already owned by someone else, that would be justice in transfer.) If I acquire title to something that was indeed previously owned, it must have been owned by someone other than myself. My title to it after all is the thing we are trying to explain. Thus if there is a historical account of my legitimate title to a holding of mine, it must be something that was previously owned by someone other than myself, or else I acquired it under the principle of justice in acquisition. In that case, the only way my title can come about under something other than the principle of justice in transfer, *and* also other than the principle of justice in acquisition, is if I acquire just title to this thing that is owned by someone else from someone who is *not* entitled to it. But this seems impossible. Thus, given the broad way in which Nozick defines it, as consisting of the two vaguely described principles, the entitlement theory is the only historical principle of justice in holdings: that is, it is the only one that is even remotely plausible.

In what follows, I will use "end-state principles" to refer to all non-entitlement principles of distributive justice. As a matter of fact, Nozick sometimes seems to do the same. More often, and somewhat confusingly, he uses "patterned principles," presumably in an extended sense, to mean the same thing.[8]

4.   The Adventures of Wilt Chamberlain

Much of what Nozick has to say in favor of the entitlement view, and against non-entitlement ones, revolves around the familiar thought-experiment involving the late basketball legend Wilt Chamberlain (160–161). Take your favorite non-entitlement principle of distributive justice – I will call it, whatever it is, P. Suppose P is perfectly realized, giving us distribution D_1. Mr. Chamberlain enters an agreement with the owners of his team to the effect that at each home game the customers will pay 25 cents that will go directly to him. The fans are glad to do so – he is very popular – and by the end of the season a million of them have paid their 25 cents, giving him $250,000 that he did not have under D_1. This increment, he tells us, is more than any other person's income. Call the new distribution D_2. It seems impossible that D_2 fits P. And yet it is hard to say that it is unjust. What he is thinking here seems to be based on something he said a few pages earlier: "Whatever arises from a just situation by just steps is just" (151). D_1 (by hypothesis) was just. The voluntary transactions that resulted in D_2 were just. The fans were acting well within their rights. Thus, D_2 must be just.

What is the point of this thought-experiment? The first point that Nozick states is rather modest: "It is not clear how those holding alternative conceptions of distributive justice can reject the entitlement conception of justice in holdings" (160). If D_2 can be just despite violating the best non-entitlement principle, then such principles can't be the whole story about justice in holdings: Entitlement must be integrated into one's view of this matter somehow or other.

So far, the argument is merely a plea in favor of a place, in the big picture of what justice is, for entitlement. After all, if D_2 is just, then what P says about it is not true, because P says that it is unjust. Further, the reason it has this false implication is that it does not respond to the just steps that led to D_2 – in other words, because it is un-historical. This would seem to mean that all end-state principles are false. Nozick does not explicitly draw this conclusion from the Chamberlain story, but it does seem to be part of his point.

Of course he has a good deal more to say against end-state principles. Of these comments perhaps the most interesting are the ones that in some cases are probably not really meant to be knock-down arguments but rather point out odd features of these principles, ones that are not obvious at first look. Nozick points out in one such observation that all these principles are "theories of recipient justice" (168). If we suppose that their function is to assign rights to holdings, then they only assign rights to receive things. They say nothing about what rights we have to give people things. They also say nothing about the rights that people who produced those things have. This is a potentially serious problem because if producers and givers do have rights (and of course they do) there is so far no reason to think they cannot conflict with recipient rights. What if P says you have no right to receive something while the best principle of givers' rights says I have a perfect right to give it to you? Which principle wins? It could be that those who advocate these principles are assuming that recipient rights override all the others. But what reason do we have to believe such a thing, other than that it would resolve the conflict between these principles? And what reason do we have to believe that this is the right way to resolve it?

Nozick also points out that, if principles like P assign rights, these rights will be profoundly different in kind from the familiar sort of property rights that are assigned by entitlement. The sort of property rights we get from entitlement are freedom-extenders. End-state principles, on the other hand, "do not give the right to choose what to do with what one has" (167). The right you get from P is a right to a position in a distribution. This right can't include the right to move out of this position. Hence there are any number of rights that a traditional property right would give you which do not come as part of this sort of right. Indeed, if you see it as a right to a place in a distribution, it begins to look at least as much like a duty as it does like a right – a duty to stay in your place. Piling one paradox on another, Nozick points out that while consuming your holdings yourself is always permitted by such a principle, gift-giving can easily be wrong. I would add that, by the same logic, a business transaction, a trade, is less likely to be a violation, at least if what P does is distribute material goods, because with a trade at least we have goods going in both directions: I give something up, but I get something back. A gift, on the other hand, is a pure transfer from one person to another and so is much more likely to move someone out of their assigned place (and the more generous – that is, the more ample – the gift is, the more likely it is to be "wrong").

These problems and paradoxes, interesting as they are, seem to be incidental to the main point that, Nozick tells us, is "illustrated by the Wilt Chamberlain example," which is that "no end-state principle … can be continuously realized without continuous interference with people's lives" (163). He claims that the notion that people can freely conform to an end-state principle assumes that three unlikely things can happen at once: first, that everyone will want to maintain the pattern (note that this means they will want the *same* pattern); second, that each will be able to discover which course of action on their part would conform to the pattern; and, third, that they will coordinate their behavior in such a way that they add up to the result of maintaining the pattern. We might call these the agreement problem, the knowledge problem, and the coordination problem. The last two objections are most plausible, once again, if one thinks in terms of a position in a distribution. One's position consists in a certain relation between one's holdings and those of others, and unless P in this case is pure egalitarianism (everyone has the same holdings) this can be difficult to find out. That is the knowledge problem. The coordination problem arises from the obvious fact that the cumulative effects upon relative positions of what multiple people do can be completely different from those of any one person's actions. If one person gives Wilt a quarter, that probably does not violate P, but if a million do it almost certainly does. Somewhere in-between, a line is crossed. The givers on one side of the line are blameless, while those on the other side are doing something wrong. P does not say what any one person should do, independently of what others are doing. It may be that your donation to Mr. Chamberlain is permissible and mine likewise, while both of them combined give him too much. Even assuming that we can find this out (the knowledge problem) we need to have some way to agree on which of us will abstain from giving to him. That is the coordination problem.

5. Assessing Nozick's Arguments

We will eventually look at other arguments Nozick presents for entitlement and against end-state principles, but there is plenty to discuss in the ones I have already reviewed. Let's look at some objections and counter-arguments.

The notion that whatever arises from a just situation by just steps is just is crucial to the reasoning that he bases on the Wilt Chamberlain story. We have already seen reason to believe that adherents of the distributive justice tradition must hold that this "principle of just steps," as for convenience I'll call it, is false. Is it?

One sometimes hears an objection to the Wilt Chamberlain discussion which would seem to imply that there is, strictly speaking, no reason to discuss this question, as this premise makes Nozick's entire argument question-begging. The idea is that the principle of just steps simply *is* the entitlement theory, so that Nozick is simply arguing in a circle, so that anyone who is impressed by this discussion as if it were an effective argument for the entitlement view, or against the alternative views, is simply confused. This objection is easily dispensed with. The principle of just steps is not identical to the entitlement view, if only because its scope is much broader: It is about justice in general, while the entitlement view is about distributive justice, justice in holdings. If we interpret the just steps principle as being about distributive justice only (which might be a good idea), the entitlement view is still not identical to it, because it identifies two specific types of just steps as being the only ones that make an outcome just. Obviously, the principle of just steps does not do that.

Further, if this objection were correct, it would be impossible to construct an argument against this principle that is not simply an argument against the entitlement view. As we shall see in a moment, G. A. Cohen constructs such an argument so, once again, the objection is ill-founded.

To be charitable, the objection might be that Nozick's argument is question-begging, not in the sense that one of its premises is identical to its conclusion, but in a broader sense: Anyone who thinks that D_1 is just already denies this premise. While this version of the objection does not say something that is clearly false, it is not clearly true either. After all, though it may be true that proponents of end-state principles should (in order to maintain a theory that is maximally coherent) deny the principle, it is not obvious that they all already know this. Indeed, given that the tension between their position and this principle was not generally known until Nozick pointed it out, this seems rather doubtful.

Let us, then, turn away from the issue of question-beggingness and back to that of truth. Is the principle of just steps true or false? First of all, it has to be admitted that it is certainly conceivable that it is false. As G. A. Cohen has pointed out, distributive justice and the justice or injustice of steps are really about different things. The former is about situations, such as the situation that is composed of the three facts I mentioned earlier: my holding $10 plus your holding $20 plus Jones holding $30. The latter is about human actions.[9] Looked at in this way, it does seem conceivable that these two sorts of justice, if that is what they are, are to some extent independent of one another. The principle of just steps gives one way in which one sort might be dependent on the other, a particularly strong type of dependence.

Cohen believes he has a counterexample to this sort of strong dependence:

> [I]magine that one of my justly held rolling pins rolls out my front door and down the hill and through your open door, without your knowledge. You innocently mistake it to be one you mislaid, and you keep it and use it. Now, so I take it, not everything is justly held, but no one has behaved, or is behaving, unjustly. And if, to vary the example instructively, you keep the rolling pin, in full knowledge of how it reached you, then you indeed behave unjustly, but whether or not what you then do counts as carrying out an unjust *step*, what you do is unjust because you are preserving a situation that counts as unjust for *other* reasons ....

Cohen admits that this is not directly a counterexample to Nozick's principle, which holds that just steps preserve justice, not that unjust ones are needed to destroy it, but he asks at this point a question that seems reasonable to me: "If unjust steps are indeed unnecessary to overturn justice, why *should* just steps suffice to preserve it?"[10]

The unjust situation at the end of Cohen's story is of course one that Nozick would agree is unjust. The judgment that it is unjust after all rests on familiar ones about property rights that he shares, and not on any principles of the sort that he is attacking. This means that the issue between Nozick and Cohen here boils down to that of whether there is an unjust step that brought this situation about. Is there?

I think there clearly is, and the likely reason Cohen does not see it is that he has conflated two things that really are different. Indeed, it is very important that they be kept distinct. On the one hand, there are issues of right and wrong. On the other, there are issues of responsibility. The former sorts of issues are settled by considerations such as duties and rights. The latter are settled in part by considerations like duties and rights, but *also* by considerations about the state of mind of the agent involved. Only after issues of the first sort are settled can issues of the last sort arise. Given that I had a duty to avoid acting as I did, can I be blamed – held responsible for – violating that duty? Issues about unjust steps are entirely of the former sort.

Once we are clear about this, it becomes obvious where the unjust step is in Cohen's story. By using Cohen's rolling pin and treating it as if it were mine without his permission, I am violating his rights, which is an unjust act. I had a duty to avoid doing this, which I am violating. Of course, I can't be blamed for this because – as we are assuming as part of the story – I am non-culpably ignorant of what I am actually doing. The situation that obtains – the rolling pin being on my land – is not unjust (i.e., does not violate anybody's rights): Nobody has a right to the rolling pin's being in any one place rather than another. It doesn't become unjust until I *do* something: that is, until I take an unjust step. Thus Cohen's example does not show that unjust situations can arise without unjust steps, only that they can arise in ways for which no one can be blamed. This is true, but does not affect Nozick's point.

Can Cohen's argument be revised or repaired in a way that makes it a threat to Nozick's point after all? I will leave this for others to decide. So far, Nozick's claim is still standing.

What should we make of those, for lack of a better word, secondary arguments – that end-state principles grant anomalous rights, that they only speak to recipient justice, and that they make pure gifts morally problematic? I think the fairest general statement one can make at the outset is that they are not equally effective against all end-state principles. Take the problem about giving. Notice that as I explained the problem,

167

I presented it as an issue about maintaining everyone's position in a structure, a position assigned to them by the end-state principle. Not all end-state principles do that. Utilitarianism, as I have already pointed out, pays no heed to the structure of the results at all, only amounts. In addition, what utilitarianism distributes is not material wealth but utility or, in other words, people's wellbeing as measured in terms of their own preferences. In terms of utility, moving wealth from one person to another can be a good thing: If a material object is transferred from the holdings of someone who values it less to those of one who values it more, utility is increased even though no material goods have been produced. Indeed, a utilitarian might well be able to approve the transactions that gave Chamberlain his $250,000. Because the transaction was voluntary, we know that all participants, unless they were making some relevant factual error, derived utility from it – the fans were glad to pay their quarters to see Chamberlain play and of course he was glad to have their money. For a utilitarian this represents, at least, a move in the right direction.

So the problem about gift-giving does not seem to apply to utilitarianism. For a different sort of reason, it does not apply to Rawls' difference principle either. Rawls' principle is about the basic institutions of society and, moreover, it is about the effects these institutions have on groups of people, not on individuals – those are the effects that make such institutions just or unjust.[11] This principle has no very direct implications about whether one man should have $250,000 that he didn't have before, and consequently Chamberlain's fans are not in any direct way running afoul of it by giving him their quarters. What Rawls calls justice is not about what individual human beings may or may not do to, or with, other individual human beings. The difference principle has a very different character from all the other principles that Nozick is criticizing in Chapter 7 and so it is a good thing, for the success of his critique, that he goes on to devote Section II of the chapter exclusively to discussing Rawls' theory.[12]

However, though the giving problem and related arguments do not apply to the difference principle or utilitarianism, they are much, much more successful if applied to what Nozick calls "patterned" (in the narrow sense) principles – the "to each according to his ..." theories, like that of Aristotle. As I tried to make plain as I was explaining these arguments, patterned principles have precisely the features that invite the sort of trouble that Nozick is trying to bring to them. In particular, they seem to face the knowledge problem and the coordination problem. These principles, as they are usually interpreted, have very specific implications as to who should have what. If the principle is, to take Marx and Engels' formulation,

"… to each according to his needs," then I am not supposed to possess more than anyone whose needs – however those are to be determined or measured – are greater than mine. If we suppose that this is indeed a requirement of justice, then the principle would indeed seem to require the sort of continuous coercive interference that Nozick warns us of.

Yet there remains one problem for Nozick's attack on end-state principles of justice in holdings. It may or may not be a very big problem. I am really not sure. It is this. The patterned principles that Nozick discusses and that Aristotle found so obvious bear little resemblance to anything that anyone, anyone who is not a philosopher constructing theories, actually seems to believe. As I just pointed out, if we interpret Marx and Engels' famous formula strictly, as a patterned principle of justice in holdings, it entails that it is an injustice if I have more than someone whose needs are greater than mine. Who actually believes such a thing? Has any important political party ever put such an idea into their platform? I seriously doubt it. I even doubt that Marx and Engels meant their rallying cry in that way.

I am not denying that many people find end-state principles, as standards for judging the justice of an entire community or an economic system, profoundly intuitive, nor am I denying that they are potent political forces in the world. The sort of end-state judgments that we do see, in public opinion polls, on placards, in editorials and elsewhere, are simply judgments to the effect that income inequality "is a problem" in America, or that income should not be distributed "too unequally." Such thinking lacks the clarity and specificity that gets real patterned principles into Nozickean trouble. In fact, if my favorite version of P is simply that "things shouldn't get too unequal," then perhaps my idea only requires coercive interference once a year – say, on April 15 – when the government takes money from people who I think have "too much" and gives it to people who I think have "too little."

This may mean that the agreement problem might not pose such a serious threat to patterned, or perhaps I should say patterned-like, principles. It is true enough that, by the time we work through Nozick's taxonomy of principles of distributive justice, the prospect of agreeing on one of them seems really daunting. (Indeed this may be part of his point in that discussion.) There are so many of them and they are so different! One principle pays attention only to quantities while another looks only at structures. Some things, like desert, which are all-important on some views (e.g., that of Aristotle) are completely irrelevant on others (as desert is on Rawls' view). But it may be that most of these principles have few adherents outside the world of people who concoct theories about these things, and there might be a very simple one, such as the "not too unequal" principle, that has relatively many adherents.[13]

To his credit, Nozick does briefly consider a class of principles that might include this one. Speaking of the voluntary transactions in the Chamberlain story that upset the pattern D_1, he says

> [P]erhaps some very weak patterns are not so thwarted. ... [G]iven the possibility that some weak conditions or patterns may not be unstable in this way, it would be better to formulate an explicit description of the kind of interesting and contentful patterns under discussion, and to prove a theorem about their instability. Since the weaker the patterning, the more likely it is that the entitlement system itself satisfies it, a plausible conjecture is that any patterning either is unstable or is satisfied by the entitlement system. (164)

The principles I have been speaking of just now are vague rather than "weak" – which I assume means easily satisfied – but just because they are vague, they can be given weak interpretations. We see here that Nozick may be prepared to say that, insofar as they are interpreted in a weak sort of way, they are likely to be satisfied by the entitlement system already. But we can also see that there might be other ways to interpret them which make them more plausible than they seem to be in the discussion of the Chamberlain example. (I will return to this issue in Section 7, below.)

This might be a good place to discuss a possible problem with the way Nozick formulates his account of the entitlement view. First, notice that, in it (see 151) principle 3 says that no one is entitled to their holdings, except through repeated applications of 1 and 2, the principles of justice in acquisition and transfer. Second, there is no stated limit to how many such applications are needed. This would seem to mean that, for any given holding of any given object to be just – for me to have legitimate property rights in the computer I am using to write this, for instance – it must be justifiable in terms of chains of just transfers that go all the way back to the original acquisition of the previously unowned natural resources of which it was made. It sounds like the chain of justifications must go back to original acquisition – the first ownership of things previously unowned. Finally, notice that Nozick adds, to the first three principles, a fourth (it is not clear whether it is a part of the entitlement view itself or merely a needed supplement), which is "the principle of rectification" (152–153). It holds, roughly, that if the first two principles were violated in the history of a holding, then the situation – apparently meaning the holdings – that would now hold had the violation never occurred must be realized.

This seems to create a serious problem, if we suppose that principles 1 and 2 are to be applied all the way back to the beginning. There are a great, great many holdings in the world today that will not pass entitlement muster, if the standard is this high. The land on which my house sits was at one time held by the Ojibway tribe. I do not know the means by which it was transferred to someone else, but it seems likely that they would not stand up, in entitlement terms, under a close examination. Where does title to my land justly belong? It would seem that, if we apply principles 1 and 2 in this open-ended way, we get a chaos of claims with people's current holdings seized and reassigned on a massive scale. The result is actually similar to the chaos and dislocation that Nozick sees as arising from a serious attempt at applying end-result principles. Do we need to go all the way back?[14]

It seems to me that an obvious *partial* answer to this question is that we need a moral statute of limitations, so to speak: Injustices before a certain point in the past do not count as such for the purposes of determining current rights to holdings. Saying this, however, is not a solution to the problem (even apart from the looming question of how far back that point in the past is). If we simply add the statute of limitations to the entitlement view in an *ad hoc* sort of way – carving out an exception to it in order to avoid some undesirable implications – we raise a major problem for entitlement itself. After all, the exception we would be carving out would be an enormous one. The first three principles are very clear about the transactions to which they are to be applied and it seems we would be suspending application in the overwhelming majority of them. If a principle cannot be applied consistently without horrendously unacceptable results, doesn't this mean there is something wrong with the principle itself? Does it mean that all principles of distributive justice have the sorts of implications Nozick finds in the case of end-result principles? Perhaps we should give up on the prospect of applying any principle of distributive justice consistently. Why not?

We can avoid all these questions if we can make a case that, far from being an *ad hoc* addition to the entitlement view, the moral statute of limitations is actually an implication of entitlement considerations themselves. How might such a case be made?

On the way to answering this question, we should first notice that any attempt to settle a question of justice in holdings that uses entitlement principles (actually any principles at all) must solve two sorts of problems, one substantive and one epistemic. The substantive problem is to

171

award rights to the parties that really (according to those principles) do have those rights. The epistemic problem is to show that one had good enough evidence for one's solution to the substantive problem. In addition, the sorts of considerations that support a case for rectification can be canceled or counterbalanced by other considerations. This is an important feature of such considerations, because it means that the reasoning that solves the substantive problem must weigh such considerations against each other. If someone lost a holding due to an entitlement-violating process, such as theft, was it rightfully theirs in the first place? If it is true that the land upon which my house sits was taken by force from the Ojibway, it is also true that they apparently acquired a significant part of their holdings in land by similar methods from the Sioux (who then moved to the west and became buffalo hunters).[15] It is not easy to think of a plot of land that has not been stolen and restolen countless times.

Part of the reason for this is that land is an extremely durable good and can have a very long history, so to an extent real estate represents a special case, but past history, if we go far enough back, can easily make it difficult to solve the substantive problem in other contexts as well. The case for reparations for chattel slavery in the old South is compelling, but what about families who have an ancestor who died in the war that freed the slaves? The lives of these family members might have gone very differently if their ancestor had not died at the age of 20. If they would have been better off, should their loss be subtracted from the amount due? Should the billions of dollars that have already been given to poor descendants of slaves over many years, in order to alleviate their poverty? The further into the past, the more likely it is that we will run into substantive entitlement considerations that can undermine a claim to current reparations in one way or another, with the result that the case for reassigning may well disappear.

More importantly, and perhaps more obviously, the further we go into the past to verify one's title to their holdings, the more difficult the epistemic problem becomes. Can we discover the means by which the precise plot of land on which I am now sitting was acquired from the Ojibway? I doubt it. Not all of the land acquired from the natives was taken by force: Some was purchased. More generally, it is certain that if we go far enough back into the past it eventually becomes impossible to know how things changed hands, surely not with the degree of certainty needed to justify a coercive reassignment of title to the thing.

I hope it is obvious that I do not mean to dismiss the legitimacy of claims for reparations by Native Americans – or of African Americans for the injustices of slavery, or of Japanese Americans whose families were "interned" by the American nation-state during World War II. (Personally, it seems very likely to me that the most recent of these three sets of claims cannot be defeated by the sorts of considerations I have raised here.) My point is merely that considerations internal to the entitlement view require some sort of limit as to how far into the past the entitlement search has to go. The moral statute of limitations is not simply an *ad hoc* attempt to dodge unattractive implications.

6. The Problem

It seems to me that Nozick's discussion of justice in holdings in Chapter 7 raises a deep and difficult issue about the nature of justice in holdings. I think it is a problem that is faced, not merely by the theorists he is attacking, but by anyone who wants to have a coherent, consistent, and plausible view of the matter. In this section, I would like to explain what the problem is and suggest a possible solution to it. First, the problem:

One thing that is made very plausible by his comments on the Wilt Chamberlain example is that the entitlement view has a very strong tendency to conflict with end-state principles. The reason is suggested by the examples of entitlement processes that I ran through above. All are activities that individuals carry out in light of their own judgment and in pursuit of their own ends, which often have little or nothing to do with factors mentioned in any particular end-result principle. If a farmer and a fisher on a tropical island are carrying out the entitlement process of trading fish for yams, they are not trying to give one another what they deserve, and they are not moving goods around because some people have unfairly large shares and things should be more equal. The farmer wants fish and the fisherman wants yams – that is all. If the results of this process satisfy some end-state principle, that is a coincidence.[16] It is true that, as Nozick points out (157), there will be "strands" of patterning in an entitlement system – people do try, by means of entitlement processes like gift-giving, to give others things they think they deserve. The point that he would insist on, and seems very true to me, is that entitlement will run afoul of end-state principles sooner or later – and probably sooner than later. But this seems to mean that the two sorts of principles will have contradictory implications, pronouncing the same things to be just and unjust at the same time. This is a problem because both sorts of principle are intuitively very plausible to most of us. We use both sorts of standards all the time. Doesn't this commit us to making contradictory judgments about justice in holdings? How is it possible for us to be consistent?

173

There are a number of ways to try to remove the inconsistency. The simplest of them seems clearly wrong. This is what might be called "nihilism": simply to deny that one of the two sorts of principle has any truth or value. One might easily get the impression – from the fact that he never says anything good about them – that this is Nozick's view of end-result principles in general. I don't think this would be a plausible position, and I doubt it represents what he actually thought. There are times – when assigning grades to students' work, for instance – when patterned principles like recognizing desert do seem to be the ones to follow. Anyone who has made the mistake of serving obviously different-size helpings of dessert to children seated at the same table will learn that there are times when humans treat equality – yes, equality of outcomes – as a norm, and that they begin to do so at a very early age. The most charitable interpretation of ASU Chapter 7 on this point, I think, would interpret it as arguing against applying end-state principles in a certain way: namely, as standards for judging the justice of the distribution (in the broad sense) of holdings across an entire society. Taking such a position would actually help somewhat with the consistency problem I am dealing with here, but it is not yet a solution. It gives one of the two sorts of principles exclusive sway in one domain (a sort of domain-specific nihilism), thus eliminating conflict in that one area, but gives no general account of how the principles themselves can be mutually consistent.

If a generalized nihilism about end-result principles is implausible, simply rejecting the entitlement view seems even more crazy. Entitlement is in fact the system we actually use, every day, to determine whether our holdings are held rightfully. I believe that the computer I am using to write this sentence is rightfully mine, and the reason I think that is that I came to hold it via one of the entitlement processes mentioned by Nozick: that is, by purchase from its previous rightful holder (which happened to be a business corporation). It seems that we always determine rightful holdings by looking at some such historical process. Admittedly, I did not check to ensure the entire history, back to some appropriate starting point, to be sure that possession of this computer came about by repeated applications of principles 1 and 2, but in situations where the cost of error in this matter would be high – for instance, when we buy a house – we do precisely that. When I bought the house in which I am now sitting, a title search had to be done that went all the way back to the year it was built (1905). When we buy a car, we ask that the title papers be signed over, which is a rough way of doing basically the same thing.

Clearly, both sorts of principle are deeply ingrained in the human psyche. The arguments that revolve around the Wilt Chamberlain discussion give us some interesting theoretical reasons for preferring entitlement principles if we have to choose between them. But do we? And is there a way to integrate the two so that they will not repeatedly trap us in contradictions?

I would like to suggest that we can do just that. I will do so by the roundabout method of setting up an example that at first sight might seem to make the problem worse than it was initially. I will then suggest a solution.

7.   A Possible Solution

In the course of his discussion of the relationship (or lack of one) between unjust steps and unjust situations G. A. Cohen presents an interesting example:

> I sell a diamond to you for a pittance (or I give it to you on a whim) a diamond that we both think is glass. By that (*ex* Nozick's *hypothesi*) just step, a situation arises in which you hold a diamond. But few would think justice is fully served if, its true character having come to light, you now hang on to it ....[17]

Now as a matter of fact, cases like this have come up in the law, and have had to be decided by judges. I think it would be helpful to recount briefly the facts of one case, in order to focus the issue of the relationship between the concept of justice and other, related concepts. An example that is more fully described than the extremely brief one just posed by Cohen will help to make the issues involved a good deal clearer than they are so far.

The case I have in mind is a classic in contract law, *Wood v. Boynton*.[18] One day in 1883, Clarissa Wood went to see Milwaukee jeweler Samuel Boynton about repairing a pin of hers. In the same box with the pin was an attractive yellow crystal that her husband had found while digging a well in the village of Eagle. She asked him if he knew what it was, saying she had been told it was a topaz. He said it might be, adding "I would buy this; would you sell it?" He offered her $1 for it and she turned the offer down. Later, when, as she said in court, "I needed money pretty badly, and thought every dollar would help," she took the stone back to Boynton and reminded him of his offer of $1. He bought it at that price. Later, when he had it professionally examined, it turned out to be a diamond worth at least $700. When she heard of this, Mrs. Wood demanded the

175

return of the stone, offering Boynton $1, plus 10¢ interest. He refused. She sued for return of the stone and lost. She appealed and lost again.

The reason she lost the case might be glossed as follows. The question is whether there is something about the sale that would enable Mrs. Wood to rescind it. There are reasons why a sale can be rescinded, but unfortunately for her none of them are present here. There was no breach of warranty, because there was no warranty (no one guaranteed that the stone was of a certain nature). There was no fraud (no one had deliberately misrepresented the nature of the stone). There was no "mistake in fact as to the identity of the thing sold" (e.g., Mrs. Wood did not deliver the wrong stone to Boynton). The legal fact of the matter, very sadly for Mrs. Wood, is that, as the judge put it, "she cannot repudiate the sale because it is afterwards ascertained that she made a bad bargain."

Cohen would say that justice was not "fully served" here. I would say on the contrary that justice is precisely the sort of thing that judges are supposed to mete out and that the judge in this case produced the only result he could have produced: The rights to the diamond belong to the defendant.

I have to admit, though, that it is difficult to say this without squirming. Both Wood and Boynton took a risk and he won big – very big.[19] Is that fair? It is certainly hard to say that it is. If I were in Boynton's place, I would have given some portion of the profits from the sale of the diamond to Mrs. Wood, especially because she only gave it up for one pathetic dollar because she "needed money pretty badly." How much I would have given her, I am not at all sure. I certainly wouldn't have given her all of it, which is what she wanted, but to give the poor woman something seems only fair.

That actually is my point, or a large part of it. The sorts of considerations that might lead someone in Boynton's position to share the proceeds with Wood are considerations of fairness. These considerations – for instance, Mrs. Wood's need and the extreme inequality of the outcome of her transaction with Boynton – are the sorts of things upon which end-result principles are based. I would like to suggest that we can consistently integrate such principles with entitlement in the following ways.

First, fairness is to be treated as an ethical category distinct from that of justice. Principles of justice determine what rights people have, while principles of fairness determine what rights people ought to have. Further, entitlement principles are principles of justice, while end-state principles are principles of fairness. In the case of *Wood v. Boynton*, the judge has to decide to whom the diamond legitimately belongs. This is a question of rights – to be more precise, it is a question of property rights. The judge decides this question – quite properly, on the view I am suggesting – on the basis of entitlement considerations. He in effect asks whether the trade transacted by Wood and Boynton, an entitlement process, successfully did what entitlement processes are intended to do: assign rights. He finds that it did. This of course leaves wide open the potentially thorny question of what Boynton ought to have done. That you have a right to do or have something does not by any means imply that you ought to do or keep it. If you have a right to do something, it does not follow that doing it would be fair. In the present case, the question of fairness is not the question whether Mrs. Wood has some of the money coming to her as her right (she doesn't): It is the question of whether Boynton should give her a right – a property right – to (some of) it.

My proposed way of integrating these two types of principles solves the coherence in a perfectly general way. These two sorts of principles only seem to be contradictory if we assume they are about the same thing – namely, justice. But there is no contradiction in saying, both, that Mrs. Wood has no rights in the proceeds and that it is unfair she does not. One statement is about what rights she has, and the other is about what rights she should have. Two statements cannot contradict each other if they are about different things.

My proposal also removes any cause for surprise that, as Nozick brilliantly shows, the logical character of the two sorts of principles are so profoundly different – that one treats producing something as giving one rights over it, while the other completely ignores producer's rights – or that one allows givers to confer just title to things while the other ignores givers entirely and focuses instead on recipient "justice." If two sets of principles are about completely different things, it comes as no surprise that they treat completely different sorts of considerations as relevant.

In a limited sort of way, the proposal might also enable end-state principles to sidestep one of the objections Nozick raises against such principles. This is one that I have not discussed yet: what might be called the emigration problem. He tells us that for some end-result principles (I would say he probably means nearly all) the question of whether to allow emigration is "a tricky matter." Suppose that a given country (I will call it country A) institutionalizes some end-state principle, such as helping the neediest, or maximizing the position of the worst-off group: "Everyone above a certain level is forced to contribute to aid the needy." Suppose there is another country (country B) that does not have this policy but other than that is "(as much as possible) identical." The only motive one could have for emigrating to country B would be to avoid participating in this arrangement. "What rationale yields to result that the person be permitted to emigrate, yet forbidden to stay and opt out of the compulsory scheme of social provision?" What can justify forbidding "internal opting-out" while permitting emigration in this case, which amounts to a sort of external opting-out (173)?

I confess that, as I have thought about this argument over the years it sometimes has seemed to me a very difficult problem indeed, while at other times it has seemed like a sophistical trick, albeit a trick that I had not managed to figure out yet. At length I have come to the conclusion that it makes a big and very relevant difference whether one takes the principle that has been institutionalized in country A completely seriously as a principle of justice, or whether one takes it simply as a notion about how things ought to be. If it really is a principle of justice, this would seem to mean that the needy have a right to a portion of the would-be emigrant's holdings. That would mean that moving from A to B is an unjust act: It violates rights.

It seems to me that whenever we seriously believe that leaving a given country is an unjust act, we do not mind preventing the act by means of coercion. Suppose that I have committed murder in country C, and that I am trying to board a plane for country D for the sole reason that D does not have an extradition agreement with C and that if I manage to get there I will not get my just deserts. Obviously, the government of C would do whatever it can to stop me from doing that, and no one would object. Why not? One way to put the reason would be to say that moving from C to D would be an unjust act on my part: the act of avoiding deserved punishment. In what way is this case different from that of countries A and B, such that coercion is justified here but not there? If the principle that is institutionalized in A is a legitimate principle of justice, then by moving to B the emigrant is denying to the needy that which is rightfully theirs. In fact, if we are really consistent about this, it would seem that the case for coercively preventing emigration is actually stronger in the case of moving to B than it is in the case of moving to D. Although it is true that *ex hypothesi* both moves are unjust, it is only in the case of moving to B that (again, by hypothesis) any rights are clearly being violated. It is not clear that my not being punished violates anyone's rights: that is, it is not clear that anyone has a right that I be punished (on this point, see ASU 137). However, the principle in A, as we are now interpreting it, does imply that emigrating to B would violate the rights of the needy.

However, (Nozick assumes) nobody wants to say this principle justifies coercively preventing the would-be emigrant from leaving. This problem disappears if we stop interpreting this principle as a principle of justice and opt instead for the alternative that is made available by my proposal: the idea that it is only (in my sense) a principle of fairness. That is, it is only about what rights people ought to have. The reason why this is true also makes it clear why, as a matter of fact, proponents of end-state principles would by and large not welcome this way of sidestepping Nozick's objection. The reason is that the judgment that a person ought to do a certain thing does not imply that anyone would be justified in coercing them to do that thing. If I tell you that I think you ought to start saving for your retirement, that does not in any way imply that anyone would be justified in forcing you to do so. The same thing is true if the "ought" involved is a moral one. It can be true that I ought, morally, to apologize for something I did and yet false that anyone may force me to do it.

Of course, this way of resolving the emigration problem concedes Nozick's main point in Chapter 7. It implies that the principle in A, and other principles like it, does not justify coercion and, consequently, does not justify a more-than-minimal state.

My proposed distinction between justice and fairness might have similar implications for another principle that I discussed earlier: the widely shared principle of distributive (so to speak) "justice" that claims, merely, that holdings should not be "too unequal." As I pointed out before, this notion is vague. Indeed, it is extremely vague. This of course is one reason it is widely shared. The more vague an idea is, the more things it can mean and, consequently, the more people can accept it.

This same vagueness, though, can be used against principles like this one. If sheer vagueness is the reason large numbers of people agree with it, are they really agreeing about the same idea? If not, the principle is not really solving the agreement problem I discussed above in Section 4. Vagueness can also be a reason for treating such principles as principles of fairness, as opposed to principles of justice. Admittedly, there are notions that might be regarded as principles of justice that are not models of clarity – the punishment should fit the crime, you should get what you pay for, treat like cases alike – but the notion that holdings should not be too unequal is orders of magnitude more vague than these. More importantly, principles that are principles of justice (in my sense) justify using coercion, typically (though perhaps not always) by assigning rights. Obviously, the notion that holdings should not be too unequal does not come close to being clear enough to justify coercing specific people and taking specific amounts of wealth from them. And yet it is only possible to coerce specific people and it is only possible to take specific amounts. In the real world, there is no such thing as a generalized person who is "too rich" and a vague amount of wealth that is "too much." A principle can only justify coercion in the world we actually live in, and that means it can only do so if it achieves a certain minimum of clarity. This is something that can be achieved – by individuals as they interpret the principle for themselves. But this happens at the expense of solving the agreement problem. In other words, a vague principle of the "not too unequal" sort either solves the agreement problem, or justifies coercion, but not both. It only justifies coercion if it is too clear to command widespread agreement.

On the other hand, this is no problem at all if we interpret the principle as one of fairness and not of justice. There is no obvious reason why our notions of what is fair should not be vague. In fact, they generally are – often extremely so. Further, since they do not directly justify coercion, there is no problem if everyone has their own interpretation of these vague notions. It will not result (not necessarily, that is) in someone forcing their own view of fairness on masses of people who do not share it. If the principle is merely a principle of fairness, it need only serve as a basis on which individuals govern their own actions and donate their own resources in pursuit of their own vision of how things ought to be.

Finally, my proposed distinction between justice and fairness might have important implications for an issue suggested by Nozick's opening comments in Chapter 7 (149). The idea of distributive justice, he says, suggests that there is an agent behind the distribution, that there is a distributor. His worry of course is that this suggestion gives the idea of distributive justice, as applied to an entire society, an unfair advantage, since if there were a distributor we would need to worry about whether they had distributed in a way that deserves moral criticism. If there is a distributor, there must be moral concern about the distribution. Is the reverse of this also true? Does moral concern require a distributor? That is, does moral criticism of the distribution *only* make sense when there is a responsible agent behind it?

The answer to the latter question is arguably different, depending on whether the criticism is based on the idea of justice or that of fairness. Is it unfair that some people are physically very beautiful while others, through no fault of their own, are actually rather unpleasant-looking? I have found that different people have different intuitions about this. It is possible to see a distribution (wide sense) as unfair without a distributing agent who is responsible for it (though I have also found that I get more "yes" answers if I frame the question as one about whether "nature" can be unfair). It seems to me considerably more difficult to find *injustice* in a distribution that has no distributor. Injustice, in my sense, is a moral offense that is morally far worse than mere unfairness. It typically is a violation of someone's rights. It justifies someone in threatening the perpetrator with a weapon, and coercing them. The "injustice" we are contemplating here would be a serious moral wrong that does not necessarily have any wrongdoer who stands behind the wrong and can be held responsible for it. Does it make sense to speak of a serious moral wrong for which no one can be held responsible? It is easier to simply say that the distribution, notwithstanding having no perpetrator, is unfair. But, as I have said, in that case one gives up or weakens considerably the case for coercion and going beyond the minimal state.

8. The Proviso

So far, Nozick's explanation of how one acquires just title to things is completely open-ended: One justly holds (so far) whatever one acquires in accordance with the principles of justice in acquisition and justice in transfer. As Locke pointed out long ago, this would seem to imply that "any one may ingross [i.e., acquire] as much as he will."[20] Nozick's response to this apparent implication is roughly the same as Locke's: He adds a "proviso" to the entitlement account of justice in holdings.[21] That is, he places a limit on one's right to acquire resources: One's acquisition may not make others worse off. As Locke puts it, one must leave "enough, and as good, ... in common for others."[22]

Worse off in what way? He offers two possible versions of this proviso, a more stringent one and a weaker one. The stronger version would forbid acts of appropriating a resource that would prevent others from either appropriating some of it for themselves or making use of it. The weaker version only forbids preventing others from using it. Perhaps the most lucid way to understand Nozick's discussion of this issue is in terms of an example he attributes to Hastings Rashdall in a footnote (179 fn.): A traveler, several miles ahead of others who will come along (apparently members of the same party) appropriates the only water in the desert.[23] The stronger version would prohibit this, while the weaker would permit it, provided that the first traveler shares the water with the others (or sells it to them, though not charging whatever he pleases for it – see 179 and 180).

Nozick gives two reasons for preferring the weaker version of his proviso. One of them seems very sensible to me, while the other, though more interesting, is less plausible. The more sensible reason is that it "is arguable that no one legitimately can complain if the weaker provision is satisfied" (176). I would add that the step that the stronger version takes beyond the weaker one seems arbitrary. The point of the proviso, after all, is to prohibit acquisitions that make people worse off. The desert traveler is made worse off by not being able to drink the water. Why should we add that, in addition to not preventing others from drinking the water, the first traveler should also not prevent them from owning a share of the oasis?

The other reason he gives is more complex. His initial account of it is presented in terms of the strong proviso:

> Consider the first person Z for whom there is not enough and as good left to appropriate. The last person Y to appropriate left Z without his previous liberty to act on an object, and so worsened Z's situation. So Y's appropriation is not allowed under Locke's proviso. Therefore the next to last person X to appropriate left Y in a worse position, for X's act ended permissible appropriation. Therefore X's appropriation wasn't permissible. But then the appropriator two from the last, W, ended permissible appropriation and so, since it worsened X's position, W's appropriation wasn't permissible. And so on back to the first person A to appropriate a permanent property right.

This is a reason for preferring the weaker requirement, he says, because with it "we cannot zip back so quickly from Z to A, as in the above argument, for though person Z can no longer *appropriate*, there may be some for him to *use* as before" (176).

The first thing to be said about this is that this talk of not zipping back "so quickly" is rather sloppy writing on Nozick's part. The effect that Z has on A here, if there is one, is a logical effect, not an event in time: It supposedly *implies* that A had no right to appropriate. This is not something that happens either quickly or slowly. Actually, as far as this argument is concerned, the superiority of the weaker version consists in the fact that it "zips back" less often, simply because it is easier to satisfy. With respect to the zipping back problem, its being easier to satisfy is the *only* difference between them. However, it is still true that, if it is ever violated with respect to a given resource, then the zipping back argument would seem to mean that nobody ever did rightfully appropriate that resource – ever, back to the beginning. This seems a terrible implication for a principle to have, even if it has it less often than any alternative principle. It also seems terribly counterintuitive to say that the proviso, whether in the weaker or stronger version, ever does have this implication. It seems to me that the best response to the zipping back problem is, not to opt for the weaker proviso, but to try to get rid of the problem itself. Is there a way to do that?

I would like to suggest that there is. Notice the striking similarity between the zipping back argument and the reasoning of the student in the celebrated Paradox of the Unexpected Examination.[24] In case you are not familiar with it, it generally goes like this. A teacher makes the following announcement to his class: "I will be giving a surprise examination in this class. It will be on one of the five days – Monday through Friday – that we meet next week, but when I give it, it will be unexpected. What I mean by that is that at the beginning of the school day on which I will give the examination, you will not yet know that it will be given on that day." One of the students raises her hand. When called on, she says: "I'm afraid you won't be able to do what you've just said you will do. After all, the exam can't be on Friday, because at the beginning of that day we will know that it will be given on that day. So if it is unexpected it can't be on Friday. But for the same reason, it can't be on Thursday either. At the beginning of that day, if the exam hasn't been given yet, we will know it has to be given today, because it can't be given on Friday. But then it won't be unexpected. But then it can't be given on Wednesday either, nor on Tuesday or Monday. You can't give an unexpected examination next week."

This is regarded as a paradox because it seems counterintuitive that with five possible days there is no day on which an unexpected examination can be given. I say the zipping back argument should be treated as a paradox for an analogous reason. Even assuming the stronger version of the proviso, it seems counterintuitive that, given that a certain resource exists in abundance and it would take us centuries to collect all of it, there is no bit of it that anyone can legitimately appropriate and make her or his own, simply because some day in the distant future someone will appropriate the last bit of it.

I also claim that we can escape the counterintuitive conclusion by a rather simple means. Without suggesting that I have the solution to the unexpected examination paradox up my sleeve (to this day there is no generally agreed-upon solution!) I can point out one feature of the student's reasoning that is needed in order to reach her startling conclusion. This is the fact that the concept of "a day on which we know the quiz would be today (if it is given)," which is set up by the teacher's definition of "unexpected," can in principle be applied to indefinitely many different days. This is needed for the student to reason in the recursive way she does, applying the concept to each item in the series, from the end all the way to the beginning. By contrast, the thing that Y is not supposed to do – appropriate the last share of the resource – is a unique event. The concept, "appropriating the last share of the resource," cannot be truthfully applied to more than one event. However, Nozick quietly replaces this concept with one that *can* be applied to more than one event by treating two different events – (a) making it impossible for someone to appropriate by taking the last share and (b) making it impermissible for them to appropriate – as the same. This is necessary if he is to reason in the recursive way he does, eliminating every legitimate act of appropriation in the series. We can avoid this implication by the simple means of making the proviso mean what we originally thought it meant, so that (putting it in terms of the strong version) it is about making it impossible for others to appropriate by appropriating the last available share.

Having said this, I must admit that Nozick's argument raises the interesting issue of the ethical status of acts of appropriation that make it impermissible for others to appropriate. Is it always wrong? If not, when is it wrong? I have no suggestion to offer as to the best answers to these questions, except that they can be handled by means of principles distinct from the proviso. Setting aside the question of how these issues are handled, we do not at present have reason to think they will have the counterintuitive implications that Nozick attributes to the proviso in the "zipping back" argument.

I should also admit that, for simplicity, I have focused on the stronger version of the proviso. It seems likely though that an argument like the one I have just given can also be applied, perhaps in a more complicated form, to the weaker proviso. Even without doing that, though, we can see that the zipping back argument is not (or at least not without settling the separate issue of making appropriation impermissible) a reason for rejecting the stronger version of the proviso.

9. Where is the Baseline?

In addition to discussing the way in which our acquisition may not make others worse off (whether by preventing acquisition of the resource or merely by preventing use), Nozick also discusses the matter of magnitude: The proviso prohibits us from making others *how much* worse off? Where is "the baseline" below which our acquisitions may not push them? At first, the answer to this question might seem obvious. Consider this statement, which is probably his clearest single statement of his favored (i.e., weaker) version of the proviso: "A process normally giving rise to a permanent bequeathable property right in a previously unowned thing will not do so if the position of others no longer at liberty to use the thing is thereby worsened" (178). This might suggest to a casual reader that the baseline is wherever a person was an instant before the acquisition: One's acquisitions cannot make others, with respect to use of the resource, worse off thereby acquired – period.

It turns out though that he regards the degree to which one may not be "thereby worsened" to be an open question and even adds that "fixing the baseline needs more detailed investigation" than he is able to give it here. However, his brief comments (at 180–182) on a wide array of examples do convey a rather clear impression that he actually is fixing the line in one specific location. He gives a set of examples of situations where he thinks that the weaker version of the proviso "takes effect" – that is, requires one to either share the resource or to sell it (and not at just any price). It takes effect, as we have seen, (1) if you come upon the only water hole in the desert, several miles ahead of other pioneers, and appropriate it all. It also applies to you if (2) everyone has their own water hole but everyone else's dries up due to natural causes while yours happens to be unaffected, (3) you own the only island in an area and a castaway lands on it, (4) you purchase all of a resource, and (5) the patent on your invention excludes a simultaneous inventor (though it is not clear whether this is meant as a case to which the proviso itself applies or an analogous case illustrating the reasoning that lies behind it).

On the other hand, he tells us that the proviso does *not* take effect if (a) everyone else's water hole dries up due to natural causes but yours does not because you took some special precautions to prevent this, (b) you synthesize, from readily available materials, a new substance that cures a previously incurable disease, and (c) you did not invent this substance but you purchased the entire supply from the person who did. It may not be obvious at first sight what distinguishes (1) through (5) from (a) through (c), but I think we find a clue in a comment he makes about a case concerning which he is less certain than these others: that is the case of a person who discovers a previously unknown natural substance in a remote location and discovers that it cures a previously incurable disease and appropriates the entire supply. His comment on this is that it might be right to make this individual's property right end after a while (perhaps limiting his or her right to bequeath it to others) because as time passes it becomes more likely that others would have discovered the substance. This is relevant, I would think, because it is only after the moment when there *would* have been another discoverer that the original discoverer's appropriation can prevent people from using it. This suggests that Nozick's baseline is something very much like this: being made worse off than one would have been, with respect to using the resource, but for the appropriator's appropriating it and subsequent behavior. This, for example, would distinguish case (2), the water hole that is naturally immune to the drought, from case (a), the artificially immune one. In the latter case, your water hole would also have been dry, and useless to the

185

others, if it weren't for your behavior subsequent to appropriation; thus your appropriation and subsequent behavior do not make others any worse off than if you had not appropriated the water hole in the first place. In the former case, your non-dry water hole would have been available to others if you had not appropriated it; thus your appropriation makes them worse off than they would have been, with respect to using this resource (unless you do something about it).

Having said that, I should mention that Nozick makes some other comments about the proviso that seem to have given rise to a very different interpretation of his position among some of his critics and commentators. Michael Otsuka and others have read him as fixing the baseline in a position that is extremely low. Otsuka formulates his conception of the Nozickean baseline like this: "You may acquire previously unowned land (and its fruits) if and only if you make nobody else worse off than she would have been if she had instead been free to gather and consume food and water from this land and make use of it but not to privatize the land itself."[25] Jonathan Wolff maintains that it says merely that you may not make others worse off "than they would have been had there been no appropriation at all."[26] This seems to mean that the baseline is the level of wellbeing we would enjoy in some sort of hunter-gatherer state of nature before the invention of private property. On Wolff's interpretation, the proviso apparently only prohibits making people worse off than they would be if they still lived in the Paleolithic Era. That would be a pretty lax standard.

What might have given rise to this interpretation? Neither author tries to quote Nozick actually saying what they are making him say, but there is at least one passage in ASU that might suggest this way of understanding him. Because this seems to me a serious misunderstanding, it may be worthwhile to quote the passage at length. Speaking of examples like the water hole case, he says:

> Considerations internal to the theory of property itself, to its theory of acquisition and appropriation, provide the means for handling such cases. The results, however, may be coextensive with some condition about catastrophe, since the baseline for comparison is so low as compared to the productiveness of a society with private appropriation that the question of the Lockean proviso being violated arises only in the case of catastrophe (or a desert-island situation). (180–181)

In this rather awkwardly written passage, I read the part that begins "since the baseline" in terms of the phrase "may be coextensive with some condition about catastrophe." In other words, it means that the proviso *may* be equivalent to a condition of catastrophe in that the baseline *might* be so much lower than the productiveness of a society with private appropriation that it only applies in catastrophic situations (etc.). (I will say more about catastrophe principles in the next section.)

This passage seems to be related to a long paragraph a few pages earlier that begins with this question (177): "Is the situation of persons who are unable to appropriate (there being no more accessible and useful unowned objects) worsened by a system allowing appropriation and permanent property?" Here he is asking whether the system of private property might itself violate the proviso. He then wonders, briefly, what the "appropriate baseline for comparison" might be for the purpose of answering this question and considers the possibility that the percentage of current income that is based on untransformed resources might be crucial here. This is clearly a different baseline from the one involved in the idea that individuals may not make "the situations of others worse than their baseline situation" (180). There seem to be (a point that he unfortunately never makes clear) two baselines, a macro one and a micro one. In the above-quoted passage (from 180–181), he seems to be entertaining the possibility that the micro one might be identical to what he has earlier suggested might be the macro one. There are a number of ambiguities and vague points in his discussion of these matters (which an editor should have asked him to clear up) but I think it is fairly clear that at this point in the text he is only viewing this possibility as just that – a possibility. Further, in his comments on the array of examples I have been discussing here, he clearly leans toward taking a different approach, thus ruling this possibility out.

10.   Why this Proviso?

What is the proviso based on? As we have seen, Nozick presents it as a prohibition against worsening the situations of others. This might make the idea intuitively appealing at first – until we remember that not every way of worsening the situations of others, including completely innocent others, is wrong or a violation of rights. If you take some of my market share by offering the consumers the same product at a lower price, that worsens my situation in a perfectly straightforward sense, and yet it is not wrong. As Nozick would agree, I have no right to my customers' being stuck with my high prices. To offer them a better deal than I do is not a boundary crossing. But then, appropriating the last share of a resource and failing to share it with others does not seem to be one, either.

The proviso gives people a very specific sort of right: It is a certain right to (use) a resource, just because it is a resource. Why? Is there something special about resources, something that is relevant here? In Locke there is a potential answer. He held that before resources are developed in some way that makes them useful to human beings – while, that is, they are strictly nothing more than resources – they are the common property of all of the human race, which has collective ownership of them. Thus it makes sense that he would think that to appropriate in a way that does not leave enough and as good is "to intrench upon the right of another": This right might be explained as based on others' participation in these collective property rights over resources that have not yet been appropriated by individuals.[27]

Nozick of course does not share this assumption that resources start out in a common pool. What, then, is the basis of his proviso? It is not easy to see what it would be. Failure to share something, apart from a special relationship (e.g., a contract or promise) that might serve as the basis of a right to that thing, is not the sort of thing he treats as a rights-violating act elsewhere in ASU.

The proviso actually does not seem to me to be a terribly plausible principle. Consider one particular resource – namely, diamonds – and for simplicity let us begin with the strong version of the proviso. Suppose that I know that there is one unmined, unowned diamond left on Earth, and that I know just where it is. Suppose further that we apply the proviso as Nozick applies it in the zipping back argument: that it takes effect when someone has the opportunity to appropriate the last share of something. This would seem to imply that it would be wrong of me – of anybody – to appropriate that diamond. Because only one can have it, no one may have it. Apparently, it has to stay right where it is – in the ground. This seems to me problematic in itself, quite aside from the alleged problem of zipping back. I don't think one need be a utilitarian to think that the diamond's staying in the ground is a pointless waste. No one may enjoy its beauty, simply because only one could. I am not sure what sort of argument could bring me to accept a principle that has implications like this, but it would have to be a powerful one, I should think.

Of course, the weaker version does not imply that I should leave the diamond in the ground, and this makes it seem immediately more plausible than the stronger one. However, if we assume, as we did with the stronger version, that this version too takes effect in cases like this, then it would limit my rights to this diamond. I would have an obligation to pass it around, perhaps, or rent it out (at a price people can afford). Perhaps, in the absence of such behavior, the principle would require me to otherwise compensate diamond-lovers who, unlike me, were unable to appropriate the last unappropriated diamond. All this, especially the idea that failing to do any of these things would violate the rights of others – seems very odd to me. What reason is there to believe such things, apart from a Lockean assumption that makes the property status of resources special (by making them collective)?

One possible response to this might be to say that the above reasoning seems to work against the proviso because of the particular resource I pick to apply it to – diamonds. Maybe the proviso doesn't apply to some resources, like diamonds, but does apply to others, such as water. But I don't think it even works for water, in all cases. Consider the following example, which actually is a real case. There is a two year college in California, Deep Springs College, which is located in the middle of a vast desert valley on top of a mountain range. It is the only human habitation in the valley, and for miles beyond in every direction. Within the modest perimeters of the college's property is the only water source, the epony-mous spring. (This may be *why* it is the only human habitation in the valley!) That means that the college monopolizes this valuable resource throughout a rather large area. Now suppose that someone develops a plan to build a house in the valley, thinking that Deep Springs College is obligated to share its water with them. Does the college have to agree with that assumption? I really don't see why. I suppose that, if officers of the college were to hear that some person had indeed hatched such a hare-brained scheme as this, and if they had no intention of sharing the water on a permanent basis, they ought to warn the person of that fact. Even that, though, is not clearly a matter of the observing the would-be immigrant's rights. The clear, definite, obvious rights here all seem to be theirs.

Of course, there are details in the above example that help make this view of the matter plausible. It seems relevant that the interloper is planning to relocate to the valley while knowing perfectly well that the only source of water is already private property. It also might be relevant that the planned move is intended to get "rights" for the mover to things that do not belong to him. Arguably, the move would itself be an unjust act. But this is actually my point, or part of it: To bring about anything like the limits on the right of appropriation that Locke and Nozick envi-sion, more factors are relevant than the bare fact that something is a resource and the additional bare fact that someone has appropriated all of it, or all of it in a certain area, or the last share of it.

To form some conception of what things really are relevant, I suggest we take a look at the point of the proviso itself. As I have already mentioned, Locke introduces it as a problem inherent in his theory of appropriation. That problem was that it seems to imply that "any one may ingross as much as he will." Nozick appears to agree that this is indeed a problem for the sort of view that he and Locke hold on these matters. In effect, I have just rejected that idea. The mere quantity of a resource that has been appropriated is not a problem.

However, some of the examples that Nozick presents in the course of his discussion of the proviso do seem to pose serious problems for the theory of property, problems that have to be taken very seriously indeed. These include cases like the island castaway situation, where a mariner is marooned on an island owned by someone else, and in addition *some* of the situations where someone appropriates the entire supply of something necessary for life, such as the case of the desert traveler who arrives at the water hole ahead of the others. Nozick offers the fact that the proviso can "handle correctly" cases like these as a great advantage of that theory (178–179). If we were to drop the proviso, how *would* theories like Locke's theory of acquisition handle these cases?

The first thing to say about this is that, unlike the alleged problem of ingrossing as much as one will, these problems are ones that are faced by any theory of property. If I am marooned on an island with no resources of my own, it makes no difference whether the island is the property of an individual, a hunter-gatherer tribe, or a nation-state. It also makes no difference what the alleged moral or legal basis of their property right might be. *All* property rights exclude in one way or another the non-holders of those rights, and that immediately raises the ethical issue of what the holders may/must do to/for me and likewise it raises the issue of the ethical status of my behavior toward them. Just as all theories of property must show how property rights legitimately originate (see 178), so they all must face these problems as well.

The second thing to say is that, just as these problems arise independently of any particular theory of property, so there may be no need to build their solution into the theory of property at all. Nozick's proviso, on the other hand, is internal to his theory of property. He seems to think this is an advantage, suggesting at one point that at least this indicates that handling of problem cases is not simply *ad hoc*. It seems to me that it is his proviso that commits the sin, so to speak, of adhocery. Unlike Locke's version of the proviso, which might be based on his common pool assumption, Nozick's is simply an exception to his view of property rights which is introduced for no reason other than the fact that it saves the theory from unpalatable implications that it seems to have. If our handling of problem cases is to avoid being *ad hoc*, we must have some reason for our solution other than that it saves a theory from itself. How then should we handle these cases? Obviously, I will not be able to devise a real solution here, but I would at least like to suggest where a solution might be found.

In a real-world castaway or desert traveler situation, there would normally be no worry about whether the appropriator would force the castaway back into the sea, refuse to share water, or do some other horrific thing. People are for the most part not like that. The worry of course is about the person who is like that. The proviso would imply that people in situations like that of the castaway would be justified in using coercion. For both Locke and Nozick, the reason for this has to do with limits on the property rights of the appropriator. Perhaps we would do well to look instead at the situation of the desperate castaway and the thirsty desert travelers. Surely it is reasonable to think that someone in such circumstances might use coercion, because of the very desperation of the circumstances themselves. In criminal law there is an old idea called "the defense of necessity," which holds that one may be blameless in breaking the law, if the alternative is sufficiently dire, such as imminent death or serious injury. Similar moral or metaethical theories might be brought forth here. One might theorize, for instance, that in certain extreme situations non-moral considerations, such as the need to survive, *override* moral considerations such as the rights of others or one's own duties. Another possible theory might appeal to a naturalistic explanation of the function of morality. On this view, morality serves as a framework of rules that enable us to cooperate in order to survive and flourish. When all cooperation breaks down and civilized relations are no longer possible, the view might hold, the constraints of morality *no longer apply*. Such a view would embrace what Nozick considers at one point (30 fn.) as a mere possibility: that rights are non-absolute in the sense that they "may be violated in order to avoid catastrophic moral horror."[28]

Both the "override" and the "no longer apply" views hold out the promise of handling some of the cases that the proviso is meant to handle, and for some of them might have similar implications as to the jusifiability (or blamelessness) of coercion. However, they are different from it in a number of ways. At one point, when he is explaining that his proviso does not involve the notion of overridden rights, he remarks, correctly I believe, that overridden rights "do not disappear; they leave a trace absent [in his view] in the cases under discussion" (180). One such "trace" might be an obligation to give compensation. Suppose, for example, that I, a lone aviator, crash my plane in the remote wilds of Alaska. I head for civilization on foot, with little hope of making it. Nearing death by starvation,

I happen upon a trapper's cabin with a well-stocked larder. Out of desperation I break in and help myself to the food. With my strength restored, I make it to safety. If one takes the view that my extreme need overrides the trapper's property rights in this case, one can still hold that I have a strict obligation to compensate the trapper: for instance, that I must return (perhaps as soon as I can) and replace what I have taken. On the other hand, if we handle this case by applying the proviso (after all, if I must starve in the presence of the trapper's larder, that would hardly be a case of "enough and as good left" for me!) then, while we might think it would be nice of me to return and replace things, it does not seem I would have a strict obligation to do so. The proviso would seem to mean that my need made the trapper's property rights disappear: The food was no longer the trapper's property. Hence there is no requirement to compensate. This, however, seems to me a counterintuitive result. On this point, the proviso seems inferior to at least one alternative view.

Another way in which these alternatives, in this case both of them, differ from Nozick's proviso is that, unlike it, they are not entitlement principles. This means that, as far as they are concerned, if you have a monopoly of a resource, it makes no difference how you got that monopoly. Thus if you have the only water hole that did not go dry, it makes no difference whether this failed to happen through natural causes or because you took some special precautions to prevent it. What does matter is the direness of the need of the others. It also matters what the resource is – especially, whether it is something that is necessary for life or not.

This means that these alternatives probably will not draw the line between Nozick's cases, the line that separates those in which the principle takes effect and those in which it does not, in the same place that his principle does. This could count either in their favor or against them, depending on whether one has a good reason for thinking the line ought to be drawn in one place rather than another.

11.   Taxation, Slavery, and Demoktesis

Understanding the passage (169–172) that rather shockingly connects taxation with slavery is not perfectly straightforward. The reader's task is complicated by the fact that the passage begins by talking about forced labor – "[t]axation of earnings from labor is on a par with forced labor," he says (169) – and then shifts to being about slavery (171). These aren't the same thing, are they? After all, slavery is a (putative) property right, while the right to force labor out of someone, supposing there is such a right, is not. Or so one would think. Actually this sharp distinction is one of the things that is called into question by this passage. This potent three and a half pages raises a deep question about the nature of property itself. This becomes more obvious if one considers it together with the thought experiment that forms the central section of Chapter 8, "Demoktesis."

Both passages rest on a common idea: "The central core of the notion of a property right in X, relative to which other parts of the notion are to be explained, is the right to determine what shall be done with X: the right to choose which of the constrained set of options concerning X shall be realized or attempted" (171). This means that property rights can vary widely along several different dimensions. Given that the decision as to what shall be done with X can be made by an individual or (assuming an agreed-upon decision procedure) by a group of individuals, it follows that, as he points out immediately (171), these rights can belong to a single individual or to groups of varying sizes. Given that there are many decisions about X that can be made, the right can also vary in itself, so to speak. Can you sell X? Can you bequeath it? Can you use it to pursue a particular private purpose of your own? These are all property rights that you might have in X. One's ownership of X may be more or less full; it can vary over a wide range of degrees of amplitude. It can range from a right so narrow as barely to qualify as a form of ownership at all, all the way to the property right that Sir William Blackstone memorably called a "sole and despotic dominion which one man claims and exercises over the external things of the world, in total exclusion of the right of any other individual in the universe."[29] Nozick is thinking that ownership begins – dimly, faintly – at the beginning of this series and becomes full and complete at the Blackstonian end.

Both these dimensions of variation are fundamental to the thought experiment at the center of the "Demoktesis" chapter. There, Nozick asks us to imagine a process, decidedly non-invisible-handed but involving no unjust steps, by which his minimal state can become fully more-than-minimal. Actually, this proposal, and the title of this section, "The More-than-Minimal State Derived," turn out to be something of a prank. As the narrative progresses, people begin by retaining most of the rights they have, while selling nonetheless some "rights in themselves" (282) to others – rights to make some decisions regarding what they may do, such as drug rights, wage and price control rights, the right to decide which of their body parts will be donated to the needy ("physical equality rights"), and so forth. More and more of these "shares" are sold until all decision rights for each individual are on the market. Through a series of consolidations which he shows are conceivable despite being vanishingly unlikely, all these rights are held by one Great Corporation, with everyone holding one voting share. The decisions to be made by this include potentially all decisions about your life and that of any other person. In return for the loss of all decision-making authority each of us gets a voice (i.e., one vote) in every decision to be made (which will make a difference to the outcome in the extremely unlikely event of a tied vote). We have arrived at full, direct democracy, rule by an untrammeled General Will. (Rousseau's *The Social Contract* is quite rightly cited in fn. 6.) (Interesting that a tale which in the hands of a Kierkegaard or Nietzsche might have been worked up as a philosophical horror story is here played out as a sort of Higher Joke. Does this show us the difference between American philosophy and its Continental cousin?) To this "eldritch tale" he appends "The Tale of the Slave" (290–292). Here we imagine nine continuously varying stages though which a stereotypical case of slavery, ownership by a single cruel and arbitrary master, gradually evolves into the Great Corporation case that we have already seen. He ends with a semi-rhetorical question: "[W] hich transition from case 1 to case 9 made it no longer the tale of a slave?" I say "rhetorical" because Nozick believes the answer to the question is clear – never! – and "semi" because the reader is supposed to struggle to give some other answer, struggle in vain. The joke is on us. Of course, the point of the tale of the Great Corporation is not to derive an extra-minimal state but to draw a moral connection between slavery the fully extra-minimal state: Both commit fundamentally the same violation of human dignity. Even a perfectly just process by which such a state could come about would involve selling that dignity away.

The most perfect form of unlimited democracy would be in every way equivalent to a form of slavery. The reason for this is also the reason why forced labor and slavery are the same thing: Rights to decide what is to be done with a person – independently of voluntary acts on the part of that person that commit them to be so disposed of – would be property rights, property rights over a person. This would be especially true of a right to decide what is to be done with someone's productive efforts. This, however, raises a question: Given that forced labor and outright, full ownership of a person are forms of the same thing, differing only in degree, why is taxation on a par with either one, either forced labor or ownership (i.e., slavery)?

On this point I see two main arguments in the text, one of which is more naturally expressed in terms of force and the other in terms of a sort of property right. The former argument is the one he presents in response to the possibility of a state that only taxes people above a certain minimal level, so that one can avoid being taxed by producing no more than what is needed for bare subsistence.[30]

> The fact that others intentionally intervene, in violation of a side constraint against aggression, to threaten force to limit the alternatives, in this case to paying taxes or (presumably the worse alternative) bare subsistence, makes the taxation system one of forced labor and distinguishes it from other cases of limited choices which are not forcings. (169)

As I understand this argument, a crucial element is the idea that we are supposing a violation of a side constraint against aggression. The idea would be something like this. If I rob you at gunpoint of $20 and as a result you are unable to go to the movies, then I wrongly compel you both to give me the $20 and to stay home from the movies. If you manage to go to the movies, but only by mowing your neighbor's lawn for $20 you would not otherwise need, then I wrongly compel you both to give me the $20 and to mow your neighbor's lawn. This is not an implausible view, I think, but as I am reading it, it does assume the more fundamental idea of the wrongness of aggression. What it adds to it is the idea that the wrongful coercion involved in the forced extraction of wealth is not limited to that bare unilateral transfer. It extends to whatever it compels you to do or omit doing, and this can include the labor involved in producing it.

I see the other argument in comments like the following:

> When end-result principles of distributive justice are built into the legal structure of a society, they ... give each citizen an enforceable claim to some portion of the total social product; that is, to some portion of the sum total of the individually and jointly made products. This total product is produced by individuals laboring, using means of production others have saved to bring into existence, by people organizing production or creating means to produce new things or things in a new way. It is on this batch of individual activities that patterned distributional principles give each person an enforceable claim. Each person has a claim to the activities and products of other persons .... Seizing the results of someone's labor is equivalent to seizing hours from him and directing him to carry on various activities. If people force you to do certain work, or unrewarded work, for a certain period of time, they decide what you are to do and what purposes your work is to serve apart from your decisions. This process ... gives them a property right in you. (171–172)

I quote this passage at such length because I suspect that the idea behind it probably is one that requires a lengthy discussion, really a longer one than can be given in a book on political philosophy without wandering too far into other areas. The idea seems to be about the nature of the productive activities (labor, saving, etc.) that bring forth an expropriatable product, that they do not have the sort of isolated reality that would enable an enforceable claim to the product to extend only so far as the product and no further than that. If you work for nine hours and I coercively take the product of four of those hours away from you, what I do affects not merely the product but those four hours as well – retroactively, if you will. It is now I, and not you, who determine the purpose served by those four hours of – not my, but – your life. Of course, it is possible for you, by your action, to alienate to me the right to do that. You might have voluntarily agreed to work for me for pay, or you might have committed some crime that deserves punishment by involuntary servitude. But what we are imagining here is of course that you have done no such thing. That would seem to mean that what I am doing cannot be justified. Some people find this point intuitively compelling; others do not. Convincing those who do not, if that should be possible, would probably require some sort of inquiry into the nature of purposive human action.

Notes

1 Joel Feinberg, "Justice and Personal Desert," in *Doing and Deserving* (Princeton, New Jersey: Princeton University Press, 1970), pp. 55–87.
2 Feinberg, "Justice and Personal Desert," p. 58.
3 Feinberg, "Justice and Personal Desert," p. 57.
4 There seems to be no canonical version of this story, written by an eye witness. To tell the truth, the anecdote is most often – though not always – told with the positions of the words "unfair" and "unjust" transposed in the final witticism. This seems clearly wrong to me. Doing the same thing to everybody tends to support claims of fairness. Whether it is directly relevant to justice depends on your view of justice. (By the way, I do not mean to imply that Morgenbesser influenced Nozick on this point. The story appears to date to a period when Nozick was no longer at Columbia.)
5 I am silently switching here from speaking of current time-slice views to speaking in terms of time-slice views in light of Nozick's suggestion (155) that this category really should include ones that hold a distribution to be justified on the grounds that it makes up for something that was wrong with an earlier distribution (where both are considered in time-slice terms). In light of this, "time slice" (without the "current") seems to more accurately express what he has in mind.

6 Aristotle, *The Nicomachean Ethics*, trans. H. Rackham (Cambridge, Massachusetts: Harvard University Press, 1926), 1131a25–26.

7 Aristotle's notion of distributive justice requires that the ratio between shares (not merely their order) be identical to the ratio between the extents to which we possess the feature. Thus if the principle is "to each according to their moral virtue," then it can only be just that my shares are twice what yours are if I am twice as virtuous as you. This would seem to require us to measure virtue. See *The Nicomachean Ethics* (many editions), Book V, Ch. 3, esp. 1131b4–11. Joel Feinberg endorses Aristotle's ratio version of distributive justice and adds quite a bit of detail to it in his *Social Philosophy* (Englewood Cliffs, New Jersey: Prentice-Hall, 1973), pp. 107–117. Though Nozick disagrees with the patterned view, he is actually being rather charitable here. His version of this view would be easier to apply than the versions that Aristotle and Feinberg actually endorse: It would surely be easier to say whether Peter is more or less virtuous than Paul than it would be to say how much more or less virtuous he is.

8 He may be warning us that he will be using "patterned principle" in this extended sense in this sentence: "And we extend the use of 'pattern' to include the overall designs put forth by combinations of end-state principles" (156).

9 G. A. Cohen, *Self-Ownership, Freedom, and Equality* (Cambridge, England: Cambridge University Press, 1995), p. 43.

10 Cohen, *Self-Ownership, Freedom, and Equality*, pp. 43–44.

11 John Rawls, *A Theory of Justice* (Cambridge, Massachusetts: Harvard University Press, 1971), pp. 7–11 and 64–65.

12 I won't be discussing Section II here, as it seems to me to belong to the study of Rawls' views about justice more than to the study of Nozick's own views on the subject. It would take us rather far afield into a discussion of Rawls which would not yield proportionate results in understanding what Nozick is doing elsewhere in ASU. Needless to say, though, for those who are familiar with Rawls' theory, Section II is well worth reading.

13 Perhaps I should say that I am not dismissing the sophisticated theorists of distributive justice. I am merely discussing the relative difficulties involved in voluntarily conforming to P and, failing that, coercively enforcing it. Also, I would point out that some of these theorists seem to accept the "not too unequal" view. As near as I can determine, this is the view that Cohen holds throughout *Self-Ownership, Freedom, and Equality*.

14 Note I do not mean to imply that Nozick does not notice this problem. When he introduces the principle of rectification, he asks: "How far back must one go in wiping clean the historical slate of injustices?" (152). He adds, simply, that he knows of no satisfactory discussion of this issue (152 fn. 2).

15 Robert H. Lowie, *The Indians of the Plains* (Garden City, New Jersey: The Natural History Press, 1965 [orig. pub. 1954]), pp. 212–213.

16 The one partial exception is the notion put forth by Hayek, which Nozick calls "distribution according to value rather than merit," which, very roughly

speaking, is the way markets distribute things. Nozick presents some reasons why this is not very plausible as an account of what distributive justice is at p. 158 (for one thing, it would imply that charity is unjust!).

17 Cohen, *Self-Ownership, Freedom, and Equality*, p. 45.

18 64 Wis. 265, 25 N. W. 42 (1885). It can be found in any first-year contracts text and online. All the quotations in my narrative are from the case, which is attributed to Taylor, J.

19 The Eagle Diamond, as it is known in history, eventually became one of the most famous gems in the world. Boynton sold it to Tiffany and Co. in New York for $850, who sold it to J. P. Morgan. He donated it to the American Museum of Natural History. It ended up in the hands of a jewel thief who called himself Murph the Surf, and disappeared from history. http://wisconsinology.blogspot.com/2013/03/murph-surf-and-eagle-diamond.html

20 John Locke, *Second Treatise of Government* (Indianapolis, Indiana: Hackett Publishing, 1980 [orig. pub. 1690]), sect. 31.

21 I should add a qualification: Nozick's response is roughly the same as his interpretation of Locke's response. His interpretation could of course be incorrect.

22 Locke, *Second Treatise*, sect. 27.

23 Nozick seems to be misremembering Rashdall's example somewhat. The nearest thing I can find to it in the essay cited involves a party of travelers in an "unappropriated prairie" where the first traveler appropriates "all the available apples or acorns or dates." Must the others starve, Rashdall asks, rather than violate the first traveler's alleged property rights? Hastings Rashdall, "The Philosophical Theory of Property," in *Property: Its Duties and Rights Historically, Philosophically and Religiously Regarded (Essays by Various Authors)* (London: MacMillan, 1915), p. 44. I will stick with the desert/water version of the example, which is actually better for illustrating Nozick's point. I think Nozick's misremembering Rashdall's example is a result of confusing it with an example in Hayek, which *is* about someone who appropriates the only water hole in the desert. See F. A. Hayek, *The Constitution of Liberty* (Chicago, Illinois: University of Chicago Press, 1960), p. 136. Nozick cites this passage in Hayek at 180 fn.

24 There are many discussions of the conundrum. A very sophisticated one is R. M. Sainsbury, *Paradoxes*, 3rd ed. (Cambridge, England: Cambridge University Press, 2009), pp. 107–119.

25 Michael Otsuka, *Libertarianism without Inequality* (Oxford, England: Oxford University Press, 2003), p. 23 fn. 31.

26 Jonathan Wolff, *Robert Nozick: Property, Justice, and the Minimal State* (Stanford, California: Stanford University Press, 1991), pp. 112 and 113. Rather than quoting or citing ASU, Otsuka cites this passage in Wolff. Wolff in turn cites, not anything in Nozick's book, but an earlier paper by G. A. Cohen, reprinted as "Self-ownership, World-ownership, and Equality," in *Self-Ownership, Freedom, and Equality*, pp. 67–91. Cohen says (p. 82) that

Nozick weakens Locke's proviso "by considering not what might or would have happened tout court, absent the appropriation, but what would have happened on the special hypothesis that the world would have remained commonly owned." My impression is that Otsuka derived his interpretation, which seems to me grossly wrong, not directly from the text of ASU, but from Wolff, who seems to have gotten it from Cohen. (To be fair to Cohen, I think he is actually giving a misleading statement of his interpretation, which is actually more sensible and sensitive to the text than this declaration makes it sound.)

27 Locke, *Second Treatise*, sect. 36. On the idea of resources as being jointly owned by everyone, see Ch. 5, *passim*.

28 He denies, correctly, that his proviso is based on this sort of thinking (180).

29 William Blackstone, *Commentaries on the Laws of England* (Chicago, Illinois: University of Chicago Press, 1979 [orig. pub. 1769]), vol. 2, p. 1.

30 This is an oddly generous concession on his part: He seems to imply that this is what states normally do, whereas they actually may never behave this way. Some taxes (e.g., sales taxes) are taxes on consumption, and cannot be avoided by being unproductive. In one way or another, existing states seem to tax everybody and do not permit one to escape the power to tax.

9

The Search for Utopia

1. Introduction

Of all the 10 chapters in ASU, the single chapter that comprises all of Part III has always seemed to me to be one of the most original and interesting. In addition, in a book with many loose ends and more than a few cryptic statements and arguments, there is never any doubt what his position is, what his argument is, and in what ways (with one perhaps minor exception) the argument is supposed to support the position he takes. However, this seems to be, as far as I can see, a minority view. Part III is clearly the least discussed of the three parts of the book, and it seems to have had little influence. Some comments on it seem rather dismissive.[1]

In what follows I will comment on some features of the argument that might not be obvious and try to make a case for taking the "Utopia" chapter seriously.

2. An Unusual Sort of Utopianism

Nozick begins the chapter by explaining why he is talking about utopia. The first time I read this explanation I found it somewhat odd. In Part I he has defended the minimal state, and in Part II he has countered various reasons for thinking that a more-than-minimal state is justified. Now, he explains, he faces a problem. There is a possibility that the minimal state lacks "luster," that it might not have the capacity to "inspire" people (297). I think my first reaction to this worry of his was that there is no obvious reason why a state *should* be lustrous or inspiring, any more

Anarchy, State, and Utopia: An Advanced Guide, First Edition. Lester H. Hunt.
© 2015 John Wiley & Sons, Inc. Published 2015 by John Wiley & Sons, Inc.

than the parts or instrumentalities of states (e.g., armies, diplomatic missions, bombs, etc.) should have these attributes. In spite of such quibbles about how it might best be expressed, though, I do think that there is a real problem here and that he is quite right to address it.

I would put the problem in terms of a distinction he makes early in the book: goals and constraints. As I said at the outset, his project in this book is to examine the political from the vantage of the ethical. He has argued that it is possible that a minimal state does not violate constraints of a certain sort: namely, rights understood as a sort of moral immunity against coercion. He has also responded to various reasons for opting for a state that, in his view, would violate these constraints. In other words, though the argument is fundamentally a moral one, the only moral principles that have played a central role in his argument have been constraints.

What about goals? All the features of a thing that make it positively desirable are to be found in the goods, the values, the ideals that are goals of human action. Nozick may have shown that the minimal state is *right*, in the sense of not wrong, but other than enforcing rights, what is *good* about it? A utopia, by definition, is something good – in fact, supremely good. If Nozick can show that his state would somehow facilitate or lead to utopia, he will certainly have answered this question. Indeed, I would argue that his view implies that his minimal state would more or less force utopia to exist.

One of the factors that complicates this view is that the problem of defining "utopia" is one of the issues that is raised in an acute form by Chapter 10. You might say that, just as Part I challenged our concept of the state by defending a state that lacks features we commonly associate with states, and just as Part II challenged our concept of distributive justice by presenting a conception that does not much resemble what we thought distributive justice was, so Part III does the same for our concept of utopia by departing radically from the utopian tradition. He describes one point of departure himself: "The utopian tradition," he tells us, "is maximax" (329). This fact separates him from that tradition in a very important way.

Every human action, especially that of designing or choosing institutions, has a variety of possible outcomes and we always are subject to some uncertainty as to which one will actually happen. There are two readily discernible principles for dealing with this uncertainty. We can choose the course of action in which the best possible outcome is better than the best possible outcome of any of the alternative courses of action that face us. This is maximax. Or we can chose the course in which the worst possible outcome is better than the worst possibilities of the alternatives. This is what Nozick calls minimax.[2] We can aim for maximizing the maximum or for maximizing the minimum. As we shall see shortly, the reasoning that Nozick does in defending his sort of utopia is heavily influenced by minimax considerations.

This immediately creates an interesting theoretical problem. Nozick is definitely right in saying that the utopian tradition is maximax. Indeed, "maximax institutional design" could perhaps serve as a *definition* of "utopianism." On the other hand, minimax devices like the separation of powers and checks and balances defended in *The Federalist Papers* represent a non-utopian, even anti-utopian, point of view. For James Madison and the other authors of *The Federalist*, thinking about good government should focus on institutional devices that make it less likely that government will go wrong in various ways. True utopians don't think that way. So if Nozick's clever idea is a minimax utopia, it sounds very much like a square circle, an implicit contradiction. Is it?

I think we can save his idea from contradiction, at least the immediate threat of it, by making a simple distinction. On the one hand, there are utopian societies, however they might be defined. On the other hand, there is utopian thinking. What I have just called "utopianism" is utopian thinking. Given this distinction we can say that Nozick is defending a certain sort of utopian society on the basis of reasoning that has a decidedly non-utopian element. He believes that utopian theorists heretofore have based their thinking on the wrong sorts of principles.[3] This is not, so far, contradictory.

Of course, whether the sort of society that his theory describes can be a genuine utopia depends on what the proper definition of "utopia" is. Utopia, he tells us, cannot be a society that "simultaneously and continually" realizes "all social and political goods" because that is not possible: What we are concerned with here is the best of all *possible* worlds (297–298). But he finds "an ambiguity in the notion of the best possible world" and suggests that there are at least two definitions of the best possible society. It might be "that one of the possible ones in which things turn out best: the maximax society in which the most favorable eventuality is realized." Or it might be that which comes about "in accordance with the 'best' principles of institutional design (which build in certain safeguards against bad eventualities at a cost of making some good ones more difficult of quick attainment)" (298 fn.). This seems to me a slightly confused way to put the matter. Whether "utopia" (or, to use his somewhat metaphorical phrase, "the best possible world") can be defined in terms of the best principles of institutional design depends on what these principles are. A Madisonian might say that the best such principles are ones that forestall certain bad eventualities, such as autocracy and mob rule, and that such a society has a good chance of being *better* than any society has been so far. "Better," like "good enough," clearly falls short of utopia. I think what Nozick should have done here is to define utopia as the best possible society (or one that falls within some optimal range of possibilities) and then offer – not a definition but – his *theory* that it can only be achieved by employing certain principles of institutional design (which incorporate minimax considerations). This would be perfectly consistent with what he actually does in this chapter.

There is another important way, in addition to his minimax leanings, in which Nozick departs rather sharply from the utopian tradition. Before I can say what it is, I will need to briefly run through the first of the two main components of the argument, the "possible worlds model" (the other one being "the model projected into our world"). Like the more famous experience machine, the model of possible worlds can be seen, at least to some extent, as a thought experiment:

> Imagine a possible world in which to live. ... Every rational creature in this world you have imagined will have the same rights of imagining a possible world for himself to live in (in which all other rational inhabitants have the same imagining rights, and so on) as you have. The other inhabitants of the world may choose to stay in the world which has been created for them (they have been created for) or they may choose to leave it and inhabit a world of their own imagining. If they choose to leave your world and live in another, your world is without them. You may choose to abandon your imagined world, now without its emigrants. This process goes on; worlds are created, people leave them, create new worlds, and so on.

Perhaps I should point out before going on that these "possible worlds" consist, as far as present purposes are concerned, entirely of people. Nobody seems to be imagining a world they would like to be in because it contains an abundance of beautiful natural scenery, because the weather is always fair, or because resources are so lavishly abundant that people need only work a few hours a week. For the moment, we are to ignore the potentialities and limitations inherent in the non-human environment.

Given its exclusively human content, it is fitting that he also calls these possible worlds as so described, including their equal imagining rights (and consequent right of emigration), "associations." Perhaps some of these worlds will eventually become stable, in the sense that the current population will choose to remain in them.[4] He names three "conditions" that will be met by stable associations.

The first is that "*none* of the inhabitants of the world can *imagine* an alternative world they would rather live in, which (they believe) would continue to exist if all of its rational inhabitants had the same rights of imagining and emigration" (299).[5] This follows immediately from the definition of an association: If they could imagine an alternative they would prefer, they would already be there.

This is what I think of as the thought experiment aspect of the possible worlds model: We are meant to contemplate the model at this point and see that this indeed does answer to what "best possible" means, as applied to these associations. Not that this description is a definition of that phrase, but that it describes fully sufficient conditions for being the best possible world. To be the best for each and every person in the community: That certainly seems enough to make it the best possible. That people can move to another world simply by imagining it and yet do not do so – a fact implied by the stability of this world – seems to guarantee that it is the best for them. If there can be communities in our own world that meet some condition that sufficiently resembles this one, then surely they would qualify as utopias.

Further, if we assume that people want the best for themselves, which seems a safe enough assumption, then it would appear that the model is a process that, as people create worlds, leave them, and create new worlds, *spontaneously generates* best the best possible world – or worlds, for as we soon see, Nozick thinks there will be more than one.

The inference I believe Nozick is asking us to make here involves a couple of assumptions that it will be worthwhile to pause over briefly. First, and most obviously, we would be assuming that a good society is one that is *good for* the people in it. This in turn might commit us to some view, or some member of a family of views, about the good itself. It could commit us to the idea that what makes a thing – anything – good is that it is good for someone (or, perhaps, for some living being). This is not an implausible view, but it is a view. If Nozick is indeed committed to this idea, it is something he could be wrong about.

Further, we are taking individual choice as a strong indicator of what is good for that individual. Nozick's reasoning holds that a stable world is the best possible, and the reason given is that (given their experiences and circumstances) the people in that world choose to stay there. This seems to mean that people are capable of knowing (at least after a series of experiences passing through unstable worlds) what is really good for them. This seems to involve us in an assumption about what it is for something to be good for someone. If this assumption is to be very plausible, the good-for relationship would have to be something that is not terribly difficult for the benefitted individual to detect. This would probably have to mean that the property of being good for someone would have to depend in some relevant way on facts about that person's consciousness. For instance, to take some very simple examples, perhaps what makes something good for you is that it pleases you, or that it makes you happy, or it is that you want it, or would continue to want it if you knew all the relevant facts, and so forth and so on. These are things that everyone can know about, or have a good chance of knowing about. Again, this is not a terribly implausible assumption, but it is an assumption. It seems to involve *some* sort of subjectivism about the property of being good for someone and, when combined with the other assumption, about the good itself.

This is interesting because Nozick makes it plain throughout ASU that his view of rights is not subjectivist at all. To be an objectivist about the right and a subjectivist (of some sort) about the good: That is not a contradictory position but, as I say, it is a position and one might take issue with it.

The possible worlds model does appear to commit us to some degree of subjectivism about the good. One thing that is interesting about this is that it seems to me that authors of literary utopias by and large, perhaps all of them, take the opposite view. This is the second of Nozick's two sharp departures from the utopian tradition that I mentioned above.

It would be very difficult to prove that value-objectivism characterizes the entire utopian tradition. At any rate, it is very clear that the two most iconic authors of literary utopias – namely, Plato and St. Thomas More – share this view. Thomas More, in the book after which all utopias are named, tells us that the inhabitants of Utopia, the fictional island nation that is the subject of his book, do not lust after silver and gold as we do in our world. Indeed, they regard it as less valuable than iron. The reason, he says, is that they do not "value them beyond what the metals themselves deserve" – that is, in proportion to their real usefulness. Of course he is sure that iron is more useful than gold. Thus Utopians do use gold, but they use it, among other things, to make chamber-pots (in effect, toilets).[6] Thomas More plainly thinks that the pleasure people derive from gold, and the fact that they do want it, are entirely irrelevant to the question of its value. They merely show how corrupt and deluded people are. This is his attitude throughout his book. Plato, whose *Republic* is still the greatest utopia of them all, sets forth, in his book, an extremely objectivist view of the good.[7] It is, literally, one of the things he is famous for.

3. Two More Conditions

So much, for the time being, for the first of the three conditions that would be met by stable associations. The other two are less important and can be dealt with more briefly. They are logically linked.

The second of the three might be called "the non-exploitation condition." In the possible worlds model, you "will not be able to set up an association [that is, a stable one] in which you are the absolute monarch, exploiting all the other rational inhabitants" (300). In this sense, A is "exploiting" B if B must give up more (i.e., more utility, more perceived value) to A than B gets in return. The impossibility of one person exploiting all others, he points out, follows from a more general truth: In a stable association there can be no subset of its members who would be better off without the rest of the members. If there were, they could imagine a world they would rather be in – namely, one without the other member(s) – and they could be in it just by imagining it, which of course is what they would do. But this would conflict with the definition of a stable association.

There is a complication here that we should notice. As we will see later on, it makes possible certain objections to Nozick's case for utopia. He places a constraint on the imaginers in his model: One cannot imagine a world which is such that it follows from the description of the people in this world, either as a matter of logic or of causal laws that the imaginer knows, that they would most prefer to live in it. They cannot be *designed to* "want to live in a world with a certain (kind of) person, and will do whatever he says ..." (303). Arguably, without this constraint the non-exploitation condition will only be trivially true: The model could in that case produce worlds in which people live in conditions that we would otherwise call "being exploited," except that they have been designed in advance to like being treated that way.[8] *However*, he does allow the imaginers to imagine a world of people who all accept some general principle or other, including perhaps some definite principle of distributive justice, and he admits that some of these shared principles "might be quite atrocious" (304). He doesn't give any examples, but I notice that elsewhere he says that his utopians would be free to sell themselves into slavery if they wish (332). Perhaps he has such arrangements in mind here, as well as principles like "a wife must obey her husband in all things" or "the elders must make all the important decisions for the group." There don't seem to be any constraints on what sorts of agreed-upon principles there might be, so some could easily be patriarchal or hierarchical in some other objectionable way. (Does this let exploitation in again, through the back door, so to speak?)

The third of the three conditions is based on some of the same reasoning that produced the second one. The second followed from the fact that an inhabitant of a stable association cannot take from others more (i.e., something that those others value more) than what the inhabitant contributes to them. Can you take *less* than that? Can the others make a profit, so to speak, from your contribution? Nozick's answer is, in effect, no. For suppose that you did. Then some other world could offer you more than this one does and still come out ahead (i.e., "make a profit"). For instance, you could simply imagine a world that is otherwise like this one, except that those in it notice this opportunity to "purchase" your services in this way. If there is an exploitable interval left between what you take and what you give, another will do the same, and then another will do the same, and so on, until the interval is vanishingly small. This, as Nozick points out (302), is what is known in economics as receiving one's marginal contribution. In this way the possible worlds model rewards each member according to what they contribute to others.

This point seems to me more a curiosity than anything else. Insofar as it is meant to be a good-making feature of the model, it seems to be an appeal to a patterned principle of distributive justice. In fact, it seems to be one he has already discussed, the one he called "distribution in accordance with value" and attributed to Friedrich Hayek. Nothing he says about the possible worlds model conforming to distribution according to value conflicts, strictly speaking, with his earlier rejection of it as a principle of distributive justice. In the earlier discussion, what he rejects is the idea that this is "a standard that one should insist a society fit" (158). Now, in Chapter 10, he isn't insisting that societies fit it. He is only pointing out that the possible worlds model does fit it. What is just a little mysterious about this, though, is that he seems to be pointing it out as a good-making feature of the model, and it is not obvious why, in Nozickean terms, it would be. To be fair, though, he never does say that it is one of the reasons a stable association is a model of a utopian society. Perhaps the third condition is simply one of the reasons he finds the model "intrinsically interesting" (306).

4. Projecting the Model

Given that, as I have argued, the possible worlds model is most plausible if we assume a view of the good that is in some relevant way subjectivist, it is somewhat disconcerting to notice that, about seven years after the publication of ASU, Nozick published an account of the good (or what he

207

there calls "value") that is explicitly *objectivist*. This was in his second book, *Philosophical Explanations*.[9] This raises the possibility either that he later developed views that are incompatible with the model or that my analysis of it is simply wrong. Actually, I will make a case in the next section that the later view suggests a way in which we might combine an objectivist view with a certain sort of subjectivism and thereby reconcile the possible worlds model with the idea of the objectivity of value. Before I can do that, though, I need to say something about the rest of the case for utopia.

If we accept the first of the three conditions of stable possible worlds, that no inhabitant can imagine a world they would rather live in, and if we accept Nozick's notion that a stable world would therefore be the best possible, then the possibility that there could be something in our world that corresponds to it is certainly an exciting one. It would seem to mean that there can be something in our world that spontaneously generates good communities, and spontaneously moves in the direction of the best possible ones. Nozick tells us that such is indeed the case:

> In *our* world, what corresponds to the model of possible worlds is a wide and diverse range of communities which people can enter if they are admitted, leave if they wish to, shape according to their wishes; a society in which utopian experimentation can be tried, different styles of life can be lived, and alternative visions of the good can be individually or jointly pursued. (307)

The bare-bones legal system of Nozick's minimal state is now interpreted as a "framework for utopia." This means that most of the state functions that the Nozickean state refrains from carrying out can re-enter the picture, as features of voluntary associations. Believers in any particular end-state principle of distributive justice will be free to form communities that apply their principle (provided only that the principle is practicable in the real world). The most obvious possibility would be some form of socialism. But it would have to be a form of socialism in which non-socialists are not forced to share things they do not wish to share (though of course they may be prohibited from living in that community). The one familiar state activity that these communities would not be able to imitate is military conquest. This would be prohibited by the framework itself.

Nozick lucidly sets out four ways in which the framework differs from, and will fall short of, the model (307–309). The communities in the framework can only contain real people who have not been designed with the community in mind (people who share your vision of perfection might not exist). These communities exist in the same world together and must decide how to deal with other communities. Finding out about communities in the framework and moving to them costs you something (at least, it takes effort and perhaps a lot more than that). Finally, and perhaps most worrisomely, some communities may try to keep some members ignorant of currently existing alternatives to their way of life.

It is rather obvious how all of these features of the framework will decrease its power as a utopia-producing engine, as compared to the possible-worlds model. We should keep in mind, though, as we evaluate his argument, that the issue here is whether the framework is superior to alternative systems. The model itself is not such an alternative: Ironically, all the worlds in the "possible-worlds" model are *im*possible. The mere fact that the framework is inferior to the model, even if it is *far* inferior to it, does not mean that it is no good. The issue, as Nozick puts it, is whether the framework is superior to "alternatives even more divergent from the possible-worlds model than it" (308–309).

5. The Three Paths

The three "theoretical paths leading to" utopia are arguments that are directed against conceptions of utopia that are alternatives to his own – which would mean that they are directed against the entire utopian tradition. As we will soon see, they appear at first to suffer a frontal collision with a problem we have already run into.

The first revolves around a list of widely divergent people who have actually existed, including Allen Ginsberg, Henry Ford, Frank Sinatra, and Ayn Rand, and an intimidating barrage of questions about what the one society would be like that would be the very best for all of these people (309–311). There can't be one sort of society that is optimally good for everyone: People are just too different. Thus utopians like Plato and Moore were mistaken in trying to design such a system. The second "path" maintains, that aside from the problem of agreeing about what is good, there remains the fact that "not all goods can be realized simultaneously," so that "trade-offs will have to be made." I think by "realized simultaneously" he means realized fully and simultaneously, since the impossibility of achieving the full amount of each good is what forces upon us the decision as to how much of each we are to seek, which in turn forces the issue of their relative value. Certain forms of equality can only exist at the cost of certain kinds of liberty. If we think both are good, we still have to decide how important they are in relation to one another. Nozick denies that there is "one unique system of trade-offs" that is right for everybody. The framework is superior to single-community utopias because it can produce a diverse variety of communities, each representing "a slightly different mix" of values, thus enhancing the chances of providing something that will best approximate any given individual's "balance among competing goods" (312).

The third path relies on Nozick's discussion of invisible-hand processes in Chapter 2. The framework serves as the basis for what he there calls a filtering process (the other type of invisible-hand process being equilibrium processes – see 21–22). The filter is the process already described above, in which people enter communities, alter them somewhat to better suit them, and leave if they see something better. The filter consists in the fact that utopian plans that prove wanting in practice cannot survive if people are free to leave at comparatively low cost – something that will not be true if an entire nation-state tries to become a utopian system (following a single plan) itself. One great advantage that filter devices have over the alternative used by the utopian tradition – design devices, in which one tries to construct something single-handedly – is that a filter device makes lighter demands on one's knowledge, "including knowledge of what is desirable" (314). In fact, the filter process supported by the framework produces new knowledge: It is a process by which utopia is searched for and discovered.

Perhaps it is obvious how the third path is influenced by minimax considerations. There is always the possibility that a utopia will look wonderful on paper but work out badly in practice. A nation-state that tries to be a utopia can go horribly wrong, with its residents more or less trapped within it.[10] The third path embodies genuinely utopian striving – reconceived as the search for the best of *possible* worlds – while accommodating legitimate minimax worries about how easily dreams can become nightmares.

Interesting as they are, all three paths seem to encounter the problem I mentioned in the last section: In his second book, Nozick developed a theory of the good that appears to conflict with what he is saying here. There he defends his theory that goods, or, more specifically, "intrinsic values," are "organic unities."[11] We needn't go into what this means, except to point out what may be obvious already: that Nozick does not think that whether something is an organic unity is a matter of personal taste or in any other way subjective. The third path works best if we are entitled to assume that the people who are joining, modifying, and leaving communities can identify which ones are genuinely good – otherwise we will never get to the *best* possible worlds. It does place that much of a burden on human knowledge. The requisite knowledge of the good and the best is easiest to come by if there is something relevantly subjective about it. Further, something's being an organic unity does not seem to be a relation it has to some person or some living being. Nozickean intrinsic value is good for you, of course, but it is good for everybody. This seems to mean that, not only is value objective, it is universal as well. Apparently, we should all value the same things, on pain of some kind of philosophical error. This seems to clash with the first two paths to utopia, both of which start from the idea that people are very different in terms of what is good for them. If people are that different in that particular way, most of them are just plain wrong. Were Plato and More right about that after all?

Does the *Philosophical Explanations* view explode the three paths? I don't think it does. In the later book he discusses the possibility that "the objectivity of value" (i.e., his view) poses a "threat to individuality." By this he means precisely the issue I was discussing just now: Does his view imply that we have to value the same things, on pain of being wrong? Though he does not mention utopia in his discussion, his answer to this question suggests that, as far as the three paths are concerned, the answer is "no, not in any relevant sense." His treatment of the "individuality" problem in *Philosophical Explanations* is based on a fact that is also fundamental to his discussion of utopia: that not all values can be realized (fully and) continuously. Though truth and beauty are good "for" everybody, we must decide the rate at which we value them in terms of the other values that must be used up or passed up in pursuing them. Here, he thinks, there is indeed a certain failure of objectivity: "[T]here is no right answer (fixed by the realm of value) about which feasible mixture [of values] is the most valuable." There is a failure of universality as well: "[T]here is no one objectively correct set of weights for values."[12] Thus Nozick can both agree and disagree with More. Both can say that gold has value (More doesn't say that gold is *no* good). But More thinks there is a truth about *how* valuable gold really is, a truth that makes it less valuable than iron, while Nozick would say there is no such truth.[13] This enables Nozick to agree with the utopian writers of the past about the objectivity of value while rejecting their denial of individuality and choice.

If we interpret the three paths in light of this idea, it makes the second path, the one about people differing in their trade-offs between different goods, the fundamental one. This one explains why the differences between people that we meet up with on the first path are relevant to the question of which society is the best. Although basic intrinsic values do not differ for different people, optimal mixes of them do, and there is no single sort of community that equally supports them all. Further, if the optimal mix for a given individual is not fully determined by objective facts that they must discover, this eases somewhat the burden that the third path places on the knowledge and insight of the people who are joining and leaving communities. Easily introspectable features of the consciousness of the valuing individual, features like happiness and satisfaction, might be crucially relevant to discovering what is best (i.e., what mix of goods is best) for that individual.

6. Would We Utopianize?

Chandran Kukathas has objected that Nozick's framework contributes nothing to the utopian process: "[I]f it imposes no restrictions of the mobility of people, goods, and ideas, it is not clear in what way it is serving as a filter device." It cannot claim the authority to decide which projects are legitimate utopian experiments, because the scientific spirit that discovers things by experience denies that there are authorities of that sort.[14] (I would add that it would also violate the constraints that the Nozickean state places on itself.)

In a way, he is quite right. Kukathas is thinking of the utopia chapter as part of the answer to anarchism.[15] I have been interpreting it as a response, not to anarchism, but to more-than-minimal states that claim to advance positive ideals (equality, sharing, the Christian way of life, etc.). Part I of ASU was his answer to anarchism. Part III, like Part II, is part of his attempt to resist going beyond the minimal state. If the question Kukathas is raising is "what does Nozick's minimal state positively add, that is not already present in anarchy, to the utopian process?" then the answer might well be "nothing." It does nothing to positively promote utopian pursuits. The filter process is not the framework itself, but the social process of people entering communities, leaving them, and so forth, and of course accumulating knowledge and progressing over time as people learn from one another's successes and failures (see 316).

However, Kukathas' argument can easily be transformed into one that might come from the more-than-minimal side of the fence. This would be an objection that, on my interpretation, a defender of Nozick would need to answer. The objection would be that if his state does not do anything to positively nudge people in the direction of utopian experimentation – and it doesn't! – then what reason do we have to think that people will do it, at least in large enough numbers to have the communication, the accumulation of knowledge, and the progress over time that are essential to the utopian process actually taking place? Most people (at least in my experience) are not very utopian. The things they want from life are relatively modest: to make an honest living, raise a family, and so forth. For the most part the people in the real world do not have the utopian fire in the belly. It is possible to live in the framework itself, instead of joining an experimental community, and surely some would do so, as Nozick himself admits: "Some of course may be content where they are. Not *everyone* will be joining special experimental communities, and many who abstain at first will join the communities later, after it is clear how they work out" (312). In that case, though, how do we know that enough people would choose to live in such communities?

Before trying to answer this question, we should notice that as I think the above-quoted admission suggests Nozick is not assuming that everyone has utopian hankerings. Further, the nature of his filter device works to some extent independently of people's intentions to create utopias. Many people might be joining communities simply to improve their own lot. They may simply see something in one community or another that they find better than what they have now. As things work out in practice and people continually try to improve their own lives, they get closer and closer to utopia. Utopia will come about and not (or not solely) because it was the object of some human intention. This of course is a result of the fact that the filter is an invisible-hand process.

Further, there are a host of non-utopian reasons for joining these communities. Remember: The framework avoids performing many of the functions that are often performed by states as we know them. Canadians who move to the land of Nozickia might miss their native land's government-operated health care system. The framework does not cure diseases or provide resources to those who do. In the framework there are no public (in the sense of government) schools, museums, aquariums, sport stadiums, concert halls, opera houses, zoos, botanical gardens, astronomical observatories, or parks. The framework does not represent the Christian way of life, the Muslim way of life, nor indeed any way of life or any virtue, not excepting the virtues of sobriety, temperance, and civility. All activities that do not violate Lockean rights, including prostitution and using psychoactive drugs, will be permitted. It might be possible to provide a Nozickean reason for prohibiting such things to children.[16] However, the framework cannot declare where or when these things are done, and that means they might be done where children can see or find out about them.

Of course, government services like education will still be provided in the framework, as they were in our world before they were taken over by the state. They can be provided by business corporations, philanthropic organizations, organized religions, clubs, and mutual aid societies. But some people will prefer that some service be provided by the community itself and not merely by some organization within it (perhaps they like feeling that the community as a whole cares about this particular service). Those homesick Canadians might want to join or start a community that provides the same health insurance plan to all residents, charging them based on their ability to pay. As long as participation in the plan is clearly stated as a condition of moving there, it will be allowed by the framework.[17] Similar things are true of people who want to live a way of life that they feel would be undermined by actions permitted by the framework. Muslims could even form communities that apply Sharia law. If women freely consent to the (as it seems to non-Muslims) inferior position they would occupy in such a system, the framework would permit such a practice. Others would have reason to move to communities that have non-libertarian restrictions that are less drastic than those of sharia – pacifists who despise guns, Christians who want to keep their children far away from prostitution, feminists who hate pornography, and many others.

There are numberless reasons why people we would not ordinarily think of as utopian personalities would want to join a community. In that case, if Nozick is right about the filter process, we would be on our way to utopia. By its very inertness, the framework might force (in a non-coercive way) utopia to get started.

There is another way in which the inertness of the framework would help, which is worth mentioning briefly before going on to other matters. In our world, people do try to build utopian communities and are stopped by officials who use the complex web of regulations – including building codes, health codes, zoning regulations – while their real objection to them is that their vision of the good life is too different from ours. It is arguable that most or all of these laws would not exist in the framework (or would not be so easily exploitable if they did).[18]

7. A Stability Problem

Peter Singer introduced an issue regarding the utopia chapter that is rather reminiscent of an old bone of contention between Stalinists and Trotskyites: whether you could have socialism in one country, an island of socialism in a sea of capitalism, or whether a world revolution is necessary for socialism to succeed. Singer's problem is on a smaller scale: Would

Nozick's utopian communities collapse simply because they try to exist in a world that is based on principles that are very different from their own?

> Could a community that wanted a lot of redistribution survive the departure of wealthy members whose moral principles are weaker than their desire for wealth? ... Could a community maintain its dedication to an austere life of virtue if it were surrounded by the flashy temptations of American capitalism? Nozick would say that the choice between austere virtue and flashy temptation must be left to the individual; but doesn't this assume an ability to make free rational choices that most people simply do not possess?[19]

In an indirect sort of way, this is a reply to an argument that Nozick gives for the framework later in the chapter (317–320): The framework can serve as "utopian common ground," meaning that most other utopian theorists can endorse it because their utopias can exist within it. The one exception, he says, are "imperialistic" utopians, who insist that everyone live their way. Singer thinks he has found a whole range of exceptions: all utopias that require, for their existence, that people make sacrifices for some ideal, whether it is a political ideal like equality or an austere religious conception of sexual morality. Such communities cannot survive the presence of alternative life-styles that seem less idealistic but more fun. They would not be able to survive in the framework, which allows people to follow such temptations wherever they lead.

Actually, Nozick does address this issue, or one that is very close to it (326–327). This is the issue, as he puts it, of whether "isolated experiments are doomed to failure" if they occur in a social environment that is "hostile to the goals of the experiment." Singer must have found his answer to this question deeply unsatisfying. Speaking of a hypothetical (presumably well-planned and executed) experiment in micro-socialism, Nozick says: "As more and more people see how it works, more and more will wish to participate in or support it. And so it will grow, without it being necessary to force everyone or a majority or anyone into the pattern."

Clearly, Nozick and Singer are making assumptions that are worlds apart. As we have seen, Nozick thinks that ordinary people, at least in a free society and at least after sufficient experience and experimentation, can know what is good for them. Singer thinks people not only can be deeply deluded about this, but usually are. This may involve differing assumptions about the nature of the good, about human nature, or both. Some of the issues involved we have already discussed, and others would take us too far afield to treat here. But there is one important point raised by Singer's objection that can be dealt with fairly briefly.

Singer appears to be making an empirical prediction: That a certain type of utopian experiment – namely, the sort that asks experimenters to incur high costs for the sake of the utopian ideal – is doomed to die in a society that permits certain less burdensome alternatives. That is a genuine issue of course: We have just seen Nozick making a prediction that seems contrary to this one. There is a big problem, though, about Singer's approach to this issue. He is treating this as a matter about which we must speculate and reason *a priori*, as if such isolated utopian communities are as much a product of Nozick's fertile imagination as the framework itself. Of course, that is not true. For centuries now, there have been hundreds, perhaps even thousands, of utopian communities in the West. In the United States they have existed continuously since 1735.[20] Between the years 1735 and 1935, 277 are known to have existed.[21] We have had the Ephrata Cloister, the Shakers, the Harmony Society (the Rappists), the Zoar Separatists, the Amana Colonies, Oneida, the Icarians, the Bishop Hill Community, to name a few of the most important. With the Great Depression came a lull in utopian activity, a lull which ended with a bang in the sixties.[22]

Yes, one might say, but doesn't their very number indicate failure of a sort? It seems a testament to the human desire to start utopia, rather than an ability to bring it off. Have any of these communities really lasted?

Well, yes. The Hutterites are a very relevant case here, as they practice both the sorts of (supposed) self-abnegation that Singer seems to find highly unstable: They practice micro-socialism (everyone works and no one is paid a wage, which makes it impossible to get rich) *and* an austere conception of moral virtue (no drinking, smoking, swearing, fighting of any kind, or colorful clothing; a very old-fashioned sexual morality – and it goes on). And yet they have practiced their way of life (with comparatively brief interruptions in their practice of micro-socialism) since 1528 (an astonishing 486 years as of this writing).[23] As of 1995 they had about 390 colonies in the US and Canada, with a combined population of around 36,000 people.[24] The other great success story in the history of utopian experimentation is the kibbutz movement in Israel, which has operated continuously since 1909.[25] There are also, surprisingly enough, a number of hippie communes established in the sixties and early seventies that are still functioning today, including the Twin Oaks community in Louisa County, Virginia, Stephen Gaskins' The Farm in Lewis County, Tennessee, and Tolstoy Farms near Davenport, Washington.[26] In addition, shouldn't we consider 2,000 years of Christian monasticism as a relevant example of longevity? True enough, we don't usually think of monasteries as utopian communities, but they do involve both the sorts of austerity cited by Singer, and throughout much of their history their residents have faced the same sorts of temptations that Singer foresees in Nozick's framework. Further, we are somewhat hampered in finding examples of real-world utopias by the fact that we tend to think of them as arrangements that practice communalism (i.e., what I just called micro-socialism). Why not include the non-socialist Amish?[27] Their conception of virtue is even more austere than that of the Hutterites, and yet they are still here. In fact, their numbers in North America are rapidly increasing.[28] I think it is fair to add that they see themselves in effect as fitting Nozick's definition of utopia, because they think they have crafted the best possible association (the best, that is, that is possible here on Earth).

Still, in fairness to Singer, I have to admit that, among the sorts of communities that we usually think of as utopian (limiting ourselves, consequently to micro-socialist ones) the Hutterites and the kibbutzim are the great exceptions. Yacov Oved, in his magisterial history of these communities in the United States, finds that few have really managed to thrive beyond the first generation, apparently meaning by that the life-times of their founders (though he draws comfort from the fact that the few that have done so are thriving *now*).[29]

What are the prospects for the stability of utopia in an environment of free choice? I see a sharp difference, here, between the first generation of a utopian community, its founders, and the second generation. (For convenience, by "second generation," I will be referring to all non-first generations: that is, to all inhabitants who are descendants of the founders.) If I may indulge in some *a priori* speculation of my own, I think I can explain why utopia is much more secure in the first generation than in the second. Take Singer's case of the community that "wanted a lot of redistribution," but its wealthy member's "moral principles are weaker than their desire for wealth." First of all, the principle of distributive justice will be in the founding document, the system people agree to when they join. If members of the founding generation go through the trouble to create a community that has a distinctive principle of distribution, then it is very likely this is something they want. This is what they believe in. If it makes it impossible to be rich, they must not want to be rich. Some of them want to avoid wealth and the endless race to acquire it. If one of these people leaves the community, it is unlikely to be for the sort of reason that fits Singer's argument: that they fell back in love with making piles of money. It is more likely to be something about the community itself that they do not like. The passionate attachment of the founding generation would explain why one common cause of the death

217

of utopian communities is the dying off of the founding generation and "a dearth of suitable replacements."[30] If people leave the community, not because of the *pull* of the money, but because of the *push* of the community, then they ought to leave it. If the community cannot survive because too many people are leaving for that sort of reason, then it ought to die. The filter is working. The same line of reasoning applies (in a weaker form) to anyone who joins the community on the basis of a free and fully informed decision.

The second generation is in a significantly different position. The reason these people are here is not that they made a costly and considered decision to be here. That decision was made by their parents (or more distant ancestors). Accordingly, they are more likely to be open to influence by ideas from outside the community. This represents a problem that may be unique to experimental utopian communities. Such communities are unlike others in that they are *ideological*. By that I mean that they are what they are because their residents share beliefs that, in other sorts of community, need not be shared. The existence of the town where I live, Oregon, Wisconsin, is not threatened if residents do not all agree on what the ultimate purpose of life is. The same is not true of a certain community that exists just a short distance down the road from where I sit as I write this: the Tibetan Buddhist monastery of Deer Park. Utopian communities in general are like that: Agreement about certain things, things that other communities need not agree about, is essential. This means that interaction with "outsiders" (meaning people who do not share the founding beliefs of the community) presents a problem. Interaction can lead to influence, and this can result in abandoning those beliefs. If enough people do so, the group will cease to exist as a distinctive community.

This means that second generation communities do have a certain tendency to be unstable. History shows that this is indeed the case. There is this much truth in what Singer is saying. There are some important differences, though, between my account and the one suggested by Singer's comments. First, he presents the process leading to defection as an irrational one in which weak people violate their own principles simply because there are tempting alternatives. The process I am describing involves changing one's principles, not violating them, and can be quite rational. If it is rational, then, this is evidence that these people *ought* to defect and that, perhaps, these communities ought not to exist. Second, I am presenting this as a problem that characterizes, not the framework, but utopian experimental communities themselves, whether in Nozick's framework or in our own world.

218

Finally, history also shows that this does not imply that second generation communities are simply doomed. Given that some communities do last, there must be things that they can do to achieve a degree of stability. One such measure would be to adopt practices that establish the distinctness of the group and in some way limit or qualify interactions with outsiders. Of this nature are the distinctive dress and speech of the Hutterites and Amish, and even some of their abstinences (with no automobile at your disposal it is much more difficult to get in touch with outside influences).[31] All of the surviving hippie communes I named above are in remote locations and limit visitors to visiting hours on weekends. These practices, admittedly, can be ethically problematic. One could argue that some of them are related to the worrisome practice that we have already noticed, that "some communities may try to keep some of their members ignorant of the nature of other alternatives" (307). If deliberately concealing information is troubling, are practices that make the information feel less vivid and the alternatives less near-at-hand also troubling? Surely not all insulating practices are equally problematic. It may be that one of the trade-offs that communities must consider is the one that is involved in balancing stability against openness. You can't have it all. In the real world, including the framework if it should ever exist, nothing is perfect – including utopia!

8. The Prospects for Utopia in the Framework's Filter

Utopias can and do exist, even in a world that, outside the community's boundaries, operates on the basis of other principles altogether. But one important fact that has leapt into the foreground in the last section of this chapter places a certain burden on our attempts to predict their existence: Once a utopian community comes into existence, its continuing to exist, rather than perishing from defections, might very well require some effort. This of course is in addition to whatever factors might impede its forming in the first place. On the other hand, one factor emerged in Section 6, above, that weighs on the other side of the ledger. In particular, it is a reason to think that utopias are more likely to form, and more likely to endure, in Nozick's framework than in our world as we know it today.

This is what I have called the notable "inertness" of the framework. A broad array of functions that in our world are already carried out by a massive welfare state would not be carried out by the framework. As I have said, this would give ordinary people a powerful reason to form communities and to join ones that already exist. I would now point out that the same factors will give people a motive to work on their communities and to make them last, partly by making them better – making them worthy of lasting.

This feature of the framework is distinct from its working as a "filter," to use Nozick's illuminating term. Insofar as the framework functions as a filter, its function is analogous to that of natural selection in standard neo-Darwinian evolutionary theory. Just as natural selection eliminates from the gene pool genetic material that lacks "fitness," so this feature of the framework eliminates communities that are insufficiently attractive to individual human beings as places to live their lives. Darwin's original theory, as is well known, lacked a mechanism to explain how the different characteristics of species from which the selection was made came about. Natural selection is a mere filter and, if that is all it is, then it lacks a mechanism that positively drives the process of change. Similarly, if Nozick's framework is merely a filter device, it must rely on forces other than itself, not only for an explanation of how selected communities come into existence in the first place but also for how they stay in existence once selected.

But we have seen that it is not a mere filter. The very inertness of the framework drives the search for utopia by compelling an endless array of motivational forces to drive the search. All the human values and yearnings that are (partly) satisfied by the extra-minimal state would be directed toward forming communities and, having formed them, making them last and work. They would also lead to people who wish to leave a community opting to move to another community based on a somewhat different plan, rather than moving to the politically sparse world of the framework itself. In these ways, the inertness of the framework would support the stability of the communities.

There is another way in which it would do so. In our world, the people who go through the immense labor of building an experimental community are people who feel a powerful need to live a life that is radically different from mainstream society. This in spite of the fact that they live in a world where the state itself performs functions (or tries to) that before the twentieth century were performed by experimental communities, organized religion, and other non-coercive organizations. This means that in the world we live in, first generation utopians tend to include numbers of people who are simply misfits, madmen, dreamers, and fanatics. Such people can be interesting, even admirable, but they probably are not the best people to be building something that works and that lasts. In the framework, as I have suggested, *everyone* will have some reason to join a community. This would no doubt mean that experimental communities would be on the whole quite different from the ones that exist in our world. They would far more often be built by people who are, to be blunt, psychologically normal. For that reason, we could expect the search for utopia to find more stable and lasting results.

Notes

1 In this category I would put the objections by Peter Singer I will discuss later in this chapter.
2 Nowadays this strategy is often called "maximin," which seems more logical to me, given that what the strategy does is to maximize the minimum, but to avoid being unnecessarily confusing I will follow Nozick's usage.
3 For an account of maximax thinking gone horribly wrong, see Mikhail Heller and Aleksandr Nekritch's distinguished, and appropriately titled, *Utopia in Power: The History of the Soviet Union from 1917 to the Present*, trans. Phyllis B. Carlos (New York: Summit Books, 1986). It is a tale of aiming for the maximum thereby actually hitting the minimum.
4 Actually, he defines a stable world as one in which "the original population will choose to remain" (299), but I assume by "original population" he means population at the time it no longer has emigrants. I see no reason why worlds that evolve before they finally stabilize (in that some of the original population has left) should not count for his purposes as stable worlds. Accordingly I have amended his definition somewhat.
5 I'm afraid I don't understand the last clause of this definition. Why would unstable worlds be limited to ones that people leave in order to go to a stable one? Intuitively, isn't a world unstable just in case people are leaving it, regardless of where they are going? Or is he *predicting* that people would only emigrate to worlds they believe are stable? If this is only a prediction about human behavior, then why is it included in a definition of "stable world"? Also, if it is a prediction, it isn't very plausible. After all, a world is unstable, in his sense, if even one person will emigrate. Given that, it could be perfectly rational to emigrate to a world you think is unstable. Such "unstable" worlds might continue to exist for a long time. Whether instability is relevant to wanting to go there depends on *why* the world is unstable. Fortunately, though this idea is repeated (299–300) and comes up again briefly (305), I don't think it is important.
6 Thomas More, *Utopia*, ed. George M. Logan and Robert M. Adams (Cambridge, England: Cambridge University Press, 2002 [orig. pub. 1516]), pp. 60–61.
7 See Plato, *Republic* (many editions), 504e–509b.
8 Also, this constraint brings the model a little closer to reality, in that in our world people cannot be designed to suit the wishes of others (at least, not yet!).

Most importantly, it is needed if the model is going to spontaneously generate worlds that are genuinely the best: Without it, the model could produce worlds in which people are ecstatically happy with whatever the imaginer chooses to dish out to them.

9 Robert Nozick, *Philosophical Explanations* (Cambridge, Massachusetts: Harvard University Press, 1981), pp. 403–450.

10 See note 3, above.

11 Nozick, *Philosophical Explanations*, pp. 415–422.

12 Nozick, *Philosophical Explanations*, pp. 446–450. I should mention that he does not deny that there are *any* universal or objective truths about rankings of values. He suggests (p. 448) that "[t]here is some open range" of "partial rankings of value" that are legitimate. It is still possible to overvalue or undervalue something, even though there is no one trade-off rate that is objectively right for everyone.

13 Of course, there is such a thing as the market value of gold, which is the rate at which the market trades gold against other goods, but that is not what we are talking about here.

14 Chandran Kukathas, "*E pluribus plurum*, or How to fail to get to utopia in spite of really trying," in Ralf M. Bader and John Meadowcroft, eds., *The Cambridge Companion to Nozick's Anarchy, State, and Utopia* (Cambridge, England: Cambridge University Press, 2011), p. 397.

15 He makes this explicit at a number of places. At the end of his essay, he says: "In Part I of ASU he tried to show why leaving the state of anarchy was morally legitimate, in Part III he tried to show why leaving it would be good." Kukathas, "*E pluribus plurum*," p. 301.

16 It might be based on something like the reasoning that leads to common law notions like statutory rape or the nullity of contracts with minor children. A minor's consent does not count as consent, so doing certain things to or with a minor counts the same as forcing those things on them. "Consensual" sex with an underage person counts as rape.

17 Another proviso would be that it cannot be introduced in an already-existing community and forced on everyone without compensating the unwilling victims or remedying the injustice in some other way.

18 The pretext for the original 1993 military-style assault on the Mount Carmel Center (known in the press as the Branch Davidian Compound) in Waco, Texas was to arrest its leader for non-paying of a federal tax on some machine guns he had purchased, apparently as an investment. The tax ($200 per gun) was instituted in 1934 to discourage private ownership of such weapons. See David Kopel and Paul H. Blackman, *No More Wacos: What's Wrong with Federal Law Enforcement and How to Fix It* (Amherst, New York: Prometheus Books, 1997). Of course, the framework would not levy charges in order to discourage behavior it does not like. In the sixties and early seventies hippie communes were closed down (in one case I know of, literally bulldozed – four times) using sanitation codes and building codes. See Richard Fairfield's account of the destruction of the Gorda Mountain

commune in the Big Sur area of California and of Morning Star Ranch ("The Digger Farm") in Sonoma County of the same state in Richard Fairfield et al., *The Modern Utopian: Alternative Communities of the '60s and '70s* (Port Townsend, Washington: Process Media, 2010), pp. 15 and 68–75. Prof. Timothy Miller, a contributor to the same volume, notes that the boom in hippie communes in the sixties was facilitated by the rarity, in those days, of zoning regulations (pp. 321–322): "Gradually, however, zoning has become stricter, in some cases because upstanding local citizens were horrified at the countercultural invasion they experienced. Zoning laws not only limit land uses, but are often coupled with building codes, ensuring that simple structures cannot legally be constructed, and often specify occupancy limits – often as few as three or four unrelated persons in a given building or on a given piece of land." Some surviving hippie-style communes, he tells us, exist in violation of these laws, which is one reason they are so little-known. Publicity might bring in the government bulldozer.

19 Peter Singer, "The Right to Be Rich or Poor," in Jeffrey Paul, ed., *Reading Nozick: Essays on Anarchy, State, and Utopia* (Totowa, New Jersey: Rowman and Littlefield, 1981), p. 38.

20 Yaacov Oved, *Two Hundred Years of American Communes* (New Brunswick, New Jersey: Transaction Books, 1988), p. 3.

21 In the appendix to his book, Oved lists them by name and gives their years of operation. Oved, *Two Hundred Years*, pp. 485–490.

22 Oved, *Two Hundred Years*, p. xiii. Oved's book is the most detailed history of these communities to date. Unfortunately, it only covers the two-century period that ends at 1935. An interesting source on the hippie period in utopian experimentation is Richard Fairfield's *The Modern Utopian*, cited above in note 18. It consists of reprints from a magazine of the same name that Fairfield edited and published from 1966 to 1971, which reported and commented on then-contemporary utopian projects. A wonderful resource on the Golden Age of American utopianism is Charles Nordhoff, *The Communistic Societies of North America* (New York: Dover Publications, 1966 [orig. pub. 1875]). Nordhoff visited virtually every experimental community then in existence and his accounts of them seem scrupulously fair. He later became a distinguished political journalist, possibly the most respected of his day.

23 Gertrude E. Huntington, "Living in the Ark: Four Centuries of Hutterite Faith and Community," in Donald E. Pitzer, ed., *America's Communal Utopias* (Chapel Hill, North Carolina: University of North Carolina Press, 1997), p. 322. Huntington tells us (p. 320) they abandoned socialism for about 70 years in the eighteenth century and for 40 years in the nineteenth century.

24 Huntington, "Living in the Ark," p. 322. The most recent numbers I have been able to find are on a Mennonite website: There are "about 40,000 members in about 450 colonies today" (http://the-mennonite.tripod.com/hutterites.html). If both sets of numbers are roughly accurate, Hutterites are not only still with us, they are growing, and fast.

25 Oved, *Two Hundred Years*, p. 482.
26 Fairfield, *The Modern Utopian*, p. 320. The source here is Timothy Miller, Professor of Religious Studies at the University of Kansas. He also says that there are "several hundred" of these communes still in existence. I find this hard to believe, but he is after all the expert here, not me. By the way, part of the success of Twin Oaks is no doubt due to the fact that, from the beginning, it had something that hippie communes typically lacked: clear rules and regulations.
27 "The Amish are in some ways a little commonwealth, for their members claim to be ruled by the law of love and redemption." John A. Hostetler, *Amish Society*, 3rd edn (Baltimore, Maryland: The Johns Hopkins University Press, 1980), p. 5.
28 Recently, the Amish population in North America has been doubling every 20 years. Donald B. Kraybill and Carl F. Bowman, *On the Back Road to Heaven: Old Order Hutterites, Menonites, Amish, and Bretheren* (Baltimore, Maryland: The Johns Hopkins University Press, 2001), pp. 103 and 133–134.
29 Oved, *Two Hundred Years*, p. 475. He seems to think that people might finally be figuring out what the Hutterites and kibbutzniks are doing right. For his fascinating discussion of what that might be, see pp. 470–478.
30 Oved, *Two Hundred Years*, p. 470.
31 The oddest such practice that I know of is this: "By keeping the clock either slower or faster than [i.e., behind or ahead of] worldly time, the Amish effectively stay out of step with the world. ... When the world changes to standard time, the Amish set their clocks a half-hour ahead. ... Whether practiced consciously or unconsciously, [this] is an effective means of insulating the Amish from the activity and structures of the world." Hostetler, *Amish Society*, p. 114.

Index

Anarchy, State, and Utopia: An Advanced Guide, First Edition. Lester H. Hunt.
© 2015 John Wiley & Sons, Inc. Published 2015 by John Wiley & Sons, Inc.

Index

coercion 5, 150
  future event-based 99
  justification of 98, 106, 179–180
  risk responses 98–99
  see also force; punishment
Cohen, G. A. 16, 20–21, 38, 151,
    166–167, 175–176
collective well-being 28
compensation
  agent compensation 111–112
  for boundary crossings 88–89
  deterrent effect 94–95
  distinction from punishment 131
  extreme situations and 191–192
  fairness compensation 123
  fear and 92–96
  full compensation 89, 91–92, 111,
    119, 123
  market compensation 89–92
  objections to 90–92
  principle of 89, 107–111, 122
  for risky independents 107–111, 114
competition 79
conflict between agencies 74–75
conscription 56, 127
consent issue 80–82
constraints 14
  natural rights as 149–150
  rationality of 31, 32
  see also moral constraints
consumer-owned cooperatives 123
cooperation 143–144
coordination problem 164–165, 168
counterexample to the rule 6–7
Crow society 138–139
current time-slice principles 159–160,
    196

dangerous manufacturing 122
deductive-nomological model of
    explanation 61–62
Deep Springs College, California 189
defense of necessity 191
de jure monopoly 87, 89

democracy 194
desert 155–156, 161
  distinction from entitlement 156
difference principle 160, 168
dignity 32
discount rates concept 48–49
distribution 154
distributive justice 2, 154–157, 197
  end-state principles 161, 163–170
  entitlement principle 153, 158–159,
    163, 170–173
  "not too unequal" notion 179–180
  taxonomy of principles 159–162
  see also justice in holdings
dividing the benefits of
    exchange 89–92, 115
Divine Command Theory 25
division of labor 73
dominant protective association
    (DPA) 74–76
  legitimacy issue 130–132, 146–151
  monopoly of force feature 130–132
  protective role 133–137
  versus state 125–130
duties of imperfect obligation 19

Eagle Diamond case 175–177, 198
egalitarianism 160
emergent justification 80–81
emigration problem 177–179
emotion 95–96, 120
end-state principles 161, 163–164
  assessment of arguments
    against 165–170
  problems with 164–165
    possible solution 175–181
entitlement 155–156, 158
  distinction from desert 156
entitlement process 158–159
entitlement theory of justice in
    holdings 156, 158–159, 163
  problems with 170–175
    possible solution 175–181
  proviso 181–192

226

Index

Iroquois–Huron conflict 144–145
is/ought divide 29–30

Jollimore, Troy 51
justice 155
   distinction from fairness 156–157,
    176, 178–179
   recipient justice theories 163–164
   see also distributive justice; justice
    in holdings
justice in acquisition principle 158, 162
   see also appropriation
justice in holdings 154–155
   end-state principles 161, 163–170
   entitlement theory 156, 158–159,
    163, 170–173
    proviso 181–192
   problems with 173–175
    possible solution 175–181
   see also distributive justice
justice in transfer principle 158
justification
   of coercion 98, 106, 179–180
   emergent 80–81
   of the state 54, 85–86
   teleological 80
just steps principle 165–166

Kant, Immanuel 29–30
kibbutz movement, Israel 216
knowledge problem 164–165, 168
Krader, Lawrence 138, 139, 151
Kukathas, Chandran 212

Lakota society 145
law-defective potential
   explanation 62, 65–66,
    68–69
law of nature 147–148
legal moralism 106–107
legal system 80, 84
legislative authority 126–127
legitimacy 130, 132
   dominant protective
    association 130–132, 146–151

Lemos, John 51
libertarian constraint 11
line-drawing problem 97, 100, 122
Locke, John 9–10, 30, 61, 68, 72,
   126–127
   appropriation theory 190–191
   social contract theory 80, 86, 132
   Two Treatises of Government 9–10
long-term planning capacity 28–29

Mack, Eric 122, 123, 124, 133, 151
Madison, James 202
market anarchist 128
market compensation 89–90
   objections to 90–92
   see also compensation
markets 123
maximax institutional
   design 201–202
meaning in life 28–29
membership in society 142–143
mental state theories of welfare 42
methodological intuitionism 6–7
military conscription 56, 127
Miller, Thomas 223, 224
Mill, John Stuart 36, 39
minarchist 129
minimal state 5, 85–86, 200–201
   framework for utopia 208–209
   justification 5, 201
   more-than-minimal state
    derivation 193–194
minimax institutional design
   202–203, 210
monasteries, as utopian
   communities 216–217
monopoly
   de jure monopoly 87, 89
   state as 71
   versus oligopoly 79
monopoly of force 71, 75, 130–132, 139
   dominant protective
    association 130–132
   rights enforcement and 76
moods, versus emotions 95

228